Higher Mental Processes

Selections from
The American Journal of Psychology

Edited by Robert W. Proctor

COMMON THREADS

An anthology from the
University of Illinois Press

T0366950

© 2015 by the Board of Trustees
of the University of Illinois
All rights reserved

Printed and bound in Great Britain by
Marston Book Services Ltd, Oxfordshire

Library of Congress Control Number: 2015939449
ISBN 978-0-252-08145-3 (paperback)
ISBN 978-0-252-09811-6 (e-book)

CONTENTS

INTRODUCTION

Professor Robert W. Proctor

Higher-level, or complex, cognition has been a topic of interest in the field of psychology since its earliest days, with much of the progress in this area recorded in the pages of *The American Journal of Psychology*. As early as the second volume in 1889, the *Journal* included an article on symbolic logic by Christine Ladd Franklin (*AJP*, 2, pp. 543–567), in which she said, "It is the starting point of the immense command over intricate reasoning which is furnished by the modern developments of Deductive Logic" (p. 545). Many other articles on reasoning, decision making, and problem solving have occurred in the years since that article, several of which are collected in this e-book.

This collection of articles is centered on a 2012 review article, "The higher mental processes in *The American Journal of Psychology*," written by Richard A. Carlson for the 125th anniversary volume of the *Journal*. His article surveys research in higher-level cognition, discussing how the methods and topics of research have developed and progressed. In that article, Carlson states, "I attempt to identify the earliest contributions in the Journal, to characterize changes over the decades in how the topics have been studied, to point out contributions that I think are of special interest, and to discuss the articles that seem to me to have been most influential or best reflected trends in the field" (p. 25). The remainder of this book consists of a selection of three representative articles on each of the topics of reasoning, decision making, and problem solving, which have been selected to convey firsthand the progression of research methods and theory concerning human thought processes.

The first section contains articles on reasoning. The initial article, "Synaesthesia in the process of reasoning," by Thomas Cutsforth (1924), reports a case study of himself, the synesthetic participant for whom all sensations produced vivid visual percepts, and another psychologist who was not synesthetic. They provided detailed, introspective reports of the contents of their reasoning processes while solving analogies and other problems. Among the conclusions was that synesthesia "is essential to the cognitive activities of the subject who possesses it because it is the only structural tool he has of comprehending meanings" (p. 97). The study conducted by Chant (1933), "An objective experiment on reasoning," uses the method of much contemporary psychological research, drawing conclusions from statistical analysis of the performance of a large group of undergraduate students on a task designed to allow objective measurements of behavior. The most recent of the studies on reasoning, "How implication is understood," by Johnson-Laird and Tagart (1969) again examines undergraduate students' performance in a controlled setting, showing that deductive reasoning errors are influenced by the form of the sentence by which a logical implication is expressed.

The section on decision making begins with an influential 1948 article by Preston and Baratta, "An experimental study of the auction-value of an uncertain outcome." Their experiment studied groups of participants competing to bid on a series of opportunities to win points. The results showed deviations from predictions of normative decision theories based on objective probabilities and values, which the authors attributed to subjective probabilities being higher than objective ones for low probability outcomes but lower than them for high probability outcomes. Galanter (1962, *AJP*, 75, pp. 208–220, and in his 1990 article "Utility functions for nonmonetary events," included here) applied a direct scaling approach to derive utility functions for the subjective values of monetary and nonmonetary events. In the final article, Birnbaum (1983) examines the issue of base-rate neglect in decision making using a signal detection analysis and concludes that whether humans in fact deviate from normative predictions in this regard depends on the theory that is assumed.

The three articles selected to illustrate problem-solving research begin with Bulbrook's (1932) article, "An experimental study into the existence and nature of 'insight.'" "Insight" refers to a phenomenal experience that is supposed to occur as a consequence of reorganization of knowledge. Bulbrook evaluated whether evidence for insight could be obtained in a controlled setting, testing both psychologists trained at reporting and untrained undergraduate students. The participants attempted to solve a series of problems involving objects placed on a table, providing reports of their progress. Several psychological processes were identified from these reports, but Bulbrook concluded that there was no unambiguous evidence for the phenomenon of insight. Although Bulbrook found little evidence for insight, Buyer and Dominowski (1989, *AJP*, 102, pp. 353–363) and Dominowski and Buyer (2000) in the article included here, "Retention of problem solutions: the re-solution effect," found evidence that reorganization, whether insightful or not, benefits retention of the problem solution. Specifically, problem solutions were remembered better when the participant solved the problem initially than when the solution was provided by the experimenter. The final article is Cleveland's

(1907), "The psychology of chess and of learning to play it," which Carlson (2012) describes as "strikingly modern" and "prescient" in its analysis of this complex problem-solving skill and its acquisition.

A benefit of a journal that extends from the earliest days of psychological science to the present is that it provides a record of the progress of thinking on a variety of topics. If these readings pique your interest, you should examine other articles cited by Carlson (2012), as well as ones that have been published since his review was completed, to get a more complete perspective.

Robert W. Proctor
Editor

THE HIGHER MENTAL PROCESSES
IN *THE AMERICAN JOURNAL OF PSYCHOLOGY*

RICHARD A. CARLSON
The Pennsylvania State University

Research on the higher mental processes throughout the history of *The American Journal of Psychology* is reviewed. The domains covered include reasoning, judgment and decision, problem solving, and metacognition. Within each domain, the earliest contributions to the *Journal* are discussed, as is the development of the research domain over time. The increasing refinement of research methods and theoretical tools over time is accompanied by much consistency in research questions.

The history of *The American Journal of Psychology* (hereafter, the *Journal)* overlaps with much of the history of scientific psychology, and it is fascinating to trace that history by reading articles published in the *Journal.* For roughly the first 40–50% of the *Journal's* history, there was great concern with formulating the subject matter of psychology and with competing schools of psychology. During the *Journal's* history, there has also been great change in many of the methods of scientific psychology and in the theoretical tools brought to bear on elucidating mental processes. In this article, I trace some of this history by examining articles published in the *Journal* concerning the higher mental processes: reasoning, judgment and decision, problem solving, and metacognition.

The classification of articles into these categories is a bit arbitrary, in part because in the earlier years of the *Journal* the literatures on these topics were less distinct from one another than they have become. Nevertheless, in each category I attempt to identify the earliest contributions in the *Journal,* to characterize changes over the decades in how the topics have been studied, to point out contributions that I think are of special interest, and to discuss the articles that seem to me to have been most influential or best reflected trends in the field. I have excluded book reviews from this review, although many of those provide interesting snapshots of changing ideas in the literature on thinking. A number of other worthwhile articles have been excluded due to space limitations.

Reasoning

Since the earliest days of psychology, researchers have been interested in how, and how well, people think about implication and draw inferences. Much such research has taken formal logic as a starting point and model, and this is reflected in the earliest discussion of reasoning in the *Journal,* which focused on logic rather than the empirical study of reasoning. In what appears to be the first article on reasoning to appear in the *Journal,* Franklin (1889) critiqued Boole's approach to logic, describing his method as "a very obscure and torturous journey" (p. 560), and discussed various improvements suggested by her and others. Although Franklin presented no empirical data about how people actually reason, she referred repeatedly to the naturalness of various systems of logic and suggested that a criterion for evaluating a logical system is "closeness to the real processes of reasoning" (p. 560). From a modern psychological perspective, there is a curious tension between viewing the work of logicians on one hand as capturing the laws of thought and on the other hand viewing it as providing "an organized method for doing thinking" (p. 544).

A couple of decades later, Phelps (1918) anticipated modern two-process theories of reasoning and judgment, describing reasoning and intuition and offering a kind of evolutionary argument for their contrasting nature. As in modern theories, he described intuition as faster than reasoning. However, he rather archaically attributed these "temperaments" to men and women, respectively, and ended on what seems an odd religious note.

In general, later work on reasoning published in the *Journal* has been empirical, although Johnson (1954) and, in reaction to Johnson, Noble (1975), published discussions of the relationship of inductive reasoning to deductive logic. Noble's comments on Johnson's article also reflected a return to the sometimes acerbic tone of earlier articles in the *Journal;* for example, in a footnote (p. 546) he allowed that "perhaps Johnson was only *seemingly* opposed to common sense."

The earliest empirical investigation of reasoning reported introspections during a variety of reasoning tasks by a synesthetic participant (the author, Cutsforth, 1924) and a check observer. Although the two observers differed in the extent to which they reported visual, kinesthetic, and verbal imagery, "no functional differences" between the observers were found (p. 97). A decade later, Chant (1933) reported "An Objective Experiment on Reasoning," presenting statistical analyses of the behavior and reports of a large number of participants solving inductive reasoning problems. Again, two forms of thinking—analytic, logic-driven thinking and the use of associations to prior knowledge—were found.

Only in 1969 did an experimental study using a task based on deductive logic appear in the *Journal.* In this article, Johnson-Laird and Tagart (1969) reported data demonstrating that the phrasing of a conditional statement influences how it is understood. In particular, the phrasing of statements determined whether they were interpreted in a truth-functional manner as bearing on the truth of their antecedents. This work reflected the Zeitgeist in research on reasoning, searching for regularities in and explanations for the errors and biases in reasoning that researchers were beginning to document in laboratory settings. Although a few articles adopting this newer perspective on reasoning appeared in the *Journal* over the next decades (e.g., Politzer, 1981; Pollard & Evans, 1987), including a contribution from my own lab (Carlson, Lundy, & Yaure, 1992), the *Journal* was not to be a major outlet for such work.

Judgment and Decision

Research on judgment and decision in the modern sense was rare in the early years of the *Journal;* although articles on psychophysical judgment were common, only a handful of articles were concerned with more cognitive decisions and judgments. Moore (1921) examined the impact of expert and majority opinion on judgments, finding that people were more influenced by majority than by expert opinion, a result that would probably replicate today. Weld and Danzig (1940) studied the changes in belief as evidence was presented in a mock trial, finding that evidence was often interpreted in light of judgments reached early on, suggesting that participants formed their opinions early and interpreted evidence in ways that supported those opinions. Morgan (1945) demonstrated that the size of the hypothesis space for a problem did not appropriately influence reasoning: Participants did not report lower probabilities associated with each hypothesis as the number of hypotheses increased. Each of these early studies documented in various ways that people make judgments that deviate from normative standards. This general theme has dominated much of the research on judgment and decision since, as research methods and theoretical analyses have become more sophisticated.

In an important and much-cited article, Preston and Baratta (1948) noted the irrationality of making bets that cost more than their expected value (amount of gain multiplied by probability of gain). In attempting to explain this behavior, they noted some misconceptions about chance found in previous work. More important, they hypothesized that there were systematic deviations of subjective from objective probability and that psychological value need not correspond to objective value, thus anticipating and bringing into the realm of experimental psychology the ideas of subjective expected utility theory formalized by Savage a few years later. The specific question they addressed experimentally was whether a psychological scale of probability could be constructed on the basis of gambling behavior (bidding for the opportunity to play particular gambles). Their major result was that average winning bid was greater than the expected value for low probabilities and lower for high probabilities. Given the assumption that "psychological probability is the probability which must be used in order to bring the price paid into rational relationship with the prize" (p. 189), they presented a graph depicting the relationship of psychological to mathematical probability. The "indifference point" at which psychological and mathematical probabilities appeared to correspond was approximately 0.20. The authors speculated that this might change depending on the context of the game, such as variations in the amount of money players received at the beginning of the game, on analogy to Helson's (1947) idea of adaptation levels in psychophysical judgment. Preston and Baratta's article has been cited more than 130 times, and the essential shape of the probability function sketched by Preston and Baratta can be found in Kahneman and Tversky's (1979) hugely influential prospect theory of decision making. Galanter (1990) cited Preston and Baratta's article as the beginning of the psychological literature challenging the assumptions of "economic rationality." However, it is noteworthy that they—like many authors since—assumed that given the subjective inputs or premises, the actual thought process corresponds to the normative structure of expected value theory.

Edwards (1953) pointed out that Preston and Baratta's model assumed that "people do try to maximize monetary returns" and "do combine probabilities and values according to a simple multiplicative formula" (p. 350). However, he noted that it might instead be assumed that it is the psychological value, or utility, of money that might systematically vary from its objective value, and he cited research purported to show the nature of this variation. However, Edwards argued that these studies do not really examine how decisions are made. His alternative approach was to observe the choices made between gambles with equal objective values. The results showed that certain probabilities were disproportionately preferred or avoided and that participants much preferred low-probability bets when expected value was negative. Perhaps most important, the results point out the difficulty of inferring subjective probability or utility curves from gambling behavior. Edwards (1954a, 1954b) pursued this research question—probability preferences in choosing gambles—in several subsequent studies.

Continued interest in the measurement of subjective probability and utility, and the comparison of actual decision to variations on the multiplicative expected value model, is illustrated in a number of subsequent studies. Galanter (1962) used a direct scaling approach to measuring utility, asking participants to indicate, for example, how much money it would take to make them twice as happy as receiving $10 would. This approach led him to conclude that utility is related to money by a power function. Galanter also asked his participants to assign likelihoods to events with "vague actuarial probabilities" and found that they could do so. Most important, he demonstrated that these scalings of utility and subjective probability could be used to make good predictions of individuals' choices between pairs of alternatives. Like Preston and Baratta, Galanter assumed that the multiplicative combination of subjective probabilities and utilities provided an appropriate description of the thought process.

Komorita (1964) pointed out that Galanter's approach allowed a test of subjective expected utility (Savage, 1954) that did not require independent measurements of subjective probability and utility. He tested a formal model of choice incorporating Galanter's power function for utility, asking participants how much they would pay to play specific gambles. He obtained excellent fits to group data and very good fits to individual data.

The concern with measuring subjective probabilities and utilities continued over the succeeding decades. For example, Jamison and Kozielecki (1968) considered the interesting situation in which a person is completely uncertain how actual probabilities are distributed over possible outcomes. They found that as the number of possible outcomes considered increased, participants' subjective probabilities increasingly deviated from the normative model, indicating increasingly incoherent sets of beliefs, and they noted that the general probability-density functions they observed with large numbers of outcomes corresponded qualitatively to the function proposed by Preston and Baratta (1948) in the study discussed earlier.

Parker, Stein, Darte, Schneider, Popper, and Needel (1981) revisited the issue of measuring the utility function for money, using an interesting conjoint measurement approach based on utility (desirability) judgments of bundles of products and money. This more sophisticated measurement approach provided strong support that the power function relating utility to money proposed by Galanter (1962) two decades earlier was superior to a logarithmic function proposed by Bernoulli in 1738. Galanter returned to the topic of utility measurement in a 1990 article, reviewing efforts to measure utility and reporting several experiments aimed at determining utility functions for nonmonetary events. He noted the compatibility of his results in both this and his 1962 article with Kahneman and Tversky's (1979) prospect theory of decision. Galanter's 1990 article makes for interesting reading, offering wide-ranging comments on psychological research on utility, including critiques of some methods and of the failures of those with applied concerns to take into account the psychological value of both monetary and nonmonetary gains and losses.

The story of the evolution of thinking about decision from the objective expected-value formulation to subjective expected utility and related theories such as prospect theory is fascinating, and the role of research published in the *Journal* in this evolution has been critical. The articles reviewed, and others published in the *Journal* over the past 60 years, demonstrate the importance of psychological approaches to decision and the increasing methodological and theoretical sophistication of those approaches.

In the 1970s and following decades, the diversity of research on judgment and decision increased, and this has been reflected in the pages of the *Journal*. Other deviations from normative decision making based on objective information were studied, and the normative models themselves were studied from a psychological perspective. For example, Birnbaum (1983) examined the evidence that people neglect base rates in making judgments, arguing that an appropriate normative model for updating belief required both Bayes's theorem and an analysis of evidence interpretation in signal detection terms. For example, in the famous cab problem, experimental participants receive base rate information about cabs with different colors, eyewitness testimony about the color of a cab involved in an accident, and information about the accuracy of the witness in identifying the colors of cabs. This problem is often used to provide evidence of base rate neglect, because participants typically weigh the testimony more highly than Bayes's theorem says they should. Birnbaum pointed out that participants may apply theories of how the described circumstances would affect the reliability of a witness, thus challenging the evidence for base rate neglect. Davidson and Hirtle (1990) showed in a study of the representativeness heuristic that people are more likely to use base rate information when the they receive stereotype-discrepant information about nontarget members of a group. These studies reflect the increasing trend to examine not just how participants combine information but how they make the judgments that enter the decision process as premises.

Recently, Galotti and Tinkelenberg (2009) studied parents making decisions about first-grade placements for their children, noting that "studying everyday decision making is not a task for the timid" (p. 456). They concentrated on the early information gathering and decision structuring phases of the decision process. Their method relied on self-report measures obtained longitudinally over a period of approximately a year. Galotti and Tinkelenberg found that parents restricted the amount of information they considered, but within those constraints, their actual decisions corresponded quite well to a linear model that specified normative decisions.

These studies, and others not reviewed due to space limitations, illustrate the role of the *Journal* in the dramatic shifts in thinking about judgment and decision over the past 60 years, as understanding the cognitive processes underlying decision has taken precedence over simple comparisons of actual to normative judgments.

Problem Solving

The term *problem solving* covers a lot of territory, and in the earliest days of the *Journal* it was sometimes used to refer to processes such as identifying associates of a word while introspecting on the mental processes supporting the generation of associates. I have restricted this review to the modern sense of the term, as in the problem space hypothesis proposed by Newell, Shaw, and Simon (1958).

INSIGHT

The concept of insight was central to Gestalt psychology (e.g., Helson, 1926), and research on insight in problem solving remains popular today. The 1920s and 1930s saw a lively debate on the concept in the *Journal,* with a number of both theoretical and empirical articles on insight, often critical of the concept and its use by Gestalt theorists. For example, Fisher (1931) critiqued Köhler's use of the term *insight* as an ordinary mechanism of the mind, arguing that the instances he cited are cases of post hoc reflection on experience rather than observations of the actual mechanisms of thought. Ogden (1932) began with Köhler's classic observation of insight in problem solving by apes and argued that "insight ... states a problem rather than a solution" (p. 355). In doing so, he argued that Gestalt psychology is superior to behaviorism, which cannot even state the problem identified by the term *insight.* Ogden's view is in some ways compatible with current views, which generally hold that insight is a phenomenon to be explained rather than a mechanism to be used in explaining other phenomena. In the next issue of the *Journal,* Hartmann (1932) published a brief rejoinder in which he criticized Ogden for "the assumption that any critique of the Gestalt position, either in general or in detail, is null and void unless it first accepts the theoretical postulates on which it is based" (p. 577).

Bulbrook (1932) provided detailed protocols of people solving a number of problems designed to encourage insight or trial and error. "Our *O*s proved to be neither Thorndikean cats nor *Köhlersche Affen"* (Köhleresque apes) (p. 448). Systematic search, perceptual and gestural strategies, and hypothesis testing were all in evidence, but not blind trial-and-error or obvious flashes of insight. This study was much closer in time to Newell and colleagues' (1958) initial statement of the problem space hypothesis than current work is to that statement. In summarizing, Bulbrook wrote, "The fact is that the further experimental description and functional analysis go in the direction taken, the looser, more ambiguous, and less satisfactory the term 'insight' becomes.... In the examination of our descriptive material we have found no characteristic process, operation, form of conditioning or mode of discovery, which we could with propriety distinguish as 'insight'" (p. 453).

The phenomena suggested by Gestalt views of problem solving have continued to inspire problem-solving research. For example, Buyer and Dominowski (1989; Dominowski & Buyer, 2000) demonstrated that memory for problem solutions by participants who generate those solutions is much better than memory by participants who fail to solve the problems but are given the solutions. They suggested that this superior memory is due a restructuring process that occurs during problem solution, like the insight process discussed by Gestalt psychologists.

Fantino, Jaworski, Case, and Stolarz-Fantino (2003) presented data challenging the conventional wisdom about problem-solving set, or *Einstellung*. Participants in their study solved water jar problems, in which the goal is to measure a target quantity of water using jugs of several capacities. Two groups solved problems that could be solved using a single equation, as in the classic *Einstellung* demonstration, but one of these groups was instructed that a single rule could solve all the problems, whereas the other group had to learn the rule through experience. A third group solved problems that required different rules for each problem. Most strikingly, the instructed-rule group performed better than the other two groups when transferred to a situation in which a new rule was effective for multiple problems, and they were as likely to discover shortcuts as any other group. However, even in the induced-rule group, the *Einstellung* effect was limited to the first few transfer problems for most participants.

CHESS

Since at least the 1960s, chess has figured prominently in the study of expert performance. Cleveland (1907) published the first study of chess playing to appear in the *Journal*. He relied on his own knowledge, intuitions, and introspections about playing chess, together with references to the aficionado literature on chess, the introspections of assistants (not reported in detail), and a few references to psychological discussions of chess. His analysis ranged from speculation on the motivations for and emotional consequences of playing chess to quite detailed analyses of the cognitive processes involved. Some of Cleveland's theoretical observations sound strikingly modern; for example, he wrote, "All processes of reasoning are, as psychological facts, sequences of mental states due to shifting of the focal point of attention and to processes of association dependent thereon" (p. 291), a description that could easily be drawn from any of several modern theories of cognition. In discussing the learning of chess, he concluded that some components of skilled chess must be automatic. His proposed mechanisms for increased skill are much like those proposed in contemporary theories of skill acquisition (e.g., Anderson, 1987): "The chess player's skill is measured largely in terms of his ability to use larger and larger units of thought.... All the intermediate steps are for the moment ignored, or, in other words, 'a short circuit' has been established and the association is between the first term and the last or the total result instead of each term being revived by the one immediately preceding it" (Cleveland, 1907, p. 301).

Seven decades after Cleveland's prescient article, the analysis of chess performance in terms of memory for meaningful chunks was an active area of investigation, reflected in a pair of articles in the *Journal* by Goldin (1978, 1979). At about the same time, Engle and Bukstel (1978) published an article extending such results to the analysis of expertise in bridge. Questions about the relative roles of chunk-like knowledge, evaluation of positions, and knowledge of rules in expertise have received attention from a number of authors in the *Journal* since that time. The ability of expert chess players to remember positions was studied by Pfau and Murphy (1988), Cooke, Atlas, Lane, and Berger (1993), Saariluoma and Kalakoski (1997), and Schultetus and Charness (1999). All these authors highlighted memory skill as an important aspect of chess skill, emphasizing experts' ability to both recognize and recall meaningful game positions. For example, Schultetus and Charness argued that pattern recognition is the primary basis of chess skill. Calderwood, Klein, and Crandall (1988) explored an implication of this idea, demonstrating that time pressure had a greater effect on move quality for less skilled players, suggesting greater reliance on rapid, memory-based processes by experts. Klein and Peio (1989) used a prediction paradigm, asking skilled and novice chess players to observe expert games and predict upcoming moves. Experts were substantially more accurate, a result that Klein and Peio interpreted as supporting a recognition-based model of chess skill.

The focus on the role of memory in expertise has also been applied to domains other than chess. Hassebrock, Johnson, Bullemer, Fox, and Moller (1993) assessed memory for medical diagnosis problems at three levels of training in order to study how problem representation varies as a function of expertise. Immediately after problem solving, the groups did not differ on the amount or type of information recalled. After a 1-week delay, however, experts remembered less information but selectively recalled information relevant to the lines of reasoning used in solving the problems. Experts appeared to use diagnostic knowledge to retrieve case-specific information.

A number of authors have examined other aspects of chess skill. In addition to studying expert recognition of chess positions, Pfau and Murphy (1988) examined increases in verbal knowledge of chess with increasing skill, suggesting that expertise results from the interaction of memory skill and verbal knowledge. Holding (1989) emphasized search and evaluation, emphasizing the increase in accuracy in evaluating possible future positions with increasing skill. Reynolds (1992) also emphasized search, arguing that experts attend to more focused parts of the chess board and that their superior memory for chess positions is largely limited to these focal portions examined during search. Hassebrock et al. (1993) reported a similar finding in another domain. They assessed memory for medical diagnosis problems at three levels of training in order to study how problem representation varies as a function of expertise. Immediately after problem solving, the groups did not differ on the amount or type of information recalled. After a 1-week delay, however, experts remembered less information but selectively recalled information relevant to the lines of reasoning used in solving the problems. Experts in their study appeared to use diagnostic knowledge to retrieve case-specific information. In contrast, Yoskowitz (1991) used both chess and pseudo-chess (new rules for standard chess pieces) to examine the role of rule knowledge in early acquisition of skill, suggesting that rules play a greater role than memory for chess positions in the early development of chess skill.

Van and Wagenmakers (2005) reported a study that provides a kind of capstone to chess research in the *Journal.* They developed a psychometric test battery for assessing chess skill, including tactical components such as choosing a move from a presented board position, verbal knowledge of chess, and memory for chess positions of varying typicality. They found very good criterion validity for established standard ratings of chess skill and predictive validity for chess skill measured several years after the test battery was administered. Importantly, the accuracy and response time to select moves contributed more to prediction than did memory for chess positions, and verbal knowledge contributed very little. These results suggest that although improved memory is a consequence of increased chess skill, it is not the primary basis for such skill.

PROBLEM SOLVING AND LEARNING

In the 1950s, a number of authors considered the question of whether problem solving was involved in learning. For example, Goodnow (1955) suggested that the common but suboptimal behavior of matching in probability learning results from approaching the task as one of problem solving. She considered the interesting possibility that partial-reinforcement learning schedules be considered as cases of decision under uncertainty, in line with the work on decision and judgment discussed earlier. Participants performed isomorphic problem-solving or gambling tasks with probabilistic outcomes, making choices closer to the normative strategy of choosing the more likely outcome 100% of the time in the gambling task. Goodnow explained this result in terms of participants' likely beliefs and strategies and how they differed depending on the presentation of the task, thus providing a cognitive interpretation of what might be considered a procedure for learning in a partial reinforcement schedule.

This theme of providing cognitive explanations for learning in terms of beliefs and strategies appeared in a number of articles in the *Journal* over the next couple of decades. For example, Galanter and Smith (1958) made "a distinction ... between trial-and-error learning, on the one hand, and thinking, or sequentially integrated behavior, on the other" (p. 366). In their choice task, they argued that participants engage in thinking that consists of "constructing a model of the external world, and running this model at a faster rate than the external model" (p. 362).

Over the next couple of decades, investigators explored the role of hypothesis testing by participants in learning studies. Participants in these studies typically assigned rule-based multiattribute stimuli to categories, receiving feedback on each category assignment. Bourne (1963) reported a study in which participants reported their hypotheses on a trial-by-trial basis, demonstrating that performance—trials required to learn a concept—depended on the strategy revealed by the first hypothesis stated by the participant. The success of various strategies depended on the complexity of concepts and on how many attributes varied from one trial to the next. Andrews, Levinthal, and Fishbein (1969) provided evidence that hypothesis testing is organized by dimensions; that is, participants holding a hypothesis that correct classification is predicted by a particular value on one dimension tend to shift to a hypothesis about another attribute on the same dimension, rather than switching dimensions, after making an incorrect prediction. This tendency was not affected by the number of dimensions available. They suggested that this tendency reflected a strategy adopted to minimize memory load.

A prominent role for strategy suggests that instructions might have a powerful effect on learning, and Erickson (1971) demonstrated such an effect. He used an instructional manipulation to examine what might be considered a consequence of the tendency reported by Andrews et al., that when concept definitions are changed, shifts of attributes on a dimension (reversal shifts) are typically easier than shifts between dimensions (extradimensional shifts). Instructions succeeded in reversing this order of difficulty, suggesting that informed participants could change the pool of hypotheses from which they were sampling.

Liu (1974) also explored the role of strategies. He reported an experiment suggesting that participants adopt strategies to adjust the pool of hypotheses they sample at each stage of solving sequential (sequence construction) problems. In this study, participants solved sequential problems such as constructing word chains meeting certain criteria. Liu used a mathematical model of solution time to support a "step-squeezing" model in which participants are assumed to consider alternatives within hypothesis sets to preserve parts of the hypothesis chain they have developed before abandoning those hypotheses and starting over.

Hypothesis-testing theories of concept learning prominent in the 1970s differed dramatically in their assumptions about what information was retained by a participant after a hypothesis was disconfirmed. Halff (1975) explored these assumptions by manipulating whether the previous stimulus pair remained in view after feedback was received (i.e., after the success or failure of a hypothesis). He used a "blank trial" procedure in which a carefully chosen set of stimuli are presented on trials without feedback in order to assess the hypothesis a participant is testing. This procedure allows a researcher to verify that a participant is focusing on a single hypothesis. Halff found that the presence of the stimulus after an error, but not after a success, facilitated learning. This result supports the view that memory for previous events is crucial to the hypothesis-testing process.

Another implication of hypothesis-testing views is that the conditions of practice, not just number of trials, should affect learning. For example, Hiew (1977) conducted a concept formation study in which participants solved series of problems with rules blocked or mixed. Mixed problems resulted in longer solution latency but greater transfer to a new task. This is analogous to practice schedule effects found in motor and cognitive learning. Hiew suggested that the mechanism of this greater transfer was abstraction of a general problem-solving strategy, based on an intuitive use of truth table reasoning.

This hypothesized truth table strategy predicts that the difficulty of learning should depend on the logical structure of rules. However, Bourne (1979) examined the conditions under which concepts defined by different types of rules (conjunctive or disjunctive) were easier or harder to learn. He found that the relative difficulty of rules depends on the attributes to which those rules are applied, contrary to theories that predict rule difficulty based strictly on the inferential demands of testing the rules.

Sweller (1980) also explored the role of rule difficulty. He examined sequence effects in problem solving, showing that even very difficult rule induction problems could be solved effectively if easier previous problems encouraged induction of a rule that could be applied to the more difficult problems. He argued that positive and negative transfer could be predicted by understanding participants' hypothesis-testing behavior. Continuing the investigation of hypothesis-testing behavior, Sweller, Mawer, and Howe (1982) demonstrated that means–ends strategies resulted in less transfer than history-cued strategies in which participants use past moves as a basis for generating new moves. They suggested that means–ends strategies interfere with rule induction. A few years later, Ayres and Sweller (1990) examined the cognitive load imposed by means–ends analysis, in which problem solvers work backwards to establish appropriate subgoals. Consistent with a production system model they developed, they found that errors were concentrated in subgoal stages and that means–ends strategies were more error-prone than working-forward strategies. They concluded that the high cognitive load imposed by means–ends analysis may interfere with learning by reducing the likelihood of abstracting solution schemas.

As late as 1980, research on the role of problem solving in learning paradigms based on operant conditioning continued. Mercier and Ladouceur (1980) compared verbal operant conditioning with and without problem-solving instructions, demonstrating superior performance by participants encouraged to adopt a problem-solving approach to learning. This superiority was observed regardless of the incentive value of the reinforce and regardless of whether participants could state the rule governing reinforcement. Mercier and Ladouceur concluded that their data "argued against an automatic and direct strengthening effect of the reinforce in verbal conditioning" (p. 548).

OTHER PROBLEM-SOLVING RESEARCH
Articles published in the *Journal* have also addressed a number of other questions about problem solving. For example, Olton and Johnson (1976) attempted to determine the mechanisms of incubation by having problem solvers engage in one of eight different intervening activities during the solution process. These intervening activities were designed to encourage specific processes thought to underlie incubation, such as set breaking. They also controlled the total amount of direct work time spent on the problem. Olton and Johnson found no evidence of incubation in any of their conditions, casting doubt on the reality of the phenomenon.

Other investigators have applied ideas from earlier problem-solving research to address current topics. Garst, Kerr, Harris, and Sheppard (2002) used a classic concept formation task similar to that used by Bourne (1963) and others to examine what they called satisficing in hypothesis generation. In their first experiment, they asked their participants to generate as many rules as possible consistent with the data they were shown. One group was given an example rule as a starting point, which was sufficient to explain the observed data. That group generated fewer possible simple rules than the control group, which did not receive a rule. Similar results were found in two follow-up experiments using different procedures. They concluded that simply having a satisfactory hypothesis makes it harder to generate plausible alternative hypotheses.

Although little research on problem solving by analogy has appeared in the *Journal,* Markman and Gentner (2000) provided a detailed review of this literature. They described their structure-mapping theory of analogy, describing theoretical mechanisms and the supporting evidence. They focused on the structured nature of representations and on the roles of connectivity and semantic similarity in establishing analogical mappings. Markman and Gentner suggested that structure mapping plays a role in a broad range of cognitive tasks.

Metacognition

The term *metacognition* first appeared in the psychological literature only in the 1970s, when it was introduced by Flavell (1979). However, the questions studied in the contemporary literature on metacognition—for example, how a person's perception of his or her performance is related to actual performance—have long been of interest, and this interest is reflected in a number of early studies reported in the *Journal.* Reports of confidence or uncertainty have served as dependent variables in research on psychophysical and other types of judgment; when such reports refer to a person's own mental processes, they reflect metacognitive judgments.

The earliest report of such judgments in the *Journal* was part of a broader analysis of belief. Okabe (1910) reported an introspective study of belief, parts of which—for example, belief by the participant that they have correctly solved a mathematical equation—could be taken as concerning metacognition. Among his conclusions is that "certainty–uncertainty consciousness closely resembles that of belief–disbelief, but is in general more strongly affective" (p. 594).

Some early studies in the *Journal* examined the relationship between memory performance and confidence. Lund (1926) reported an experiment on word recognition in which participants made lexical decision judgments and reported their confidence and introspections about the judgment process. He reported that confidence did in fact vary and was positively related to performance. In summarizing his theoretical speculations, Lund wrote, "The degree of similarity which a present situation has with a previous situation, and therefore, the degree of similarity which present perceptual and associative reactions have with previous ones, determines the degree of confidence" (p. 381). Jersild (1929) reported a study in which students answered true–false questions about reading assignments and lectures, reporting their confidence in each answer. He found low correlations between confidence and actual performance but higher correlations for the confidence expressed by the same participants on two tests, suggesting that confidence was an individual trait rather than an accurate assessment of knowledge. He also found that participants were overconfident for easy ("absolutely certain") items and underconfident for difficult ("guess") items, a finding echoed in some modern studies.

Adams and Adams (1960) presented a quite modern study of metamemory, assessing confidence in the spelling of words differing in difficulty using a subjective probability scale for reporting confidence. Participants also rated their familiarity with the meanings of the words. They compared confidence to actual performance for both reproducing and recognizing spelling. They found high correlations between reported confidence and performance but systematic biases such that participants were underconfident for difficult items and overconfident for easier items. In general, calibration of confidence judgments was better for recognition than for reproduction. Overconfidence was greater for more familiar words, but this was not statistically significant.

Groninger (1979) reviewed the then-small feeling-of-knowing (FOK) literature and tested whether the FOK experience occurred only during retrieval or also during storage. He found that FOK (confidence that the word was a target) judgments made during a recognition test between study and recall predicted recall and that the quality of this prediction increased as participants became familiar with the task. These judgments were better predictors of word recall than a variety of word attributes but reflected general overconfidence. He concluded that "the feeling-of-knowing phenomenon can occur at a much earlier stage of processing than has been shown to date" (p. 55).

Since the late 1970s, more than two dozen articles reporting research on metacognition have appeared in the *Journal*. The most cited of these is a study reported by Johnson, Raye, Foley, and Foley in 1981. These authors examined reality monitoring, defined here as participants' ability to discriminate between self-generated and experimenter-provided words. They also manipulated the extent of cognitive operations required to generate items. Johnson et al. found that evoking more extensive cognitive processing increased the ability to discriminate self-from experimenter-generated words and that falsely recognized items were more frequently attributed to external sources. The finding that the nature of cognitive operations affects metacognitive accuracy has been central to the development of theory in this area.

Another focus of metacognition research has been individual differences in knowledge or ability. For example, Park, Gardner, and Thukral (1988) demonstrated that participants' level of perceived knowledge influences how they value and use new information. They managed to find 100 participants who were unfamiliar with video recorders, not having owned, used, or sought information on them, a sample that might be difficult to replicate today. This sample allowed Park et al. to manipulate both actual and perceived knowledge. In general, they found that low perceived knowledge led to more effective processing of new information. Kearney and Zechmeister (1989) demonstrated that judgments of learning difficulty made by poor associative learners were almost as accurate as those made by good associative learners, suggesting "a fundamental capability of adult learners to recognize those item characteristics that are relevant to associative learning" (p. 365).

Perhaps the most frequent topic of metacognition research published in the *Journal* is the question of what cues are used to make metacognitive judgments. For example, Calogero and Nelson (1992) provided participants in their study with base rate information about item difficulties. Participants who received base rate information appeared to adjust their FOK judgments in accord with the base rate information, and their judgments predicted performance more accurately than judgments made by participants not given base rate information, but these judgments were not significantly more accurate in predicting actual memory performance than were normative data on difficulty. They speculated about the circumstances under which FOK judgments would predict performance better than base rate data.

Carroll and Nelson (1993) examined the overlearning phenomenon, in which repetition of study items beyond a criterion increases the accuracy of FOK judgments in predicting performance. They found that a within-participant design was more sensitive to this effect than a between-participant design, suggesting that people adjust their thresholds for reporting FOK depending on the context. Widner and Smith (1996) considered participants' interpretations of the instructions given for FOK judgments, suggesting that they might focus on the feeling that the information is known or the prediction that the information can be correctly identified. They found that FOK judgments were more accurate when participants focused on the predictive aspect of the judgment. They suggested that this finding indicates the importance of task-relevant information for accurate judgments and that it is contrary to a cue familiarity account of FOK phenomena.

Florer and Allen (2000) also found evidence against a cue familiarity account. They used a short-term serial recall task with subsequent recognition test to examine the cue familiarity account of FOK judgments. In this task, short-term recall is poorer for repeated items in the strings, and Florer and Allen found that FOK judgments and recognition performance were also lower for these items, contradicting the cue familiarity account. Instead, the authors suggested, FOK is based on factors influencing recall, such as output interference.

Barnes and Dougherty (2007) used a divided-attention paradigm to examine the cues used to make global judgments of learning (JOLs) in a list-learning paradigm. They compared focused with divided attention at three stages—encoding, judgment, and retrieval—and over repeated trials. They found that participants learned to take into account the effects of divided attention on learning and that they were able to make judgments under divided attention. Their results are consistent with a cue utilization account of JOLs, and they suggest that feelings of knowing and JOLs may be based on different information.

In general, I have not included in this review studies in which confidence ratings for perceptual judgments were collected. However, in contrast to much of the literature, Petrusic and Baranski (1997) suggested that a common theoretical framework might accommodate metacognitive judgments in both perceptual and nonperceptual domains, reviewing a number of similarities in empirical results. They studied the effects of context and feedback in the calibration of confidence in perceptual judgments. Although context—the overall difficulty of a set of items—did not affect calibration, feedback improved calibration in difficult context but made it worse in easy contexts. Thompson (1998) also examined feedback and found that its effect on metamemory accuracy was limited to specific items for which feedback was received.

Several articles examined metacomprehension, participants' judgments of how well they understand text. Maki (1995) examined predictions of test performance for important and unimportant sentences, as well as for higher-order questions not specifically testing specific sentences. Predictions were most accurate for higher-order questions, but post-test confidence judgments were most accurate for questions about specific unimportant details. Johnson and Halpern (1999) and Lin, Zabrucky, and Moore (2002) compared younger and older adults. Johnson and Halpern found that that middle-aged adults better predicted memory for text material than did younger adults. Lin et al. found that both younger and older adults had more accurate metacomprehension for texts written at a moderate difficulty level than for easier or more difficult texts, with little difference in accuracy as a function of age.

As in the metacognition literature generally, most metacognition research published in the *Journal* has focused on metamemory. However, a couple of very interesting articles explored metacognition in domains in which it is rarely studied. Levin and Angelone (2008) discussed visual metacognition, reviewing research on people's understanding of the limits and illusions of visual perception and reporting the results of a questionnaire study exploring intuitions about visual perception. Anyone who has taught an introductory psychology class or a course on sensation and perception knows that naive people have a variety of misconceptions about vision, but Levin and Angelone systematically explored these misconceptions, using the Visual Metacognition Questionnaire (VMQ) they developed. The VMQ describes and illustrates situations involving detecting change, inattention blindness, the spatial character of visual attention, visual memory, and so on, and asks participants to predict their performance. For many phenomena, such as change detection and inattentional blindness, participants dramatically overpredicted performance; for other phenomena, they were fairly accurate in their beliefs. White and Kurtz (2003) published one of the very few articles on olfactory metacognition. They tested patients with olfactory dysfunctions, assessing both their beliefs about their olfactory ability and their ability to discriminate odors. They classified 42% of their participants as unaware of their olfactory losses, as indicated by overestimation or underestimation of their olfactory ability, and this proportion varied across causes of the dysfunction. Although errors in estimating ability generally were not related to age, older adults were more likely to overestimate their ability.

Conclusion

Research on the higher mental processes published in the *Journal* makes for interesting reading. It reflects both dramatic changes in perspective, method, and theory over the past 125 years and considerable consistency in the questions psychologists have found interesting. The shift to more refined empirical methods is clear, as is the rise and fall of behaviorist approaches. In some domains, clear stories are apparent. The shift from expected value to subjective expected utility formulations of decision making, and the accompanying concerns with measurement and scaling, is particularly striking. The increasing recognition of the importance of strategy and hypothesis testing in human learning is also well documented in the *Journal*, as is the debate over the role of memory in chess skill. Most intriguing in some ways are the precursors of modern views, such as Cleveland's (1907) description of mental processes in chess skill, Preston and Baratta's (1948) influential article on subjective probability, and the early metacognition studies reported by Lund (1926) and Jersild (1929).

I have spent far longer on this review project than I anticipated, in part because almost every article sent me to related literature and in part because I found myself reading many, especially early, articles that appeared alongside those that are reviewed here. The broad historical trends in these literatures, and in the field of cognitive psychology in general, extend far beyond the boundaries of the *Journal*. However, *The American Journal of Psychology* stands out from other journals in the breadth and historical depth of its content. I hope this review encourages readers to seek out some of the articles discussed here.

NOTES
Thanks to Lori Forlizzi and Christopher Stevens for helpful comments on this manuscript.

Address correspondence about this article to Richard Carlson, Department of Psychology, Penn State University, 613 Moore Building, University Park, PA 16802 (e-mail: racarlson@psu.edu).

REFERENCES
Adams, P. A., & Adams, J. K. (1960). Confidence in the recognition and reproduction of words difficult to spell. *American Journal of Psychology, 73*, 544–552.

Anderson, J. R. (1987). Skill acquisition: Compilation of weak-method problem solutions. *Psychological Review, 94*, 192–210.

Andrews, O. E., Levinthal, C. F., & Fishbein, H. D. (1969). The organization of hypothesis-testing behavior in concept-identification tasks. *American Journal of Psychology, 82*, 523–530.

Ayres, P., & Sweller, J. (1990). Locus of difficulty in multistage mathematics problems. *American Journal of Psychology, 103*, 167–193.

Barnes, K. A., & Dougherty, M. R. (2007). The effect of divided attention on global judgment of learning accuracy. *American Journal of Psychology, 120*, 347–359.

Birnbaum, M. H. (1983). Base rates in Bayesian inference: Signal detection analysis of the cab problem. *American Journal of Psychology, 96*, 85–94.

Bourne, L. E. Jr. (1963). Factors affecting strategies used in problems of concept-formation. *American Journal of Psychology, 76*, 229–238.

Bourne, L. E. Jr. (1979). Stimulus–rule interaction in concept learning. *American Journal of Psychology, 92*, 3–17.

Bulbrook, M. E. (1932). An experimental study into the existence and nature of "insight." *American Journal of Psychology, 44*, 409–453.

Buyer, L. S., & Dominowski, R. L. (1989). Retention of solutions: It is better to give than to receive. *American Journal of Psychology, 102*, 353–363.

Calderwood, R., Klein, G. A., & Crandall, B. W. (1988). Time pressure, skill, and move quality in chess. *American Journal of Psychology, 101,* 481–493.

Calogero, M., & Nelson, T. O. (1992). Utilization of base-rate information during feeling-of-knowing judgments. *American Journal of Psychology, 105,* 565–573.

Carlson, R. A., Lundy, D. H., & Yaure, R. G. (1992). Syllogistic inference chains in meaningful text. *American Journal of Psychology, 105,* 75–99.

Carroll, M., & Nelson, T. O. (1993). Effect of overlearning on the feeling of knowing is more detectable in within-subject than in between-subject designs. *American Journal of Psychology, 106,* 227–235.

Chant, S. N. F. (1933). An objective experiment on reasoning. *American Journal of Psychology, 45,* 282–291.

Cleveland, A. A. (1907). The psychology of chess and of learning to play it. *American Journal of Psychology, 18,* 269–308.

Cooke, N. J., Atlas, R. S., Lane, D. M., & Berger, R. C. (1993). Role of high-level knowledge in memory for chess positions. *American Journal of Psychology, 106,* 321–351.

Cutsforth, T. D. (1924). Synaesthesia in the process of reasoning. *American Journal of Psychology, 35,* 88–97.

Davidson, D., & Hirtle, S. C. (1990). Effects of nondiscrepant and discrepant information on the use of base rates. *American Journal of Psychology, 103,* 343–357.

Dominowski, R. L., & Buyer, L. S. (2000). Retention of problem solutions: The re-solution effect. *American Journal of Psychology, 113,* 249–274.

Edwards, W. (1953). Probability-preferences in gambling. *American Journal of Psychology, 66,* 349–364.

Edwards, W. (1954a). Probability-preferences among bets with differing expected values. *American Journal of Psychology, 67,* 56–67.

Edwards, W. (1954b). Variance preference in gambling. *American Journal of Psychology, 67,* 441–452.

Engle, R. W., & Bukstel, L. H. (1978). Memory processes among bridge players of differing expertise. *American Journal of Psychology, 91,* 673–689.

Erickson, J. R. (1971). Problem shifts and hypothesis behavior in concept identification. *American Journal of Psychology, 84,* 100–111.

Fantino, E., Jaworski, B. A., Case, D. A., & Stolarz-Fantino, S. (2003). Rules and problem solving: Another look. *American Journal of Psychology, 116,* 613–632.

Fisher, S. C. (1931). A critique of insight in Köhler's "Gestalt Psychology." *American Journal of Psychology, 43,* 131–136.

Flavell, J. H. (1979). Metacognition and cognitive monitoring: A new area of cognitive-developmental inquiry. *American Psychologist, 34,* 906–911.

Florer, F. L., & Allen, G. (2000). Feelings of knowing in the Ranschburg effect. *American Journal of Psychology, 113,* 179–198.

Franklin, C. L. (1889). On some characteristics of symbolic logic. *American Journal of Psychology, 2,* 543–567.

Galanter, E. (1962). The direct measurement of utility and subjective probability. *American Journal of Psychology, 75,* 208–220.

Galanter, E. (1990). Utility functions for nonmonetary events. *American Journal of Psychology, 103,* 449–470.

Galanter, E. H., & Smith, W. A. S. (1958). Some experiments on a simple thought-problem. *American Journal of Psychology, 71,* 359–366.

Galotti, K. M., & Tinkelenberg, C. E. (2009). Real-life decision making: Parents choosing a first-grade placement. *American Journal of Psychology, 122,* 455–468.

Garst, J., Kerr, N. L., Harris, S. E., & Sheppard, L. A. (2002). Satisficing in hypothesis generation. *American Journal of Psychology, 115,* 475–500.

Goldin, S. E. (1978). Effects of orienting tasks on recognition of chess positions. *American Journal of Psychology, 91,* 659–671.

Goldin, S. E. (1979). Recognition memory for chess positions: Some preliminary research. *American Journal of Psychology, 92,* 19–31.

Goodnow, J. J. (1955). Determinants of choice-distribution in two-choice situations. *American Journal of Psychology, 68,* 106–116.

Groninger, L. D. (1979). Predicting recall: The "feeling-that-I-know" phenomenon. *American Journal of Psychology, 92,* 45–58.

Halff, H. M. (1975). Stimulus presentation after successes and errors in concept formation. *American Journal of Psychology, 88,* 421–430.

Hartmann, G. W. (1932). Insight and the context of gestalt theory. *American Journal of Psychology, 44,* 576–578.

Hassebrock, F., Johnson, P. E., Bullemer, P., Fox, P. W., & Moller, J. H. (1993). When less is more: Representation and selective memory in expert problem solving. *American Journal of Psychology, 106,* 155–189.

Helson, H. (1926). The psychology of "Gestalt." *American Journal of Psychology, 37,* 189–223.

Helson, H. (1947). Adaptation level as a frame of reference for prediction of psychophysical data. *American Journal of Psychology, 60,* 1–29.

Hiew, C. C. (1977). Sequence effects in rule learning and conceptual generalization. *American Journal of Psychology, 90,* 207–218.

Holding, D. H. (1989). Evaluation factors in human tree search. *American Journal of Psychology, 102,* 103–108.

Jamison, D. T., & Kozielecki, J. (1968). Subjective probabilities under total uncertainty. *American Journal of Psychology, 81,* 217–225.

Jersild, A. (1929). The determinants of confidence. *American Journal of Psychology, 41,* 640–642.

Johnson, H. M. (1954). On verifying hypotheses by verifying their implicates. *American Journal of Psychology, 67,* 723–727.

Johnson, M. K., Raye, C. L., Foley, H. G., & Foley, M. A. (1981). Cognitive operations and decision bias in reality monitoring. *American Journal of Psychology, 94,* 37–64.

Johnson, S. K., & Halpern, A. R. (1999). Prediction accuracy of young and middle-aged adults in memory for familiar and unfamiliar texts. *American Journal of Psychology, 112,* 235–257.

Johnson-Laird, P., & Tagart, J. (1969). How implication is understood. *American Journal of Psychology, 82,* 367–373.

Kahneman, D., & Tversky, A. (1979). Prospect theory: An analysis of decision under risk. *Econometrica, 47,* 263–291.

Kearney, E. M., & Zechmeister, E. B. (1989). Judgments of item difficulty by good and poor associative learners. *American Journal of Psychology, 102*, 365–383.

Klein, G. A., & Peio, K. J. (1989). Use of a prediction paradigm to evaluate proficient decision making. *American Journal of Psychology, 102*, 321–331.

Komorita, S. S. (1964). A model for decision-making under risk. *American Journal of Psychology, 77*, 429–436.

Levin, D. T., & Angelone, B. L. (2008). The visual metacognition questionnaire: A measure of intuitions about vision. *American Journal of Psychology, 121*, 451–472.

Lin, L., Zabrucky, K. M., & Moore, D. (2002). Effects of text difficulty and adults' age on relative calibration of comprehension. *American Journal of Psychology, 115*, 187–198.

Liu, I. (1974). Sequential hypothesis-testing behavior. *American Journal of Psychology, 87*, 593–607.

Lund, F. H. (1926). The criteria of confidence. *American Journal of Psychology, 37*, 372–381.

Maki, R. H. (1995). Accuracy of metacomprehension judgments for questions of varying importance levels. *American Journal of Psychology, 108*, 327–344.

Markman, A. B., & Gentner, D. (2000). Structure mapping in the comparison process. *American Journal of Psychology, 113*, 501–538.

Mercier, P., & Ladouceur, R. (1980). Type of reinforcer, problem-solving set, and awareness in verbal conditioning. *American Journal of Psychology, 93*, 539–549.

Moore, H. T. (1921). The comparative influence of majority and expert opinion. *American Journal of Psychology, 32*, 16–20.

Morgan, J. J. B. (1945). Credence given to one hypothesis because of the overthrow of its rivals. *American Journal of Psychology, 58*, 54–64.

Newell, A., Shaw, J. C., & Simon, H. A. (1958). Elements of a theory of human problem solving. *Psychological Review, 65*, 151–166.

Noble, C. E. (1975). On Johnson's paradox: Hypothesis verification. *American Journal of Psychology, 88*, 537–547.

Ogden, R. M. (1932). Insight. *American Journal of Psychology, 44*, 350–356.

Okabe, T. (1910). An experimental study of belief. *American Journal of Psychology, 21*, 563–596.

Olton, R. M., & Johnson, D. M. (1976). Mechanisms of incubation in creative problem solving. *American Journal of Psychology, 89*, 617–630.

Park, C. W., Gardner, M. P., & Thukral, V. K. (1988). Self-perceived knowledge: Some effects on information processing for a choice task. *American Journal of Psychology, 101*, 401–424.

Parker, S., Stein, D., Darte, E., Schneider, B., Popper, R., & Needel, S. (1981). Utility function for money determined using conjoint measurement. *American Journal of Psychology, 94*, 563–573.

Petrusic, W. M., & Baranski, J. V. (1997). Context, feedback, and the calibration and resolution of confidence in perceptual judgments. *American Journal of Psychology, 110*, 543–572.

Pfau, H. D., & Murphy, M. D. (1988). Role of verbal knowledge in chess skill. *American Journal of Psychology, 101*, 73–86.

Phelps, A. S. (1918). The mental duet. *American Journal of Psychology, 29*, 449–450.

Politzer, G. (1981). Differences in interpretation of implication. *American Journal of Psychology, 94*, 461–477.

Pollard, P., & Evans, J. S. (1987). Content and context effects in reasoning. *American Journal of Psychology, 100,* 41–60.

Preston, M. G., & Baratta, P. (1948). An experimental study of the auction-value of an uncertain outcome. *American Journal of Psychology, 61,* 183–193.

Reynolds, R. I. (1992). Recognition of expertise in chess players. *American Journal of Psychology, 105,* 409–415.

Saariluoma, P., & Kalakoski, V. (1997). Skilled imagery and long-term working memory. *American Journal of Psychology, 110,* 177–201.

Savage, L. J. (1954). *The foundations of statistics.* Oxford, England: Wiley.

Schultetus, R. S., & Charness, N. (1999). Recall or evaluation of chess positions revisited: The relationship between memory and evaluation in chess skill. *American Journal of Psychology, 112,* 555–569.

Sweller, J. (1980). Hypothesis salience, task difficulty, and sequential effects on problem solving. *American Journal of Psychology, 93,* 135–145.

Sweller, J., Mawer, R. F., & Howe, W. (1982). Consequences of history-cued and means–end strategies in problem solving. *American Journal of Psychology, 95,* 455–483.

Thompson, W.B. (1998). Metamemory accuracy: Effects of feedback and the stability of individual differences. *American Journal of Psychology, 111,* 33–42.

Van, D. M., & Wagenmakers, E. (2005). A psychometric analysis of chess expertise. *American Journal of Psychology, 118,* 29–60.

Weld, H. P., & Danzig, E. R. (1940). A study of the way in which a verdict is reached by a jury. *American Journal of Psychology, 53,* 518–536.

White, T. L., & Kurtz, D. B. (2003). The relationship between metacognitive awareness of olfactory ability and age in people reporting chemosensory disturbances. *American Journal of Psychology, 116,* 99–110.

Widner, R. L., & Smith, S. M. (1996). Feeling-of-knowing judgments from the subject's perspective. *American Journal of Psychology, 109,* 373–387.

Yoskowitz, J. (1991). Chess versus quasi-chess: The role of knowledge of legal rules. *American Journal of Psychology, 104,* 355–366.

REASONING

SYNAESTHESIA IN THE PROCESS OF REASONING

THOMAS D. CUTSFORTH
University of Oregon

The investigation here reported is a continuation of the work on the synaesthesia of a blind subject commenced by Wheeler[1] in 1920 and carried on jointly since then by Wheeler and Cutsforth.[2] The object of these studies has been to make an intensive survey of the mental content of a highly synaesthetic subject, and to compare his mental content with an asynaesthetic subject as check observer. During the earlier part of the investigation an asynaesthetic blind subject was available whose detailed introspections could be compared with the data on synaesthetic processes.

In the present investigation the author was, as before, the synaesthetic subject. In the absence of a trained and asynaesthetic blind subject as check observer, comparative data were obtained from introspections by R. H. Wheeler. The material consisted of analogies, absurdities, simple and difficult abstract problems, all of which had been selected for the purpose of initiating reasoning processes of varying length and complexity. Analogies such as "table is to furniture as dog is to?" or "city is to town as elephant is to?" were designed to initiate reasoning processes of a minimum complexity. Of a slightly more complex nature, perhaps, were the processes of reasoning in locating the absurd features of such statements as: "The road from my house to the store is down hill all the way to the store and down hill all the way back home." Among the simpler problems of a more abstract nature were the following: "If an electric fan were attached to the rear of a boat and the air current from the fan directed toward the sail, would the boat move?" "Does the water line of a boat rise or fall as the boat passes from fresh to salt water?" Finally, more difficult problems were employed, such as: "Justify this statement: 'A first cause is logically inconceivable';" "Justify the statement: 'Being is doing'."

Any problem was discarded whose solution was stereotyped for the reason that the material happened to be too familiar or too easy. The results upon which the following discussion is based were gathered from data on 25 successful problems for the synaesthetic $O(A)$, and 20 from the check $O(W)$. The problems were presented to the O orally, with the following instructions: "I shall present a problem to you. Solve it as rapidly as you can and then give as complete an introspective account as possible of your mental processes." The experimental work was performed under optimal laboratory conditions and with the usual precautions employed in an introspective study.

The following are typical introspective data.

Observer A. Problem: Table is to furniture as dog is to what? Response: animal. "As *E* said 'table' my consciousness of the word consisted first of a fan-shaped and yellowish-black cloud appearing in the center of the visual field and moving immediately upward and to the right into the periphery; and secondly, of a fragmentary visual image of a table, with one distinct corner pointing toward me. The first image was a synaesthetic consciousness of *E's* voice. The second image came into the visual field from the right and beneath the first image; it was colored a faint yellow, partly from the color of pressure sensation, and partly from the dull drab of the word, table. The resulting color was a light gray-brown. From this point on, the synaesthetic awareness of *E's* voice did not enter into the perception of the problem. Next there appeared a synaesthetic image, bright brown in color, which shaped itself in the form of bars, criss-crossed. It took its place beyond the corner of the visualized table, but within the limits of the angle formed by the two visible table-edges. This was my consciousness of the word, furniture. Between these two sets of imagery for table and for furniture there developed a triangular patch of white, frosty brightness. This meant to me the relationship 'is to.' While it is difficult to describe this latter experience, its mental content was simple. In appearance this frosty-white patch was a structural link between the imagery of table and furniture, relating them spatially at the apex and openings of an angle. For the moment my visual attention centered itself upon this angle, which shortly tended to open a little wider. These latter experiences constituted the anticipation of the meaning 'genus-species.' Then, immediately beyond this angular form, appeared synaesthetic visual imagery of the word, dog—a smoky-blue bar. This changed almost at once into the greyer blue of the abstract concept, dog. With lightning-like rapidity and with no conscious purpose, the frosty-white and triangular image of an 'is to'-relationship developed just beyond the color-patch which stood for dog. This constituted an anticipation of the response. Attention lingered for a moment at the opening of this newly formed angle. No color filled this space. It was a neutral grey. My attention then returned to the first part of the analogy, present to consciousness in terms of an angular form with the color for table at the apex and for furniture at the right of the opening. The color for dog took the place of the color for table at the apex of this form. In terms of eye-movement and shift of visual regard from dog to furniture and back again, I searched for a response-word which might have had the same relation to dog as furniture had to table. My attention would also shift to a void place—neutral grey—to the left of the coloration for furniture where the response-imagery should appear. After a brief hesitation of this sort there appeared, without warning, a yellow synaesthetic image for 'animal.' This yellow patch was my response just as the *word*, animal, would be your response. I then became conscious of vocal-motor imagery for the first time in this experiment. I was trying to translate the yellow synaesthetic imagery into words. This vocal-motor imagery was synaesthetic. The problem for me was solved with the appearance of the yellow visual imagery for animal."

Observer A. Problem: A first cause is logically inconceivable. Response interpreted into words: Correct; a cause is always the effect of a cause. "I perceived the word, first, in terms of visual attention to the 'one'-section of my digits number form. *E* hesitated for an instant in reading the problem, during which time the remainder of the number form was rapidly rising in focality. Then, in response to the word, cause, there was very rapid eye-movement to the right and slightly upward, consciousness of which came to me in terms of a black streak which contained numerous internal movements resembling tiny currents of rain-water running down a window-pane. This experience meant 'cause.' The meaningfulness of this imagery lay in the rapid fashion with which the movement appeared and in the blackness. Out at the end of this movement (for, at the time, the experience meant to me 'movement' and not 'streak') there was nothing in visual attention save neutral grey. For a brief time the visual line of regard wandered over this blank area, turning back from time to time to the region where the imagery of 'first' had gone, and was just fading out. Here there appeared a faded-out, brickish-red-brown, synaesthetic image which by its color meant 'effect.' From this point on visual synaesthetic imagery began to move about rapidly. The imagery which stood for 'effect' slid over as if pushed into the position of the former imagery of 'first', whereupon this latter imagery lost its whiteness—a color which meant 'one'—and took on a faded-out brown. In this fashion the meaning, first cause, had turned into the meaning, effect. There was no attempt to utilize this imagery further. Synaesthetic imagery of 'one' together with eye-movement had meant 'first cause.' When no change came over this imagery at the outset, and eye-movement shifted to a place just below it where there appeared the change of coloration just described, the problem had been solved, implicitly. The temporal and spatial relations of this synaesthetic imagery meant 'cause is the effect of a cause.' The reddish image of 'effect' blotted out the whitish image of 'first cause.' Immediate relaxation set in, and the flow of imagery pertaining to the problem stopped."

Observer W. Problem: Justify the statement that being is doing. Response: Isn't true: cannot be justified. "Consciousness of *E*'s voice at first focal in auditory terms, together with marked attention to and recognition of the words 'being' and 'doing.' Before attention had entirely left the auditory perception of *E*'s voice—while auditory qualities were tapering off in consciousness—there developed a very sudden and rapid comprehension of the problem-situation. The first stage of this was a fleeting visualization of the word, being, in front of me and slightly to the left, typewritten and projected upon a blurred brown and black background. Just to the right and on the same line with the word, being, appeared the other word, doing. Momentarily there was a rapid shift of the visual line of regard from one word to the other, left to right, with attentional emphasis upon the 'ing' part of each word. This was the first stage, or a consciousness which failed to develop further just at this time, namely, that both words had to do with something dynamic. At this juncture there was a momentary tendency to relax, a motor attitude of acceptance of the solution. Apparently, I had taken my beginning recognition of the meaning, dynamic, as a solution of the problem. But this tendency to relax was suddenly interrupted. Attention returned, visually, to the words again, and with a very rapid sweep of the line of regard across the word, doing, there appeared the syncopated verbal imagery 'doing is action,' 'the real is action.' In this imagery hardly more than the word 'doing,' the 'act' of the first 'action' and the word 'real' stood out with any degree of clearness. Then completely relaxed and attention slumped. Could not progress any farther for a time. There was a developing consciousness that the problem had not been solved; could not say why; this was a motor attitude of questioning, together with a verbal repetition of the problem several times and tendencies to frown. No meanings developed. Verbal imagery seemed detached and meaningless, when suddenly I found myself visualizing the word, being, in large black and white letters in space before me, followed at once by focal auditory-verbal and visual imagery of the word 'state.' There was exceedingly rapid eye-movement from one to the other. This entire procedure was interpreted to mean 'being is static.' Then there was flashy visual imagery of the first part of the word, becoming; very rapid and syncopated vocal-motor-auditory imagery, 'becoming-action.' then implicitly meaning and later explicitly interpreted to mean, 'it is becoming which is action (not being).' Meanwhile there was a very marked growth of bodily strains, particularly about the throat and chest, a tendency to sit more erectly in the chair, followed by a return of the visual line of regard to focal, visual imagery of the word, 'doing'. This sequence implicitly meant that doing belongs with becoming. There was then a complete relation, as if the problem had been solved. Then the meaning developed: 'Isn't so.' verbally and with slight return of visual attention to the position in space occupied previously by the two words, being and doing. This was followed by a momentary tenseness with verbal imagery, 'mistook being for becoming;' whereupon there was set up a long train of very clear-cut vocal-motor-auditory processes: 'It is becoming which is action, or doing; it is not being which is action.' Meanwhile attention was turning toward the task of introspection, and the final meaning developed visually and verbally, 'to become means to do,' 'being means simply to be.' With this came a motor attitude of acceptance."

Summary of Introspective Data

For practical purposes we shall divide the process of reasoning into two developmental stages: (1) comprehension of the problem; (2) development of the solution. The second stage involves, characteristically, the application of an abstract concept to the present situation.

A's procedure consisted first of perceiving *E*'s voice in terms of visual, synaesthetic imagery. The color, behavior and form of this imagery were invariably determined in part by the quality of *E*'s voice and in part by outstanding letters of the words. Secondly, there very rapidly developed the meaning of the problem, likewise in terms of synaesthetic imagery, and generally with the aid of a 'reasoning form' or some schema by means of which the synaesthetic imagery took on definite spatial relationships. Thirdly, *A* then proceeded toward a solution by altering or modifying this schematic and synaesthetic imagery. A solution invariably consisted of fitting visual imagery of the appropriate shape and color into his schema, a process which always involved easily observed eye-movements, changes in the line of regard, and highly focal movements of imagery. These latter movements always contained a certain amount of blackness, which represented kinaesthesis.

Both in comprehending a problem and in solving it meanings accrued to the color, spatial relationships and mobility of synaesthetic imagery. As a datum of consciousness the meaningfulness of an experience was referred to the mobility of synaesthetic imagery. The development of a 'form' was an important feature in the comprehending of any problem as well as in solving it. For example, *A*'s procedure in completing the analogy: City is to town as elephant is to what? began with the schematization of the problem in the form of an angle with its apex in his direction. Colored imagery, meaning 'city,' took its position within the apex of the angle. Another blotch of color, meaning 'town.' took its place at the opening of the angle. Between these spatialized images appeared the frosty-white color which always meant an 'is to'-relationship. But no sooner had all this imagery appeared than the fact stood out, in terms of visual attention, that this arrangement of imagery did not fit the analogy. City was at the small end of the angle and town at the large end, while a city is generally larger than a town. From this point on *A* found it necessary to reinterpret the entire problem by rearranging his schematic imagery. The opening of the angle closed in and the apex widened out, thus reversing the situation. It was in this fashion that meanings developed in terms of image-behavior. *A* then constructed a second angular form in which elephant appeared at the opening of the angle. The process of searching for the final answer consisted in trying to fit some color into the apex of this angle. As usual the response did not appear in verbal terms but in patches or clouds of synaesthetic coloration. Various species of animals appeared in terms of synaesthetic imagery, localized beyond and above the position of the angular schema. The fact that none of this colored imagery migrated to the apex of the angle, and the subsequent disappearance of the entire schema, constituted a failure to solve the problem. *A* then found himself reattending to the schema by means of downward eye-movements. At the apex of this reconstructed angle there developed a patch of neutral grey which meant 'nothing,' and to which *A* responded in verbal fashion with the word 'nothing.'

The process of arriving at a conclusion in such cases consisted of a progressive course of visual, synaesthetic imagery whose spatial arrangements, coloration and movement were implicitly meaningful. That is, they functioned as meanings without a conscious recognition of the meaning. The schema acted as a core. If visual imagery distorted the schema, the solution of the problem was delayed. In other words, if a conclusion was to be reached, the problem-form must have developed and operated characteristically, smoothly, without misplacement of imagery and without conflicting movements of imagery. The use of problem-forms seemed to be a means of attenuating and mechanizing the operation of visual imagery. It provided for economy of attention and facilitated the use of abstractions. One complex situation could be associated with another with marked facility. The entire procedure of using these forms was *A*'s substitute for the more common methods of attenuation and mechanization that are made possible by the use of verbal imagery.

A's procedure in solving the simpler problems not presented in the form of analogies was quite similar to that described above. In the boat and fan problem the conclusion that air-pressure from the fan impinging against the sail would not move the boat but would bend or break the sail appeared in the very simple visual imagery of seeing the sail bend over. The instant the sail was seen to bend, *A* relaxed. The *Aufgabe* had been fulfilled. Before the solution could be explained to another person, however, it was necessary to elaborate upon this mental content.

In solving the more complex and philosophical problems we still find this marked tendency to schematize and simplify. For example, in the first-cause problem meanings first developed as in the simpler problems. The solution consisted in the use of domino-like forms, colored to mean causes and effects. Relationships were present to

A's consciousness in terms of movements of these forms. A segment or section colored to mean 'cause' moved ahead, taking the place of the segment colored to mean 'effect.' To the left of this series of moving patches appeared a section colored to mean 'first cause.' That there is no such first cause, logically, came to *A* in the reddish-brown color which took the place of the 'first' cause, moving it toward the right. Implicitly this meant a solution of the problem. Explicitly this was interpreted by means of verbal-synaesthetic imagery 'a cause is always the effect of a previous cause.'

In every instance of such use of moving forms watery grey marks of kinaesthesis bordering the edges of variously shaped colorations gave to the experience a synaesthetic-kinaesthetic character. In certain instances the kinaesthetic symbols resembled comet-like streamers trailing behind the moving forms.

W's procedure in reasoning did not differ functionally from *A*'s. *W* comprehended the problem by means of auditory-visual perceptions, incipient verbal processes, and motor attitudes of familiarity or acceptance. He solved his problems in terms of fleeting schematizations, vocal-motor imagery, visual-verbal imagery and kinaestheses of recognizing. As with *A* certain meanings failed to develop explicitly, yet the problem was solved; *i.e.,* the reagent relaxed as if he had explicitly solved the problem. For example, in the being-doing problem, eye-movement from the visualized word 'being' to the visualized word 'state' at its right meant implicitly in this setting and connection that 'being' was synonymous with 'state.' But the explicit relation, synonymous, came to consciousness only with the appearance of additional imagery. In *A*'s case the majority of meanings were implicit. Images behaved as if they constituted fully conscious meanings. A maturing process, however, was necessary before these implicit meanings became recognized data of consciousness.

The greatest difference between *W*'s and *A*'s experiences in reasoning lies in the patterns of mental contents used. In *W* auditory, kinaesthetic and other non-visual qualities became focalized and operated as such along with various motor attitudes. In *A* mental contents were confined to the visual modality with the exception of those vague, indescribable sensory experiences with which the synaesthetic imagery was associated. On the other hand there are numerous resemblances in the mental processes of *A* and *W*. Both reagents used visual schemata. *W* was synaesthetic in the sense that visualizations of words oftentimes enriched his auditory-verbal perceptions. Both *O*s solved their problems in implicit fashion without definitely recognizing the meanings of their own mental processes, as long as interpretative periods failed to develop. Both found that such interpretative periods as did develop extended into their introspective procedure. Both found that implied meanings matured in terms of incipient motor reactions—motor attitudes of familiarity and acceptance together with verbal imagery on *W*'s part, and visual-synaesthetic verbal imagery with eye-movement on *A*'s part.

The process of reasoning in both Os has suffered a short-cutting in its logical steps, so that the noting of similarities, the relating of one situation with another, the transition from simple to complex meanings, shifting from one logical step to another and the like all take place in terms of shiftings in the line of visual regard from one part of a schema to another, or in a change in size of colored imagery, or in eye-movement from one focalized region to another. This short-cutting means that, unless an anticipated stage in reasoning develops rapidly, the preceding stage upon which it is based may vanish before the succeeding step matures sufficiently to carry on the process. In this way, if one set of imagery disappears before its successor appears, the entire process of reasoning is halted. Frequently the process of reasoning took place so rapidly, in this fashion, that the individual did not have time to interpret the meaning of what he was doing. He relaxed as if he had solved a problem without knowing what the problem was that he had solved.

In both Os logical steps were a matter of mobility of imagery—the change from one image to another, involving shifts in position and size. There were found no imageless processes or relational elements.

By far the most complex part of A's process of reasoning had to do with the conscious identification of meanings. This process of identification may be called the transition from implicit to explicit meaning. After a fashion A identifies the meanings, implicit in his behaving colored imagery, by attending to the changes which there take place. Because A is so dominantly visual, this consciousness of change turns out to be hardly more than attention to an altering of position or to an increase in brightness and size. Such changes, however, are very numerous and complex. On the other hand W identified implicit meanings, in a general way, by having recourse to motor attitudes of familiarity, and in a concrete fashion by means of verbal imagery together with focal attention upon a particular detail of his visual or other concrete imagery. Only when the process of identification is extremely sudden, vigorous and complex do kinaesthetic processes function in A as they do in W.

Here we find an interesting difference between A and W. While in both Os implicit meanings become explicit by processes of elaboration, W's procedure is always kinaesthetic and A's procedure is always visual. While W's contents become motor in responding to meanings, A's remain visual although some change must always take place in the visual imagery. For example, familiarity in W's case is a motor attitude; in A's case it is an enlargement and brightening of a synaesthetic visual image. W refines his meanings by verbal processes. A refines his meanings by changing the visual setting of a colored synaesthetic image. In W's case difficult identifications of meaning are strongly verbal. In A's case they are strongly eye-motor.

Certainty, uncertainty, doubt, acceptance and rejection do not consist of motor attitudes in A as in W, unless they rise to a very high degree of intensity and complexity. Like familiarity, they are represented in terms of image-behavior. Certainty, for example, consists of a definite standing-out, a focalization of the brightness of visual synaesthetic imagery together with an increase in qualitative detail. Motor phenomena are here confined to focalized eye-movements of scrutinizing these changes. Uncertainty consists of searching movements of the eyes and of changes in the line of regard when synaesthetic imagery fails to mature in any given situation. Doubt is like uncertainty until it becomes intense, when bodily kinaestheses develop. But at this point a peculiar thing happens. The instant the attitude becomes kinaesthetic, the synaesthetic visual imagery by means of which A becomes conscious of this attitude either blurs or entirely blots out the visualized object of the doubt. This fact holds quite as well for all the motor attitudes in their intense forms. This explains why localized bodily kinaestheses play so small a rôle in A's consciousness. Their presence is invariably a condition for the obliteration of any consciousness of the object. The synaesthetic visual imagery aroused in the attitude claims the O's attention to the exclusion of all else at the time. In this way motor attitudes obscure A's thinking and even prevent the normal course of imagery.

Acceptance consists of a very slight nod of the head, a leaning forward toward the visual field, and the sudden dropping of projected imagery toward the lower portions of the visual field. Rejection is a rising of imagery in the visual field with a slight upward jerk of the head or an incipient tendency to tilt the head backward. In case the kinaestheses of either attitude become widespread or intense, A's attention is claimed by the visual synaesthetic imagery of the resulting strains. The first stage of this shift is the appearance of very active, black-brown synaesthetic representations of kinaesthesis along the borders of projected visual imagery. The second stage is the focalization of visualized bodily strains, localized upon the body. A finds it impossible to attend to these latter strains and maintain imagery in the projected visual field; hence the interference of motor attitudes with projected visual imagery used in carrying on a process of thought.

It is interesting to note that there is a marked difference between a synaesthetic visual image detached from its indescribable sensory associate and one attended by such an associate. The former is invariably static, in the sense that there is no visual disturbance within it. It is motionless, internally. For example, A may have an auditory image of a locomotive whistle; but that it is an auditory experience, in meaning, is merely a matter of subsequent and explicit interpretation from its setting and context. On the other hand, A may experience an auditory image of a locomotive whistle with the auditory meaning present. One feature alone identifies the experience as auditory. It is a certain dynamic aspect of the image. Within its own boundaries there takes place a continuous disturbance likened to the swirling movements of smoke rising from a chimney. The image appears phenomenologically as a seething mass of amorphous coloration. It is this dynamic feature of the imagery which gives to it the quality of meaningfulness, and is traceable to kinaesthesis.

The act of attending, in A's case, is a visual act whose kinaesthetic features are usually confined to eye-strain and movement, both of which are present to A's consciousness as whirlings, spirals and lines of various degrees of blackness, all projected into the visual field. For this reason it often happens that the facts of eye-movement and strain are not noticed or are given little attention.

Summary and Conclusions

There were no imageless or non-sensory contents of consciousness either in A or in W. In A's case no reasoning takes place in the absence of synaesthetic imagery. Synaesthetic imagery is an invariable and an essential component in the development of meaning. Under the *Aufgabe* to solve problems, relationships develop by means of problem-forms and in the shifting of synaesthetic colorations in these forms. Logical steps develop in terms of changes in spatial relationships of imagery, changes in coloration, and in movements of the line of regard. There is found no structural criterion for reasoning beyond a uniformity in the use of schemata. The functional criterion of reasoning consists in the application of a concept to a present problem. We were not interested in making a contribution to the process of reasoning as such. We were merely interested in tracing, further, the rôle of synaesthesia. As in all of our other experiments, no functional differences were found between our synaesthetic and asynaesthetic data. In connection with the process of reasoning we have pointed out that the difference between implicit and explicit meaning holds in reasoning as well as in the simple development of meaning.[3]

We find, in reasoning, no exception to the general rules laid down in our previous researches; that, so far as observer A is concerned, synaesthesia is a mechanism in the normal development and use of meaning; that synaesthesia is not an extraneous form of association; that it is essential to the cognitive activities of the subject who possesses it because it is the only structural tool he has of comprehending meanings; that it varies from any ordinary process of perception or conception only in the type of imagery which dominates and in the degree to which the imaginal component dominates the sensory component; and that synaesthesia is not alone a perceptual phenomenon. It has to do with the development of meaning, and is quite as conceptual as it is perceptual. It pervades the subject's entire mental life.

NOTES

1. *Uni. of Ore. Pubs.*, 1, No. 5, 1920; *Psych. Rev.*, 27, 1920, 313–322.

2. *Uni. of Ore. Pubs.*, 1, No. 10, 1922; *Journ. of Exp. Psychol.*, 4, 1921, 448–468; *Psychol. Rev.*, 29, 1922, 212–220; this JOURNAL, 33, 1922, 361–384.

3. R. H. Wheeler, The Development of Meaning, this JOURNAL, 33, 1922, 231.

HOW IMPLICATION IS UNDERSTOOD

P. N. JOHNSON-LAIRD and JOANNA TAGART
University College London, England

Conditional sentences of the form "if p then q" are often difficult to evaluate, as students of logic well know. The conditional is clearly true when both antecedent (p) and consequent (q) are true, and false when the antecedent is true but the consequent false. But what truth-value should be assigned when the antecedent is false? Logicians, working with a propositional calculus that permits only values of truth or falsity, stipulate that the implication is true in this case—regardless of the truth-value of the consequent. However, it seems that the conditional sentence might fail to do justice to this notion of *material* implication.

Conditional sentences have been found to present difficulties to both children and adults. Matalon and Peel suggest that children tend to interpret the conditional as a material equivalence ("if and only if p then q"), which is true when antecedent and consequent have the same truth-value and false when their values are different.[1] Wason, however, argues that adults do not treat the conditional in a truth-functional manner: they consider it to be *irrelevant* when its antecedent is false.[2] For example, when someone says, "if it's raining, then I'm going to the cinema," the statement is neither true nor false but merely irrelevant if in fact it is *not* raining. The layman is unlikely to consider the statement to be true just because it is not raining. Indeed, logicians have long recognized, and argued about, this way of interpreting conditional sentences.[3]

The question naturally arises as to the extent to which the interpretation of implication is influenced by the manner of its expression. The present experiment was designed to examine the effect of statements of these types:

1. If p then q.
2. There isn't p, if there isn't q.
3. Either there isn't p, or there is q (or both).
4. There is never p without there being q.

To the logician, these sentences may be interpreted as expressing material implication.[4] On Wason's hypothesis, however, we expected that Sentence 1 would be

TABLE I. Predicted Classifications of the Four Types of Sentence

Sentence type	Situation			
	pq	p$\bar{q}$	$\bar{p}$q	$\bar{p}\bar{q}$
1. If p then q.	T	F	?	?
2. Not–p if not–q.	?	F	?	T
3. Not–p or q.	T	F	T	T
4. Never p without q.	T	F	T	T

Note: T, F, and ?, respectively, denote judgments of truth, falsity, and irrelevance; $\bar{p}$ denotes not–p.

considered irrelevant to any situation that falsified its antecedent. Similarly, Sentence 2, which was derived from the contrapositive "if not q, then not p," would also be considered irrelevant when its antecedent is false, *i.e.* when q is true. But Sentences 3 and 4 were not conditionals: they lack the conditional term *if*, and it was predicted that they would be treated as expressing material implication and elicit fewer judgments of irrelevancy. It will be noted that Sentence 3 contains the term *either* which tends to suggest exclusive disjunction[5] but that this is countermanded by the presence of *or both*, which is an explicit statement of inclusive disjunction. The predicted classifications are summarized in Table I.

There are a number of ways in which an antecedent or consequent may be falsified. For example, an antecedent like "if there's a letter A," which was used in the present experiment, can be falsified by the occurrence of a letter B, or of a geometrical shape, or of nothing whatsoever. Logically, these would be equivalent falsifications; psychologically, they might not be equivalent. This point was examined by using a suitable selection of stimuli.

METHOD

Each S was shown an array of stimuli and a sentence referring to them. The S's task was to consider each stimulus in turn and to decide whether it indicated that the sentence was true or false, or was irrelevant to the truth-value of the sentence. Ss served as their own controls and performed the task with the four different sentences expressing implication. The order of presentation of the sentences was counterbalanced over Ss: each of the 4! possible orders was used once.

Materials

The sentences presented were variations of the four basic types: *e.g.* (1) If there is an A on the left, then there is a 7 on the right. (2) There isn't an A on the left, if there isn't a 7 on the right. (3) Either there isn't an A on the left, or there is a 7 on the right (or both). (4) There is never an A on the left without there being a 7 on the right. In order to reduce residual effects, the numbers and letters in each sentence that S received, and the corresponding arrays of stimuli, were different. There were four such sets of material, involving different letters and numbers, and their order of presentation was independently counterbalanced over the Ss. The 16 sentences (4 types × 4 contents) were typed in capital letters on separate 6 × 2 in. cards.

Each set of stimuli consisted of 16 4 × 2 in. cards which were divided into two halves by a heavy ink line. On the left of the line there was a letter (either the one mentioned in the sentence or one other letter), or a geometrical shape, or nothing whatsoever; on the right of the line there was a number (either the one mentioned in the sentence or one other number), or the geometrical shape, or nothing whatsoever. Four such sets of stimuli were constructed with different numbers, letters, and shapes.

Procedure

The first set of stimuli was spread out in an arbitrary array in front of S, and the general purpose of the experiment was described. The S was told that although any stimulus must fall into one of the three classificatory categories ('true,' 'false,' 'irrelevant'), he must not assume that there would necessarily be cards in all three categories. When S understood what he had to do, the stimuli were gathered together and shuffled. S was told that he was going to classify the cards one at a time, each card being placed in an appropriate pile, and that he would be timed. S was timed from the moment that he received the sentence until he had completed the classification of the stimuli. The sentence remained on view throughout the classification. The subsequent classifications followed the same procedure except that the initial display of stimuli was omitted.

Subjects

Twenty-four Ss were individually tested. They were all students at University College London, and native speakers of English.

RESULTS

There were four stimuli which were crucial in evaluating the results. They consisted, for a sentence of the form "if there's an A …, then there's a 7 …," of the items A7, A8, B7, and B8, *i.e.* pq, p$\bar{\text{q}}$, $\bar{\text{p}}$q, and $\bar{\text{p}}\bar{\text{q}}$. Table II shows the six common classifications of these stimuli, and the frequencies with which they occurred for each type of sentence. None of the remaining classifications occurred more than twice throughout the whole experiment. There were 28 different types of classification altogether, 6 common and 22 miscellaneous ones, out of a total of 81 possible classifications.

The most frequent classification, for Sentences 1, 2, and 3, was the predicted one; and the actual frequencies were all significant ($p < .01$), assuming independent classifications, on binomial tests based conservatively upon the actual number of different types of classification for each sentence. Contrary to expectation, Sentence 4 tended to be classified in the same way as Sentence 1. Fifteen Ss produced the same classification for these two sentences, whereas there were only four other occasions when an S produced the same classification for two sentences. The chance probability of obtaining the same classification for Sentences 1 and 4, with 2 and 3 being different and different from one another, is conservatively 1/28. Clearly, the similarity of the classifications of Sentences 1 and 4 was not due to chance.

The mean number of 'irrelevant' judgments of the 16 stimuli and the mean classification times are given in Table III. The difference between the sentences of the number of 'irrelevant' judgments was significant on a Friedman analysis of variance ($\chi^2_r = 32.3, p < .001$). Sentences 1 and 4 tended to elicit 'irrelevant' judgments when their antecedents were false, and this was also the case to a lesser extent for Sentence 2. There was no tendency in any condition for 'irrelevant' judgments to increase

TABLE II. Classifications of the Four Crucial Stimuli and Classification Frequencies of Occurrence for Each Type of Sentence

	Stimuli				Sentence type				
	pq	p̄q	p̄q	p̄q̄	1	2	3	4	Total
Common classifications	T	F	?	?	19	1		14	34
	T	F	T	T	1	1	8	3	13
	?	F	?	T		5		5	
	F	F	T	T		2	4		6
	F	F	T	?		1	2		3
	T	F	?	T		2		1	
Miscellaneous classifications					4	12	10	6	32
Totals					24	24	24	24	96

Note: Miscellaneous classifications are those which did not occur more than twice throughout the whole experiment.

TABLE III. Mean Number of 'Irrelevant' Judgments and Mean Classification Times for Each Type of Sentence

	Sentence type			
	1	2	3	4
'Irrelevant' judgments	10.2	5.1	1.6	9.3
Classification times (in sec.)	45	96	107	60

when falsification was due to a geometrical shape or a 'blank' rather than to a letter or a number. On this point the Ss' rationality was vindicated.

The classification times for the four sentences were also significantly different on a Friedman analysis of variance ($\chi^2_r = 34.5$, $p < .001$). Although there was a significant learning effect for classification times ($p < .003$, Jonckheere group test for predicted trend), there was no such effect for logical accuracy.

DISCUSSION

This experiment showed that the way in which implication is expressed exerts a decisive influence upon what it is understood to denote. When expressed in the form of a conditional "if p then q" or "not p if not q" it was, as predicted, treated in a non-truth-functional manner. Unexpectedly, the same interpretation—in which stimuli falsifying the antecedent were regarded as irrelevant—was elicited by the sentence "there is never p without q." Hence, the term *if* is by no means necessary to elicit the non-truth-functional interpretation; and in the absence of an account of the semantics of these sentences, such necessary conditions remain obscure. Similarity, it seems likely that *if* cannot be taken as an unequivocal marker of the antecedent of conditionals: a sentence of the form "p only if q" is likely to receive the same interpretation as "if p then q." To what extent is the non-truth-functional interpretation due to the implicit invitation to classify stimuli as irrelevant? Performance on the disjunctive sentence suggests that Ss were able to resist the 'irrelevant' category, and it is plausible to assume that the classifications did reflect the spontaneous interpretations of the sentences. Likewise, it seems improbable that the specific content of the sentences and stimuli should have exerted any major distorting influence upon performance.

The sentence which was most often classified as material implication was the disjunction. This was never treated as exclusive disjunction, but an interesting error proved most persistent. Such was the force of the phrase "either there isn't p ..." that a number of Ss produced a truth-functional classification appropriate to the simple proposition "not p" (see Table II).

The manner in which the conditionals were interpreted, considered in conjunction with the findings of Matalon and Peel,[6] raises certain difficulties for Piaget's account of intellectual development. Preadolescent children tend to treat conditionals as expressions of material equivalence; adolescents at the level of propositional operations treat them as expressions of material implication; yet, undergraduates in the present experiment failed to treat them as any sort of truth-functional connective. Piaget believes that an individual tests a putative causal relation by expressing it in the form "if p then q" and then searching for its counterexample, formed by negating the material implication.[7] But adults evidently do not readily interpret "if p then q" as material implication. Even if they did, further doubt is cast upon Piaget's position by an unpublished experiment by Wason and Johnson-Laird, in which subjects were presented with four cards bearing values of p, p̄, q, and q̄. They were told that every card had a value of p or p̄ on one side, and q or q̄ on the other side; and they were asked to choose those cards which it was necessary to turn over to test whether a given conditional rule was true or false. There was, indeed, a consistent tendency for subjects to choose the cards which fulfilled the antecedent: p in the case of "if p then q," and q̄ in the case of "if not q then not p." However, subjects were reluctant to choose those cards which falsified the consequent, especially in the case of "if p then q." Yet such cards are a required choice on any reasonable interpretation of the conditional, including even the non-truth-functional interpretation of the present experiment.

Such a result makes a stark contrast with Piaget's views, and with the findings of Stewart and Hill that adults and children correctly evaluate inferences of the form "if p then q; not q, therefore not p."[8] It would seem therefore that there are crucial psychological differences between *making* inferences and merely *evaluating* them. Not only do Ss fail to make the inference in the card-turning test, but their failure, as Wason has shown, is resistant to a number of "therapeutic" procedures.[9]

Finally, we may ask how implication is best expressed in the English language. There is no readily available answer to this question: we are faced with a dilemma. On the one hand, disjunction yields an implicational interpretation more often than the conditional sentences, but it takes longer to process and has a tendency to produce diverse and labile interpretations—a finding which has been recently confirmed.[10] And such ambiguities are likely to be reflected in tasks involving the evaluation of inferences.[11] On the other hand, performance with "if p then q," though faster and more stable, is not consistent with material implication. However, this departure from the logicians' calculus has an unexpected advantage. It breaks the logical relation between the conditional and its contrapositive: they no longer imply one another. This does away with the paradoxes of material implication[12] and the paradoxes of confirmation,[13] at least for the conditionals of everyday language.

SUMMARY

Students classified stimuli according to whether they indicated that a sentence was true or false, or were irrelevant to the truth-value of the sentence. Four different sentences were used, with Ss acting as their own controls, and each sentence was logically equivalent to a material implication. The results showed that disjunction ("not-p or q") yielded the greatest number of classifications in accordance with the truth-values of implication. The remaining sentences ("if p then q," "not-p if not-q," "never p without q") were not classified in a truth-functional way: stimuli were judged irrelevant when they falsified the antecedents of these sentences. The results would seem to raise some difficulties for Piaget's notion of the developmental level of formal operations.

NOTES

Received for publication August 20, 1968. The authors express their gratitude to Dr. P. C. Wason for his advice and encouragement, and for a critical reading of an earlier version of this paper.

1. B. Matalon, Etude genetique de l'implication, *Etudes d'epistemologie genetique: XVI, Implication, formalisation et logique naturelle,* 1962, 69–95; E. A. Peel, A method for investigating children's understanding of certain logical connectives used in binary propositional thinking, *Brit. J. math. statist. Psychol.,* 20, 1967, 81–92.

2. P. C. Wason, Reasoning, in B. M. Foss (ed.), *New Horizons in Psychology,* 1966, 135–151.

3. W. V. O. Quine, *Methods of Logic,* rev. ed., 1956, 12; W. Kneale and M. Kneale, *The Development of Logic,* 1962, 128–138.

4. P. F. Strawson, *Introduction to Logical Theory,* 1952, 35–40.

5. A. Naess, L'emploi de la disjonction chez les adolescents, *Etudes d'epistemologie genetique: XVI, Implication, formalisation et logique naturelle,* 1962, 151–158.

6. Matalon, *loc. cit.;* Peel, *loc. cit.*

7. E. W. Beth and J. Piaget, *Mathematical Epistemology and Psychology,* 1966, 181.

8. D. K. Stewart, Communication and logic: Evidence for the existence of validity patterns, *J. gen. Psychol.,* 64, 1961, 297–305; S. Hill's findings reported by P. Suppes, On the behavioral foundations of mathematical concepts, in L. N. Morrisett and J. Vinsonhaler (eds.), Mathematical learning, *Monogr. Soc. Res. Child Dev.,* 30, 1965 (No. 1), 60–96.

9. P. C. Wason, Reasoning about a rule, *Quart. J. exp. Psychol.,* 20, 1968, 2732–81.

10. P. C. Wason and P. N. Johnson-Laird, Proving a disjunctive rule, *Quart. J. exp. psychol.,* 21, 1969, 14–20.

11. P. N. Johnson-Laird, On understanding logically complex sentences, *Quart. J. exp. Psychol.,* 21, 1969, 1–13; P. N. Johnson-Laird, Reasoning with ambiguous sentences, *Brit. J. Psychol.,* 60, 1969, 17–23.

12. Strawson, *op. cit.,* 88.

13. C. I. Hempel, Studies in the logic of confirmation, *Mind,* 54, 1945, 1–26, 97–121, reprinted in C. I. Hempel, *Aspects of Scientific Explanation,* 1965, 3–46.

AN OBJECTIVE EXPERIMENT ON REASONING

S. N. F. CHANT
University of Toronto

The purpose of this investigation was to analyze by a method of continuous observation some of the characteristics of the reasoning process.

METHOD AND PROCEDURE

The materials were eleven 5 × 8 cards on each of which was drawn a fictitious coat of arms. Each coat of arms was composed of 6 separate drawings. Beside these were printed 6 items of information concerning the family to which the coat of arms supposedly belonged, and each drawing in any particular coat of arms stood for one of the items of family information printed on the same card. No rules of heraldry were followed. In all there were 14 drawings which were repeated in different groupings, along with their respective items of family information, throughout the series of 11 cards. The complete series, with Card 1 shown as a sample and the remainder with the drawings indicated by name instead of diagrammatically, was as follows:

Card 1

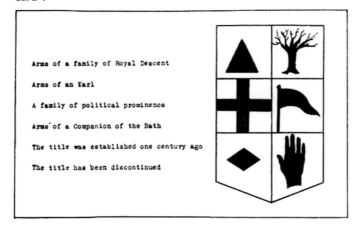

Arms of a family of Royal Descent

Arms of an Earl

A family of political prominence

Arms of a Companion of the Bath

The title was established one century ago

The title has been discontinued

FIGURE 1. Card 1. (A sample of the material used in the experiment.)

Card 2

Sword	2 Triangles	Arms of a family of Royal Descent. Arms of a family of Scotch origin.
Tree	Bar	Arms of a Baron. A family of scientific prominence.
Flag	Snake	The title was established 2 centuries ago. The title has been discontinued.

Card 3

Snake	Flag	Arms of a family of Scotch origin. Arms of a family of noble descent.
Cross	Rose	Arms of a Baron. A family of political prominence.
3 Triangles	Sword	The title was established 3 centuries ago. The title has been discontinued.

Card 4

Sword	Cross	A family of noble descent. Arms of a Baron.
Anchor	Flag	A family of seamen. A family of political prominence.
Rose	4 Triangles	The title was established 4 centuries ago. The title has been discontinued.

Card 5

Fish	4 Triangles	Arms of a family of Scotch origin. Arms of a family of noble descent.
Snake	Cross	Arms of a Viscount. A family of political prominence.
Rose	Flag	The title was established 4 centuries ago. The title has been discontinued.

Card 6

Snake	Hand	Arms of a family of Scotch origin. Arms of an Earl.
Flag	Diamond	A family of commercial prominence. A Companion of the Bath.
Elephant	Triangle	The title was established one century ago. The title has been discontinued.

Card 7

Cross	Snake	Arms of a family of Scotch origin. A family of noble descent.
Hand	4 Triangles	Arms of an Earl. A family of commercial prominence.
Flag	Rose	The title was established 4 centuries ago. The title has been discontinued.

Card 8

Cross	Sword	Arms of a family of noble descent. Arms of a Baron.
Flag	2 Triangles	A family of political prominence. A family of literary prominence.
Rose	Bell	The title was established 2 centuries ago. The title has been discontinued.

Card 9

Rose	Hand	Arms of a family of noble descent. Arms of an Earl.
Elephant	Anchor	A family of commercial prominence. A family of seamen.
Triangle	Flag	The title was established 1 century ago. The title has been discontinued.

Card 10

Elephant	Cross	Arms of a family of noble descent. Arms of a Baron.
Rose	Flag	A family of political prominence. A family of commercial prominence.
Sword	3 Triangles	The title was established 3 centuries ago. The title has been discontinued.

Card 11

Bell	Flag	Arms of a Baron. Arms of a Companion of the Bath.
Sword	Diamond	A family of literary prominence. A family of seamen.
Anchor	3 Triangles	The title was established 3 centuries ago. The title has been discontinued.

*The S*s, 69 in number, were all undergraduates who had completed an introductory course in psychology. Each *S* was observed individually while he worked at the problem for one half hour. The 11 cards, an answer sheet, and the following printed instructions were provided each *S*.

> On each of these cards is a coat of arms composed of 6 separate drawings. On each card are also 6 items of information concerning the family to which the coat of arms belongs. Each drawing on any particular coat of arms stands for one of the items of family information given on the same card. You are to determine which item of information each drawing stands for. You may use the cards in any manner you wish.
>
> On the record sheet in column 1, name or make a rough sketch of the drawing from the coat of arms. In column 2 record opposite each drawing the particular item of family information it stands for. In column 3 record at the same time as you answer your reason for giving your answer. You may correct any answer at any time by marking it "w," and recording the correct answer.

Two *S*s out of 69 misunderstood the instructions and their results are not included.

A continuous record in 15-sec. intervals was made of the *S*'s behavior while working at the problem. This record was made on a sheet that was ruled into 120 columns to serve as time divisions, and into 7 horizontal divisions to provide sections for recording 7 characteristic types of behavior in this setting, which were determined by preliminary experimentation. The 7 possible records were as follows: Recording by number (1) any cards examined individually; (2) any two or more cards compared; (3) any cards examined in serial order; (4) any cards and answers compared; (5) the answers as they were written; and recording (6) any apparently random examination of the cards; and (7) any apparent periods of inaction.

The timing of those records was arranged as follows. A rack and pinion, operated by the ratchet wheel of the line-spacer of a typewriter, moved a vertical metal strip across the record sheet the distance of 1 time division whenever the spacing lever was pressed. In *E*'s line of regard when observing the *S* was an Eastman Timer. The record was made by placing a number or check in the appropriate behavior division of the time column, as indicated by the metal strip. Every 15 sec., as shown by the timer, the spacing lever was pressed and the metal strip moved forward one time division. After some practice the record could be made without diverting *E*'s attention from *S*.

RESULTS

The method of recording described above made possible an analysis of the time spent by *S* in each of the 7 types of behavior recorded, as well as a detailed analysis of the behavior that preceded each answer given. Only 3 of the several possible time-analyses of these data are required for purposes of this study, namely: (1) the time devoted to the overt comparison of cards with cards, or of cards with answers, including sections 2, 3, and 4 of the record outlined above; (2) the time spent in the examination of individual cards, *i.e.* section 1 of the record; and (3) the time spent in recording answers, *i.e.* section 5 on the record.

Fig. 2 shows the distribution of cases for time spent in comparison in 15-sec. time-units. Note that the first class interval extends only from 0 to 1.

Fig. 3 gives a similar distribution of cases for time spent in the examining of individual cards.

Fig. 4 gives a similar distribution of cases for time spent in recording answers.

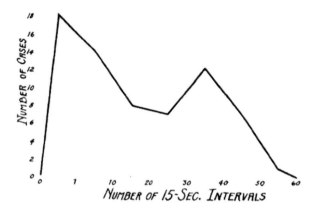

FIGURE 2. Distribution of the reports according to the time spent in comparing the cards and the answers

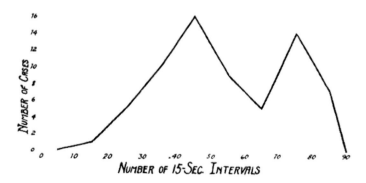

FIGURE 3. Distribution of the reports according to the time spent in examining the individual cards

The bimodal character of the distributions shown in Figs. 2 and 3, as compared with the more normal shape of that shown in Fig. 4, indicates that with reference to both time spent in comparison and time spent in the examination of individual cards, the Ss can be divided into an upper and a lower group. That this division is a function of the variables dealt with, and not common to all time studies in this experiment, is shown by the fairly normal nature of the distribution for the time spent in recording answers.

That the upper modal group in one distribution corresponds roughly to the lower modal group of the other distribution is evidenced by the negative coefficient of correlation, −0.86, P.E. 0.02, between time spent in comparison and time spent examining individual cards. The Ss therefore can be divided into two groups: (1) those who devote considerable time to the comparison of cards or of cards and answers and little time to the examination of individual cards; and (2) those who devote little or no time to comparison and relatively much time to the examination of individual cards.

Fig. 5, giving the distribution of scores in terms of the percentage of correct answers to the number of answers given, shows a bimodality similar to that seen in Fig. 2 and 3. This suggests a relation between the answers given and the distribution of time.

It is obvious from the nature of the experimental material that correct answers can be obtained rather easily by comparison. Answers obtained in any other manner may not be correct.

Table I, showing the answers given for each drawing of the first coat of arms by Ss who had examined no other card previously to recording these answers,

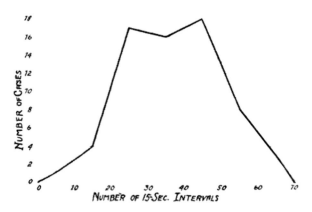

FIGURE 4. Distribution of the reports according to the time spent in recording answers

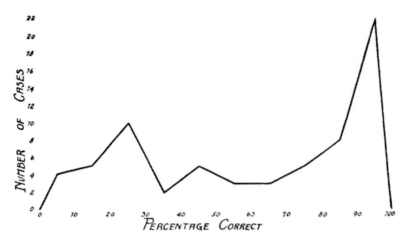

FIGURE 5. Distribution of the reports according to the percentage of correct answers

TABLE I. Showing the Answers Given for the Drawings on the First Card by 21 *S*s

	Answers					
Drawings	Royal Descent	Arms of an Earl	Political Prominence	Companion of Bath	Antiquity of Title	Title Discontinued
Triangle	2	8	0	2	3*	6
Tree	17*	0	0	0	2	2
Cross	2	9	2*	4	1	3
Flag	0	3	11	3	1	3*
Diamond	0	1	4	1*	11	4
Hand	0	0*	4	11	3	3

* Indicates correct answers in each instance.

indicates that these answers are not merely a chance arrangement. Accordingly there is some factor other than chance that is operative in determining answers not derived by comparison. The basis for these answers can be found in the explanations given by the *S*s. To illustrate, the reasons are listed below for the 4 instances shown in Table I in which over half of the *S*s agree in assigning the same answer to a particular drawing, namely: (1) the 17 answers in agreement that are correct for tree; (2) the 11 answers in agreement that are incorrect for flag; (3) the 11 answers in agreement that are incorrect for diamond; (4) the 11 answers in agreement that are incorrect for hand.

(1) Reasons given for assigning, 'Arms of a family of royal descent' to tree, which is correct:

It is a family tree (5 times).
The tree is a royal oak (3 times).
A tree stands for descent (twice).
A family tree representing descent (twice).
Royal Families can trace their descent, hence a tree.
The tree has many branches like the Royal Family.
The tree is deeply rooted like the Royal Family.
The tree is firmly rooted in the land like the Royal Family.
The tree is an oak indicating uprightness, strength and age; the Royal Family would be stronger, older and above any other family.

(2) Reasons given for assigning, 'A family of political prominence' to flag, which is incorrect:

Flag stands for patriotism (3 times).
Flag stands for the country (3 times).
Banner signifies leaders of political party.
Banner is a political symbol.
The banner would be waving for everyone to see.
The flag is the symbol of the country.
The only inference left.

(3) Reasons given for assigning, 'The title was established one century ago' to diamond, which is incorrect:

The diamond stands for a century (3 times).
Only answer left (3 times).
Conventional sign for 100.
Diamond sign of age.
The diamond has 4 quarters like a century.
The diamond represents a complete whole like a century.
The diamond has completed sides like a century.

(4) Reasons given for assigning, 'Companion of the Bath,' to hand, which is incorrect:

The hand stands for comradeship (4 times).
The hand suggests washing (twice).
The hand indicates a companionable order.
It is the hand of comradeship.
It is the helping hand of comradeship.
The hand is used in bathing.
It is the mailed fist of a military order.

These examples, which could be multiplied many times, indicate that in the great majority of instances answers derived without comparison are based upon previously established associations.

For purposes of comparison the following reasons are listed which were given by all Ss assigning the correct answer to hand, which is 'arms of an Earl.'

By comparing cards 1, 6, 7 (22 times).
By comparison (5 times).
By comparing cards 1, 6, 7, 9 (3 times).
By elimination.
A hand stands for the power of an Earl.

Here only one answer out of 32 is based upon a previously established association, the other 31 being based upon an analysis of the experimental material by means of comparing various cards.

The answers, therefore, on the basis of the reasons assigned for giving them, can be divided into (1) those based upon previously established associations; and (2) those derived by an analysis of the experimental material by means of comparison. Similarly the Ss can be divided into 2 groups: (a) 32 Ss who gave predominantly answers based upon previously established associations. In this group are 26 Ss who gave only answers based upon previously established associations, and the smallest percentage of such answers given by any one S in this group was 64% of all the answers given by that S; and (b) 35 Ss who gave predominantly answers based upon the analysis of the experimental materials by comparison. Twenty-five members of this group gave not more than one answer each based upon previously established associations, and the smallest percentage of answers derived by comparison given by any one S in this group was 78% of the total answers given by that S.

That this division of S agrees remarkably well with the time analysis given above in Figs. 2 and 3 is shown by the superimposed graphs shown in Figs. 6 and 7.

Fig. 8 shows the 67 Ss in an array based upon the time spent in the examination of individual cards, shown by the strokes. The time spent by each S in the comparison of cards and answers is shown by the dashes. The numbers along the base line show the division of Ss based upon the nature of their answers: 1 indicates that the S belongs to the group which derives answers from previously established associations; 2 indicates that the S belongs to the group which derives answers by comparison.

The pronounced agreement between the division of the Ss on the basis of their answers and the time studies justifies the division of the Ss into (1) those who emphasize almost entirely the examination of individual cards and derive their answers from previously established associations, and (2) those who emphasize

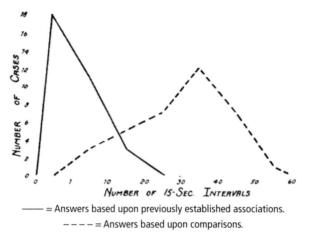

—— = Answers based upon previously established associations.

– – – – = Answers based upon comparisons.

FIGURE 6. Distribution of the reports according to the time spent in comparing cards and answers

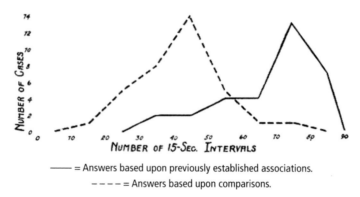

—— = Answers based upon previously established associations.

– – – – = Answers based upon comparisons.

FIGURE 7. Distribution of the reports according to the time spent in examining the individual cards

the comparison of cards or cards and answers and derive their answers through an analysis of the experimental materials.

Conclusions

The above division of *S*s clearly supports the conclusion that there are two well-defined methods of reasoning exemplified in this setting. The first is an interpretative approach, by means of which answers are derived from previously established associations that are remote from the experimental setting itself. The second is analytical, by means of which answers are derived by comparing cards or cards and answers and therefore within the experimental setting.

The first of these, the interpretative, appears to be the more elementary or basic type, while the second, the analytical, appears to be largely a product of training, as indicated by the three following evidences:

(1) One drawing was intentionally introduced into the experimental material which obviously was related to its particular item of information by a very common previously established association; namely, an anchor standing for a family of seamen. This drawing appeared on cards 4, 9, and 11. The time-records show that 77% of the group employing comparison forsook the method of comparison in this case and derived the answer from some previously established association, whereas an examination of the records shows only 31% of this group giving even one other answer that is not preceded by comparison. Hence there is a tendency to revert from the analytical to the interpretative approach when the previously established association is so obvious.

(2) The errors made by the group employing comparison show the influence of previously established association in that, as a rule, they are in agreement with the answers given by the first group. For example, assigning 'Order of the Bath' to hand and a 'Family of Scotch origin' to sword accounts for 45% of all the errors of

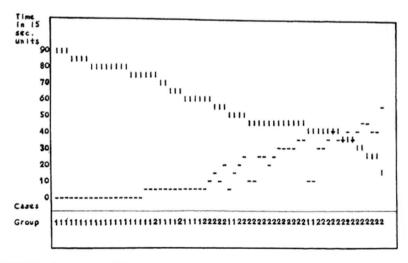

FIGURE 8. Scattergram of 67 cases

Time spent in examining individual cards indicated by vertical lines; time spent in comparing cards and answers indicated by horizontal lines; answers based upon previously established associations designated by 1; answers based upon comparisons designated by 2.

the group employing comparison, and these are the most frequent answers given by the group employing previously established associations, in both instances.

(3) The third evidence for this conclusion is that 87% of the group employing comparison have studied some experimental science in addition to psychology, whereas only 42% of the group depending upon previously established associations have done so, which indicates that the analytical approach is probably the product of academic training along scientific lines. This is the only striking difference to be found with reference to the content of courses taken by these Ss, nor did one group appear to obtain better grades than the other in any courses with any degree of consistency.

Since this experiment was undertaken as an initial attempt to investigate by objective methods the nature of scientific inference, the writer feels justified in adding the following brief note to be considered more thoroughly after a further study of the entire problem. Both of the approaches indicated in this investigation find a place in scientific inference. The analytical approach, which establishes relationships within the experimental setting itself, is representative of that type of inference which is characteristic of Mill's Canons of Induction. The interpretative approach, which goes beyond the experimental setting and relates the problem to previously established associations, is representative of that type of inference which characterizes scientific theories of a general nature, as for example some of the theories of nerve action which employ previously acquired information concerning electrical phenomena.

NOTE
Accepted for publication June 1, 1931. Reported at the 1930 (Iowa) meeting of the American Psychological Association.

JUDGMENT AND DECISION

AN EXPERIMENTAL STUDY OF THE AUCTION-VALUE OF AN UNCERTAIN OUTCOME

MALCOLM G. PRESTON and PHILIP BARATTA
University of Pennsylvania

Students of elementary probability theory will recall that a prize with a known value V, for which the probability of winning is known to be p, is said to have a mathematical expectation equal to the product of its value and its probability, *i.e.* Vp. The mathematical expectation has a certain usefulness in defining 'rational' behavior. It can be shown theoretically, and it is often demonstrated by experience, that a long series of plays will result in systematic losses, if the player characteristically pays in excess of the mathematical expectation for the privilege of playing. Equally, systematic undervaluation of the privilege of playing will result in systematic gains for the player fortunate enough to find such a game to play. It goes without saying that, irrespective of the rationality of playing games which involve wagering, the payment of amounts in excess of the mathematical expectation for the privilege of participation is peculiarly irrational.

In addition to whatever the player may possess of the theory of mathematical expectations, his play is undoubtedly affected by other considerations. Thus, many players hold unsupported convictions about the dependence of chance events, *i.e.* a long run in black at roulette is believed by many to signify that the probability for a red on the next play has been thereby increased. Goodfellow[1] and Fernberger[2] have shown that the Zenith radio public, as well as university students, believe that roulette wheels will give repetition and simple alternation much less frequently than, in fact and in theory, such sequences will appear. In addition to such beliefs about probability, affecting the price paid for the privilege of playing games of chance, are such considerations as the peculiar value which often attaches to a given winning because it completes a larger whole, *i.e.* the special value attaching to the last fifty points necessary to win a game in competition with others, the tendency towards contagious bidding characteristic of games in which several people compete against each other, and the limitation upon the amount offered which sometimes is observed when funds run low.

American Journal of Psychology
April 1948, Vol. 61, No. 2, pp. 183–193

The foregoing considerations may be systematized by examining them relative to three parameters of the game situation. These parameters are the probability of a win, the prize value and the price paid. Thus, there are certain of the considerations which imply that failure of the price to correspond with the mathematical expectation is due to peculiarities of the player's notion of the meaning of a given *probability*. Players for whom a probability of 0.01 means that they have a fair chance of winning are behaving as if a probability of 0.01 was a probability of 0.10 or more. It is understandable if such a person pays in excess of the mathematical expectation for a chance to win the prize.

A second set of the considerations previously mentioned implies a difference between the objective value of the *prize* and its psychological value. The player who needs 50 points to complete his game may value that particular set of 50 points more than is justified by the purely local circumstances. It is understandable that he will pay in excess of the mathematical expectation to win the prize.

Finally, we may note that failure of the price paid to match the mathematical expectation may be due to the fact that the *price* may have a psychological value other than its objective value. Players with plenty of funds may, on that account, regard a small price as smaller than it is by objective standards, and under that circumstance will characteristically offer too much for a given opportunity.

The foregoing possibilities raise questions of both practical and theoretical importance in an area more general and more important than the relatively specific and trivial area of games of chance;[3] namely, the area of the concept. This fact is equally clear in the instance of each of the three possibilities just discussed. In the matter of the meaning which attaches to a given probability of a win, for example, we may inquire as to whether one can identify a *psychological* scale of probabilities to which mathematical probabilities correspond.[4] The present research will present evidence on this point. It will also present evidence on the accessory question as to the extent to which knowledge and experience with the mathematical theory of probability effect a reconciliation with what might be called the *psychological* probabilities.

Procedure

The data of the present experiment were obtained from a game invented for the purpose. The game was played with 42 cards. Each card offered an opportunity to win a certain number of points at certain odds. The number of points was one of six *i.e.* 5, 50, 100, 250, 500, or 1000. The odds offered were one of seven, corresponding to probabilities of 0.01, 0.05, 0.25, 0.50, 0.75, 0.95 and 0.99. With six prize quantities and seven probabilities, it is clear that there were 42 combinations of prize and probability. Each combination of prize and probability appeared once in the series of 42 cards. Each of the combinations was presented in a story-setting which, it was hoped, would enlist accessory interest in the proceedings, and thereby diminish the monotony of the game.

In principle the game could be played by any number of players; the present data, however, were obtained from pairs and from sets of four players. In either case the procedure was the same:

(1) Each player was given play money totalling 4000 points. This sum was known as the endowment. The amount of the endowment in the present experiment was fixed at approximately 67% of the amount resulting when the 42 mathematical expectations were summed.

(2) The cards were placed in random order by use of Tippett's Tables. This order was the same for all games.

(3) A set of cards was in the possession of each player; the players faced each other around a table.

(4) The first card was turned up and was read aloud by the experimenter. The opportunity offered by the card was then auctioned off to the highest bidder.

(5) The successful bidder was then permitted to roll a set of dice in an effort to make a point, the probability for which corresponded to the probability stated on the card.

(6) If the point was made, the successful bidder received the prize, less his bid. If the point was not made, the successful bidder paid for his bid from his endowment.

(7) This procedure was continued throughout the 42 cards.

(8) The player with the most play money at the end of the game received his or her choice of candy, cigarettes, or cigars.

(9) The data of the experiment consisted in the set of 42 winning bids.

Subjects

Data were collected on 20 games. Five games were played by pairs of men and five by pairs of women—all the players being undergraduate students. Five additional games were played by groups of four undergraduates; and finally, five by pairs of faculty members. The faculty members were, for the most part, of professorial rank in the departments of mathematics, statistics, and psychology. It should be pointed out that the latter group included men with substantial acquaintance with probability theory, at the levels of both theory and practice. It may be remarked that in many cases they were observed making active use of this theory.

RESULTS

The results of the experiment will be presented in such a way as to bear upon the following matters:

(1) The existence in the game situation of a scale of *psychological probability* and its functional relationship to the scale of mathematical probability.

(2) The lack of existence in the game situation of scales of *psychological* prize value and price as distinct from the numerically defined prize values and prices.

(3) The presence of an indifference point in the psychological probability scale, when it is plotted relative to the scale of mathematical probability.
(4) The effect of the size of the prize upon the indifference point.
(5) The extent to which psychological probability is independent of formal experience with mathematical probability.
(6) The effect of the number of players upon the indifference point.
(7) The effect of the number of players upon the prices paid at extreme probability values.

Table I gives the mathematical expectation, the mean winning bid, and the ratio of mean winning bid to expectation, from the data of the entire set of 20 games. The

TABLE I. Mathematical Expectations (E), Mean Successful Bids (V), and Ratio of Expectation to Bid (R), for Each Play

Probability		Prize					
		5	50	100	250	500	1000
.01	E	.05	.50	1.00	2.50	5.00	10.00
	V	.51	4.44	4.86	12.75	19.59	59.96
	R	10.2	8.88	4.86	5.10	3.92	6.00
.05	E	.25	2.50	5.00	12.50	20.00	50.00
	V	.98	2.66	5.52	27.27	27.85	85.40
	R	3.92	1.06	1.10	2.16	1.11	1.71
.25	E	1.25	12.50	25.00	62.50	125.00	250.00
	V	1.06	10.21	14.74	35.53	114.95	231.25
	R	.85	.82	.59	.57	.92	.93
.50	E	2.50	25.00	50.00	125.00	250.00	500.00
	V	1.93	21.84	41.56	110.47	242.80	488.50
	R	.77	.87	.83	.88	.97	.97
.75	E	3.75	37.50	75.00	187.50	375.00	750.00
	V	3.73	29.98	71.88	168.30	304.70	716.40
	R	.995	.80	.96	.90	.81	.96
.95	E	4.75	47.50	95.00	237.50	475.00	950.00
	V	3.41	37.71	73.48	161.00	397.80	790.75
	R	.72	.80	.77	.68	.84	.83
.99	E	4.95	49.50	99.00	247.50	495.00	990.00
	V	3.67	41.72	84.25	226.35	384.20	913.18
	R	.74	.84	.85	.92	.78	.92

rows of the table are governed by the probabilities and the columns by the prizes. Using the set of upper left hand entries for purposes of illustration: with a probability of 0.01 and a prize of 5 points, the mathematical expectation, denoted by E, is 0.05, the average winning bid was 0.51 points and the ratio of 0.51 to 0.05 is 10.02.

Various trends are apparent in the table. (1) For all values of prize from 5 to 1000, the mean winning bid exceeds the mathematical expectation for small values of the probability and is less than the mathematical expectation for large values of the probability. To see this, note that for p = 0.01 or 0.05 the ratios uniformly exceed 1.00; for $p \gtreqless 0.25$, the ratios without exception are less than 1.00.

(2) The probability for which the mean successful bid can be presumed to equal the mathematical expectation is uniformly between 0.05 and 0.25, *i.e.* the indifference point of the probability scale is somewhat less than 0.25.

(3) The ratio shows little evidence of systematic variation with the value of the prize (across the rows of the table). If the table is examined carefully by noting the variation of the ratios across the rows, it may be concluded that there is *some* tendency for the ratios to be large at extreme values of the prize. The lack of consistency in this respect forbids, however, any clear-cut conclusion, and we prefer to leave the tendency for later investigation.

Since we have systematic variation from the mathematical expectation in the columns of Table I, with little evidence of the same in rows of the same table, we can exclude the size of the prize as a factor in the variation. No matter what the prize, the same tendency is evident, *i.e.* prizes with small probabilities are paid for too generously and prizes with large probabilities are taken as bargains. That this is not due to any characteristic of *price* paid follows from the design of the experiment. In the experiment the various opportunities were given in random order. Any theory which supposed that the peculiar variability of Table I was due to the price being misconceived uniformly when p was low or high would have to show that the p-values of a given kind appeared uniformly with conditions which produced over- or undervaluation of the price. One such condition might be the size of the largest sum in the possession of the players. This quantity would have to be uniformly large with $p \leq 0.05$ and uniformly small with $p \gtreqless 0.25$ to account for the data of Table I. The random ordering of the opportunities eliminates such an hypothesis from serious consideration. Hence, we are left with the hypothesis that when $p \gtreqless 0.05$, players uniformly conceive the *probability* as somewhat higher, while with $p \geqq 0.25$ players uniformly conceive the *probability* as somewhat lower. How much higher and how much lower can be estimated by taking the ratio of the price paid to the prize, assuming we are correct in our conclusion that no great effect exists in either the price itself or the prize. The ratio of the price paid to the prize gives an estimate of the psychological probability. For example, if a prize of $50 is

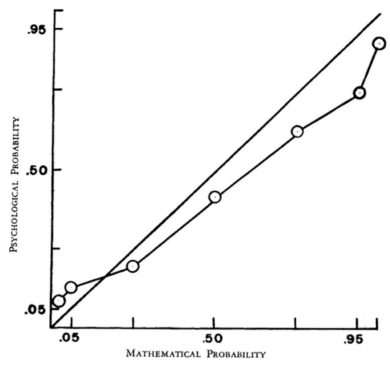

FIGURE 1. Functional Relationship Between Psychological and Mathematical Probability

won by a price of $4.50 when p = 0.01, we may say that such a person is behaving as if a p of 0.01 were a p of 0.09. The p of 0.09 we call a psychological probability. The psychological probability is that probability which must be used in order to bring the price paid into rational relationship with the prize.

Having defined a psychological probability we may inquire as to its functional relationship with mathematical probability. Fig. 1 shows the functional relationship of psychological probability and mathematical probability as it appeared in the mean results of our game, *i.e.* from the data of Table I. This figure plots average psychological probability (the mean has been taken over the six prize values) for each of the seven mathematical probabilities. The figure discloses clearly that psychological probability exceeds mathematical probability at low values of p and is exceeded by it at high values of p.

Both Fig. 1 and Table I show an indifference point in the scale of p at a point somewhat below 0.25. Table I indicates (within the limits of precision inherent in

TABLE II. Ratios of Mean Successful Bid to Mathematical Expectation for Sophisticated (S) and Unsophisticated Male Pairs (UM) and Unsophisticated Female Pairs (UF)

(Each mean based on five games)

Probability	S	Prize 5	50	100	250	500	1000
	S	7.4	11.1	1.6	4.8	1.03	11.0
.01	UM	1.2	1.1	2.6	4.7	3.2	2.5
	UF	11.0	11.7	7.2	4.8	4.5	4.2
	S	3.7	.44	.33	4.1	.80	2.8
.05	UM	1.2	1.2	.45	1.1	1.09	.48
	UF	5.8	1.5	1.9	2.4	1.2	2.3
	S	.76	.68	.46	.43	1.1	.85
.25	UM	1.0	.46	.44	.85	.81	.87
	UF	.80	.75	.54	.38	.83	.71
	S	.69	.72	.66	.84	.98	.90
.50	UM	.80	1.2	1.02	1.03	1.2	1.1
	UF	.68	.50	.62	.66	.71	.70
	S	1.1	.89	.96	.93	.86	.87
.75	UM	.80	.91	1.09	1.07	1.01	1.05
	UF	.67	.47	.81	.67	.51	.76
	S	.41	1.00	.80	.82	.91	.90
.95	UM	1.02	.95	.93	.75	1.01	.99
	UF	.83	.40	.56	.51	.48	.54
	S	.87	.91	.92	.94	.86	.98
.99	UM	.85	.96	.97	.99	.97	.98
	UF	.53	.64	.65	.85	.43	.78

the experiment) that the indifference point is *not* a function of the size of the prize offered, since it appears uniformly in all columns within the interval $p = 0.05$ and $p = 0.25$.

Table II gives ratios from the data of the three types of Ss used in pairs, *i.e.* the sophisticated, the unsophisticated men and the unsophisticated women, at each combination of probability and prize. The data show clearly that the sophisticated Ss exhibit the same phenomena as do the unsophisticated, *i.e.* the indifference point is below 0.25, where the probability is in excess of 0.25 the prize is undervalued, and

TABLE III. Ratios of Mean Successful Bid to Mathematical Expectation for Groups of Two and Four Players

(Each mean based on five games)

Probability	S	5	50	100	250	500	1000
				Prize			
.01	two	1.2	1.1	2.6	4.7	3.2	2.5
	four	21.4	11.6	8.0	6.1	6.9	6.2
.00	two	1.2	1.2	.45	1.1	1.2	.48
	four	5.0	1.1	1.7	1.1	1.3	1.2
.25	two	1.0	.46	.44	.85	.81	.87
	four	.83	1.4	.93	.61	.98	1.3
.50	two	.80	1.2	1.02	1.03	1.2	1.1
	four	.95	1.05	1.02	1.00	.95	1.2
.75	two	.80	.91	1.09	1.07	1.01	1.05
	four	1.4	.92	.97	.92	.88	1.14
.95	two	1.02	.95	.93	.75	1.01	.99
	four	.61	.84	.80	.65	.91	.90
.99	two	.85	.96	.97	.98	.97	.98
	four	.73	.87	.86	.92	.84	.96

where the probability is less than 0.25 the prize is overvalued. Clearly knowledge of the theory of probability, while it may reduce them, does not eliminate the effects.

Table III permits a comparison between data obtained from unsophisticated Ss playing in groups of two and four. This table indicates that the effect of increasing the number of players in the game appears to consist in increasing the amount of over- and undervaluation of the prize at extreme values since in all cases at $p = 0.01$ the ratio is *larger* for groups of four and in all cases at $p = 0.99$ the ratio is *smaller* for groups of four.

DISCUSSION

One of the obvious results of the experiment, requiring additional consideration as well as additional investigation, is the presence of an indifference point in the scale of the probabilities. This point is in many respects analogous to the classical indifference points studied by Hollingsworth, Woodrow, and others. It is not, however, a reflection of a time error or a time-order error since there is nothing in the design of the experiment which permits the appearance of errors of this kind. A more useful analogy perhaps may be drawn between the present fact and the fact of the adaptation level recently used by Helson in the study of frames of reference.[5] This analogy recommends itself on several grounds. In the first place, Helson has shown the adaptation-level concept to be applicable not only to the problem of predicting the apparent brightnesses of figures seen against backgrounds of brightnesses of various compositions, but also to the problem of predicting the outcome of judging intensities in other sense modalities. In the second place, he has shown it to be a function essentially of the logarithms of the intensities of the elements in the perceptual field. In the present experiment, the indifference point is not at 0.50, the center of the range of the series and the arithmetic mean of the probabilities used, but is rather between 0.05 and 0.25. The geometric mean of the series is 0.24. This fact suggests that an additional experiment should be performed in which the range of p should be constricted, the game played a second time and observation directed to the new indifference point. Such an experiment is now in process.

A third ground on which Helson's theory of the adaptation-level recommends itself is related to the function of the initial endowment in the experimental situation. In the present investigation, the players were endowed at the outset with an amount equal to 67% of the sum of the 42 mathematical expectations. Other endowments could have been chosen, and one may speculate on the outcome of possible choices. Increase in the endowment, for example, should result in increase in the average amount paid per play, since it is well known, particularly in these days, that prices go up when money is plentiful. Such a consequence would result in an increase in the indifference point. On the other hand, if the endowment were reduced, the average price should go down, resulting in a decrease in the indifference point. In short, the indifference point in this situation under certain circumstances may be a function of the original endowment. General increase of the endowment would undoubtedly change the atmosphere of the game. Psychologically it might be thought of as changing the background of the game. The theory of the adaptation level states that background contributes heavily to the location of the indifference point. With the indifference point known at two values of background (endowment), the constants can be determined by means of which a quantitative statement could be made as to the indifference point at a third background. In other words, the applicability of the theory of the adaptation level is capable of an experimental test. Such an experiment is in process.

The fact that the slope of the curve of psychological probability as a function of mathematical probability appears to vary systematically at the extremes, depending upon the number of players, is also a fact requiring further consideration. Such a fact suggests that at low probabilities increasing the number of players also increases the willingness of the players to play recklessly, while at high probabilities an increase in the number of players also increases the conservatism of the players. That the outcomes are not due to mere increase in variability due to increase in the number of players is shown by the fact that both effects occur. If increase in the number of players increased the likelihood of a reckless player appearing in the game, the overvaluation of p at values less than 0.05 would be explained; however, such an explanation would also require an overvaluation of all values of p, unless some peculiar interaction were at work. Such is not observed. On the contrary large p values are systematically undervalued.

Summary and Conclusions

(1) The phenomenon of the indifference point is demonstrated in the field of the concept.

(2) The indifference point in the scale of probabilities, under the conditions of the game studied in this investigation, is in the neighborhood of 0.20.

(3) The indifference point appears in the range of probabilities in the neighborhood of the geometric mean of the probabilities used.

(4) Probabilities of less than 0.25 are subject to systematic overestimation. Probabilities of more than 0.25 are subject to systematic underestimation.

(5) The foregoing effects are characteristic of the behavior of mathematicians, statisticians, and psychologists of many years acquaintanceship with the theory of probability as well as of the behavior of college students of various degrees of naïveté in this respect.

(6) Increase in the number of players of the game used in the experiment does not appear to affect the indifference point in the scale of probability but increases both the amount of overestimation of low probabilities and the amount of underestimation of high probabilities.

(7) The foregoing facts are interpreted with the help of a recently published theory of the adaptation level formulated from work on the perception of brightnesses.

NOTES
Accepted for publication November 14, 1947.

1. L. D. Goodfellow, A psychological interpretation of the results of the Zenith radio experiments in telepathy, *J. Exper. Psychol.*, 23, 1938, 601–632.

2. S. W. Fernberger, 'Extra-sensory Perceptions' or Instructions? *ibid.*, 22, 1938, 602–607.

3. This fact is not surprising in view of the frequency with which games of chance have been studied for general rather than specific reasons, not only by psychologists (*e.g.*, E. M. Riddle, Aggressive behavior in a small social group, *Arch. Psychol.*, 1925, #78), but also by purely social

scientists (*e.g.* J. von Neumann and O. Morgenstern, *Theory of Games and Economic Behavior,* 1944, 1–641). Von Neumann and Morgenstern have examined games of chance from the point of view of set-theory as a basis for identifying optimal strategies to be pursued in economic ventures. It is interesting to note that these writers appear to hold the understanding of economic phenomena without recourse to psychological theory as a worthwhile ideal (a familiar theme for those acquainted with the efforts in psychology to understand psychological phenomena without recourse to physiological theory).

4. Teachers of elementary courses in statistics will recognize this question (perhaps with mixed feelings) as a paraphrase of a question about the precise meaning which attaches to the statistical significance associated with a given probability, often asked by their students, and upon which the text books are sometimes as silent as the students are vocal.

5. Harry Helson, Adaptation level as frame of reference for prediction of psychophysical data, this JOURNAL, 60, 1947, 1–29.

UTILITY FUNCTIONS
FOR NONMONETARY EVENTS

EUGENE GALANTER
Columbia University

Six experiments are described that use magnitude estimation methods to characterize a nonlinear (approximately square root) utility function for money. These same methods can be used to assign utilities to nonmonetary events and objects. The procedures permit a translation between the utility of such events and their monetary equivalents. The measure represents the incremental utilities of outcomes from a current neutral position. Positive returns grow more slowly than negative—it is a pessimist's world. These utility measures are consonant with the form of the utility function hypothesized by Kahneman and Tversky (1979).

Psychologists have been busy since 1948 (Preston & Beratta), showing experimentally that several assumptions of "economic rationality" are empirically false (cf. Tversky & Kahneman, 1981). Yet—perhaps because some theoretical economists appear to hold their theories immune to accidents of fact, and practical economists and business people see no clear application for abstract theory—this blow to economic thought has had only minor repercussions.

This point has clout. Even psychologists who study motivation and motivated behavior may not be prepared to address such questions as a just wage, fair taxing, retirement benefits, wage/price relations, and social welfare costs. There is a lack of empirical work that would lead to useful models to explicate the relations among the many factors that contribute to these issues. Even in those areas that are given attention, such as job satisfaction, work incentives, group effectiveness, and consumer preference, the underlying theoretical support is weak or nonexistent (Crespi, 1977, Curtin, 1982; Weinstein, 1972). From top to bottom, the analysis of these economic issues rests on beliefs about what people will do for an extra dollar, and what they will do to avoid losing that dollar.

Few if any past or current analyses of business and finance have used anything other than dollar amounts in calculating and projecting the economic behavior of people or nations. The results of such attempts to capture the economic consequences of various political or financial happenings are often inaccurate, as they would be if, say, a measure of value for nonmonetary events that is linear with money is inappropriate. Obviously, the main qualities of value measurement are roughly monotone with price. It is the strange results (e.g., gambling and insurance or mixtures of outcomes) that, like visual illusions, argue for subtlety of analysis. Efforts to accommodate the obvious are like those of pre-Galilean physicists who tried to relate the velocity of falling bodies to distance. A simple change in the independent variable by Galileo regularized the empirical observations and provided a law of motion that opened the way to Newton's mechanics (Galileo, 1638/1954, p. 367).

The point taken here is that these problems arise, as Bernoulli suggested over 250 years ago (1738/1954), from an inadequate representation of the psychological value of gains and losses of money in particular, and on the lack of experimental procedures to determine these "utilities." Aside from early studies by Mosteller and Nogee (1951) and Davidson, Suppes, and Siegel (1957), which unlike Bernoulli's conjectures could be interpreted to support a linear utility function for money, most recent work (see the short review in Kornbrot, Donnelly, & Galanter, 1981, p. 443) supports a diminishing marginal utility function—for example, a power function of money with exponent less than one. Early magnitude estimations of the utility of hypothetical gains of money (Galanter, 1962) yielded just such nonlinear concave downward utility functions.

Economists had recognized the scientific potential of better variables than money to represent human desire and aversion at least since Ramsey (1936/1980). Von Neumann and Morgenstern revised their original exposition of game theory in 1944 to include an appendix on utility measurement and its representations (1951), and Schumpeter (1954, p. 1058) explicitly noted Stevens's scaling work (Stevens & Galanter, 1957). However, this theoretical tilt toward utility scales has not been reflected in the world of finance. There has been a continued use of dollars as the prime measure of value in every context. One reason may be that most decisions require only ordinal information. Another is that the business of business is to maximize profit; the business of people is to maximize utility. Recognizing this difference of intent is called entrepreneurial acumen.

This report then is aimed not only at showing again in various ways that the utility of money is nonlinear, but also how one's desires and aversions toward or about any arbitrary objects and events can be linked to this utility function of money. The utilities of such nonmonetary events are a numerical representation of just those things that constitute the bases of human value, and consequently of human choice. The primary purpose will not be to propose a theory of human choice and judgment, but rather to demonstrate simple empirical procedures that yield numerical data whose interpretation conforms to some of our ideas concerning human preference. Numerical utilities will be assigned experimentally both to arbitrary familiar events, such as losing one's keys or seeing the first robin of spring, as well as to monetary gains and losses. These values can then be converted easily from one representation to the other. The utilities themselves are theoretically neutral. In other words, the psychological entity these utilities represent may be thought of as a result of, or caused by, needs, tensions, or any other simple or complex facet of human nature. The source of such motivational vectors may be psychic, or biological, or both. Once these utility functions are experimentally established, several applications will be reviewed.

Because the experimental contexts for the measurement of utility frequently involve scaling hypothetical events, one may question whether the assessed utilities are equivalent to those that would be observed in real situations. For example, the incremental utility induced by finding a real dollar may be different in magnitude from the utility of an imagined dollar. Ultimately, this problem will have to be solved first by reserving judgment on the relevance of our utility measures of hypotheticals, and finally by real validation in appropriate and convincing contexts. Our fourth experiment (and Figure 2) is an initial attempt at such validation; a field study of U.S. Army retirement benefits described later in this report is another (Macpherson, 1979).

We examine first the application of direct utility assessment to monetary gains and losses. In this case, psychic objects (gaining and losing money) have physical or stimulus representations that are clear and exhaustive. It does not matter whether the money is coinage, checks, or paper specie; the amount is the controlling variable.

An early experiment that used magnitude estimation methods to assess the utility of money was a utility scaling study (Galanter, 1962). In this study, students were asked to name the amount of money they should receive to double the happiness that a gift of $10 (or $100, or $1,000) would bring them. The result in that experiment, and in many replications in many contexts (e.g., Breault, 1983), shows that doubling the amount is not sufficient to double the happiness. One needs to add about five times the base amount to double the effective utility. The result for positive increments can be represented by a power function of the form $U = aMb$, where the slope parameter, b, is about $0.43 = \log 2/\log 5$.

A next step was to assess the parameters of the negative branch of the utility function. This negative limb, it had been conjectured, would "grow as some power greater than one" (Galanter, 1962, p. 220). Indow (1961) reported results of an experiment in which subjects judged the fair price of watches that had been previously scaled for desirability. If one assumes that spending money is the psychological equivalent of a negative utility increment, then Indow's data support an exponent greater than one. Indeed, some textbooks suggest such an exponent (Coombs, Dawes, & Tversky, 1970). However, these conjectures and our own indirect determinations were not convincing, and following our earlier procedures, Patricia

Pliner obtained data in 1968 (unpublished) that was replicated in its essentials in six separate experiments by John A. Owens during the academic year 1973–74 (unpublished). Pliner's original procedures and data are reported in Experiment 1.

EXPERIMENT 1

METHOD

Subjects

Subjects were 30 male Columbia College students whose names were chosen by a random procedure from the student directory. They were contacted by telephone and an appointment for an additional telephone interview was made. They were unaware of the purpose of the interview until the second call.

Procedure

During the second telephone interview, the subjects were given the following introduction and instructions:

> I would like to talk to you about money—specifically about losing money. Of course you are not really going to lose any money, but I want you to imagine as realistically as you can that you have lost the amounts of money I will mention to you. First I will ask you a general question, and then I'll get more specific.
>
> Obviously $10 is exactly twice as much as $5 in terms of dollars and cents. But if you lost $10, do you think you would be exactly twice as upset as if you lost $5, or more than twice as upset, or less than twice as upset? [Get answer.]
>
> Now could you tell me how much money you would have to lose to make you exactly twice as upset as losing $5?

Each subject was also asked the same two questions regarding $50 and $500. For one-third of the subjects the order of the questions was $5, $50, $500; for one-third the order was $50, $500, $5; and for one-third the order was $500, $5, $50. This procedure was used so that 10 subjects would be free of response contamination for each of the money amounts.

RESULTS

Subjects' responses averaged for the first of the questions for each of the amounts of money are shown in Table 1. Regardless of the order of inquiry, most subjects believed that if the amount of the monetary loss were doubled, the experienced upset would be less than doubled. Table 2 shows the responses made by the subjects to the question "[H]ow much money would you have to lose to make you exactly twice as upset as losing $5 ($50, $500)?" The numbers summarizing the responses are the geometric means of the subjects' judgments.

TABLE 1. Number of subjects responding to the question, "Would losing $10 (or $100, or $1,000) upset you *twice* (or *more* than twice, or *less* than twice) as much as losing $5 (or $50, or $500)?"[a]

Response	Amount of money lost		
	$10 vs. $5	$100 vs. $50	$1000 vs. $500
More than twice	1 (0)[b]	8 (1)	9 (2)
Twice	4 (0)	3 (0)	4 (1)
Less than twice	25 (10)	19 (9)	17 (7)

[a] *All answers averaged (N = 30).* [b] *Numbers in parentheses are number of subjects (n = 10) who responded for the first time to the question.*

TABLE 2. Geometric means of the amount of money judged necessary to make subjects twice as upset as the loss of $5 (or $50, or $500)

Response	Amount of money lost		
	$5	$50	$500
Averages across all judgments	$21	$160	$1850
Averages of first judgments only	$25	$226	$2100

The ratio of monetary loss required to double the experienced upset remains quite stable for each base amount of money, as a power function requires. Based on the nonsignificant chi-squared test for an effect of the order of presentation of the various monetary amounts shown in the first question, the exponent that we estimate from these ratios is the arithmetic mean of all exponents by all subjects, and is equal to 0.54.

With the original edition of this surprising result in hand, we went forward to assess the negative limb in a variety of cross-modality matching experiments reported in Galanter and Pliner (1974). Since that experiment was reported, many additional data for both the positive and the negative exponents of the utility of monetary gains and losses have been collected. Table 3 represents the values of the exponents for a variety of different experiments.

In every case, the exponent for negative utility increments is a bit larger than 0.5, and that for positive increments is a bit smaller, except for the values based on conjoint measurement (but see discussion, Parker et al., 1981, p. 571). In general, incremental losses are larger than gains; we live in a pessimist's world.

Experiments like this are open to a wide class of complaints. For example, can we really believe that the power function is the correct representation of the perceptual

TABLE 3. Values of the exponent of the conjectured power law incremental utility function of money for a variety of experiments

Standard	Median	Minimum	Maximum	Reference
$10	0.46	0.30	1.00	Galanter (1962)
$100	0.51	0.33	1.49	"
$1000	0.43	0.25	0.60	"
CMM dB (pos.)[a]	0.45			Galanter & Pliner (1974)
CMM dB (neg.)	0.59			"
CMM NaOc (neg.)	0.62			"
£1	0.43	0.30	1.00	Kornbrot (unpublished)
£10	0.43	0.10	1.00	"
£100	0.34	0.16	1.00	"
PPL (pos.)[b]	0.44			Galanter et al. (1977)
PPL (neg.)	0.55			"
Double monetary utility	0.43			Breault (1983)
Embedded money	0.42			"
Conjoint measures	0.87			Parker et al. (1981)
NASA (neg.)[c]	0.57			Galanter (1986a)
CSM (neg.)[d]	0.62			Galanter (1986b)
Conjoint measures	0.64			Parker & Schneider (1988)

[a] CMM refers to cross-modality matching experiments. [b] PPL are exponent estimates from psychophysical detection experiments. The average exponents in this table are a judgmental composite by the author (positive increments, 0.45; negative increments, 0.60). [c] NASA experiments involve annoyance judgments of noises with embedded monetary values. [d] CSM data are from Experiments 3 and 4.

(or motivational) value of the objects that are judged? An excellent review of this and comparable questions by a multitude of critics (see Krueger, 1989, commentary) may be summed up in the words of McGill (cited in Krueger, 1989, p. 283), "[No one is] able to suppress judgment research simply because it conflict(s) with their axiomatic positions." One line that we have followed to address these issues is to show that the power function is compatible with simple psychophysical judgments in signal detection contexts. Utility judgments from this experiment are concordant with psychophysical utility functions estimated from the payoff matrices of liminal detection experiments, and therefore possess a strong form of construct validity (Galanter & Holman, 1967; Kornbrot et al., 1981).

Another question that arises concerning such judgments is based on comments concerning sources of bias in magnitude estimation experiments (Stevens & Galanter, 1957). Magnitude estimation procedures can give rise to judgments that may be distortions of the subject's actual impressions. These biases can result from such variables as stimulus spacing, the value of the modulus, and other stimulus properties (cf., e.g., Birnbaum, 1980). Sometimes the bias is thought to reside on the response side; for example, the responses show too many (in the statistical sense) round numbers. In this utility measurement context, judgments may be forced to conform to simple (round number) ratios because the object of judgment, U.S. currency, is decimalized. U.S. coinage and notes may predispose subjects toward a "round number" bias.

To assess this possibility, Kornbrot performed an experiment (unpublished) requiring magnitude estimation of money increments among English subjects during the summer of 1968, just before the British government switched to decimalized currency. Her exponents agreed with their American counterparts for positive increments (ca. 0.43), and are also shown in Table 3.

These results lead to the conclusion that it is justifiable to represent the incremental utility of money as a nonlinear function of the form $U = aMb$, with an exponent for positive monetary increments about 0.40 to 0.45. Exponents for losses are near 0.60. One might hazard the conjecture that the average evaluation of the utility of money is the square root, but in the real world, monetary gains grow more slowly than losses. If some practical way to add and subtract such gains and losses of utility could be found, it might explain some of the puzzling aspects of human economic endeavor such as gambling, insurance, and consumer behavior. Toward this end, more experiments were done to connect the utility of money to the utility of assorted events and objects in a person's life.

NEW EXPERIMENTS

In the fall of 1972, experiments were undertaken to measure through psychophysical scaling techniques the annoyance of aircraft overflight noise (Galanter, 1986a; Galanter, Golding, & Haber, 1978). In these experiments, and others conducted for the Federal Aviation Administration with regard to supersonic jet and helicopter noise (Galanter, Popper, & Perera, 1977), the problem of validating relative magnitudes of annoyance against some objective standard had to be faced. To this end, questions about monetary loss were embedded into contexts involving variations in sound levels of aircraft overflights. The utility measures conformed to expectations based on the previous experiments. That such odd constellations of judgmental objects could be assessed in the same context led to the following studies.

EXPERIMENT 2

METHOD

Subjects

In the three replications of this experiment, groups of from 19 to 34 Columbia College undergraduate male students (17—22 years of age) participated. All were members of an introductory course in human psychology and participation was voluntary.

Procedure

The subject was seated in a comfortable chair in a small seminar room. The following instructions were given:

> I am going to ask you to make a number judgment about a series of unpleasant hypothetical events much like the judgments you made in the class magnitude estimation experiment on the loudness of noise. Do you remember how we did that experiment? [Wait for answer—if *yes* continue, if *no* review the experiment.] First I want you to use the following event as your modulus that you should set equal to 100 (or 10, or 1, or 1000): "Your ten-speed bike has been stolen." When I ask you to give a number to another event, if you think it is three times worse, call it 300 (or appropriate value), whereas if it is only one-quarter as bad, call it 25.

> Nineteen events were presented to each subject using different irregular orders for each subject. Eight of these events were monetary losses. Each of the three replications used slightly different monetary amounts. Some monetary losses were expressed simply as "You have lost $35." Others were in contexts such as "You are fined $60 for speeding." The nonmonetary events included such things as "You get chewing gum on your shoe," or "You have a flat tire on your way to an appointment."

RESULTS

The median magnitude estimates for each event were normalized for each modulus. For each of the monetary events, the log of the normalized median judgments are plotted against the log of the monetary loss for each of the three separate experiments. The results are shown in Figure 1. Overlapping data points account for the apparent loss of data. The different symbols represent the different experiments. The solid line (from Galanter & Pliner, 1974, Exp. 2) represents an exponent of 0.59. When this number is compared with the other negative utility exponents in Table 3, the agreement is excellent.

DISCUSSION

That the various monetary events yield judgments that conform to values obtained in a variety of other contexts supports the reliability of the utility scale. However,

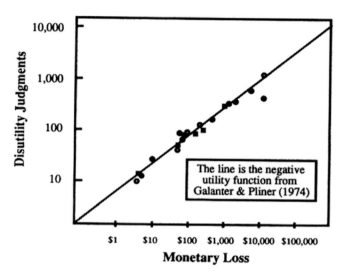

FIGURE 1. Medians of judged disutility of monetary losses from three experiments in which money losses were sprinkled among other negatively valued events or objects that were also being judged

more is at stake here. Eleven of the judgments in this experiment measure the utility of arbitrary non-numerical events. It is both reasonable and plausible to conclude that all the judgments are comparable. On this assumption, the numbers assigned to the nonmonetary events have a utility that is commensurable with the utility of the money judgments.

EXPERIMENT 3

The result of the preceding experiment is startling in its simple interpretation. These data suggest that we have devised a "universal solvent" for value, a solvent that converts the utility of an object or event into its equivalent monetary utility. The natural implication is that desire and aversion can be embedded into a one-dimensional continuum of utility. If such an interpretation is shown to be correct, we can assert that the utility of a nonmonetary item can be converted into its utility equivalent in cash and vice versa. The ability legitimately to perform such translations can be regarded as a powerful tool for the study of human motivation as well as economic transactions.

To generalize the applicability of the previous experiment, a set of descriptions of events was needed that possessed certain properties. In particular, the events should be at least moderately unambiguous and should represent culturally homogeneous objects of desire and aversion. To this end, 205 stimulus items were constructed, each of which described an object, event, or outcome that might vary in preference among individuals.[1]

METHOD

Subjects

Subjects were undergraduate or graduate students in Columbia University who were cajoled into participating for the sake of science and the amusement they might find in understanding the nature of the experiment. Some received a small gratuity for their participation. For the first filtering of the 205 stimuli, 11 subjects participated (8 graduate or professional students, 3 undergraduates; 5 female). For the second filtering, 29 male undergraduate students were drawn from a course in experimental psychology given in the spring term of 1973.

Apparatus

The 205 event descriptions were typed separately on 3" × 5" cards. After the initial filtering, the 106 items that were retained were cast into a questionnaire form.

Procedure

The deck of cards containing 205 event descriptions was given to respondents individually, and the experimenter read the following instructions:

> You will be presented with a number of verbal items, each denoting an object or event. How would you rate each of these items on a scale of +5 to −5 such as the one shown here. [Show a drawing of a bipolar numerical scale with descriptive terms ranging from *highly aversive* at −5 through *moderately aversive, slightly aversive, neutral,* to *highly desirable* at + 5.] Use only integral values. For example, an item rated +5 might be "winning the Irish Sweepstakes"; an item rated −5 might be "having terminal cancer." Zero on the scale would be neutral. We want your personal opinion or evaluation of these items. A few of the items are sex-linked and will obviously not be applicable. For example, "your wife has twins" would be answered by males only.

Of the items, 190 were nonmonetary. Fifteen monetary items were distributed irregularly throughout the 205 items, and except for one oddball, were in either of two formats: (a) "You've won $_____ in the state lottery," or (b) "You've lost a civil suit for $_____."

After a routine statistical analysis to find items that spanned the range of value ratings and had similar variability, 90 of the nonmonetary items were retained and added to 16 monetary items of various magnitudes to form a new questionnaire. Minor syntactic changes were made in some items; several underwent semantic manipulations based on intuitions that the revised wording would produce less ambiguity in their interpretations by the respondents. These 106 items were then administered to a second group of 29 subjects for a second evaluation on an 11-point bipolar scale. The same instructions were used with this new group.

RESULTS

Means and standard deviations were computed for each of the item descriptions. The distribution of standard deviations for the nonmonetary items ranged from 0.3 to 3.8, with most of the items in the range 0.5 to 2.5. About half of the items exhibited a range that fell at or below a value of 1.2. We should note in passing that the distribution of the standard deviations for the monetary items was much narrower, the deviations ranging from 0.0 to 1.4. Half of the monetary items had a standard deviation of less than 0.9.

Items were selected for inclusion in the second questionnaire so that the whole range of ratings was sampled. Additionally, stimuli were chosen from among the set of items with the smallest variability. The standard deviations for nonmonetary items from the second questionnaire ranged from .3 to 2.9, with most of the values between 1.0 and 2.0. Mean scale values for the items in the second questionnaire were correlated with scale values for similar items for the original 205-item sorting. A correlation $r = 0.94$ was obtained.

EXPERIMENT 4

After the second filtering of stimulus items, 20 of the most consistent nonmonetary descriptions were selected that spanned the range from −5 to +5. These 20 items were cross-checked in a series of informal magnitude-estimation calibration studies, which resulted in the elimination of 2 items from the list and the addition of 4 others. These 22 items were divided into two groups of 11 items, one group with positive preference ratings, and the other with negative values.

METHOD

Subjects

Subjects were undergraduate students drawn from an introductory psychology course at Columbia University. The positive items were scaled by 152 students; 55 students assessed the negative ones.

Item descriptions

The 22 nonmonetary items that had been winnowed from our original 205 were divided into 11 positive and 11 negative descriptions. To each of these were added eight gains or losses of money for a total of 19 items that made up each questionnaire scale. The monetary amounts in the negative list were altered slightly from their counterparts in the positive list.

To provide a modulus for the magnitude estimation scale, an item was selected at the low end of the range and called *10*. For the positively valued list, the item was "You are given a brand-new bicycle." For the negatively valued list, its complement "Your brand-new bicycle is stolen" served as the standard of comparison for the other 19 items on the list.

Procedure

Each group of subjects received answer sheets containing 20 spaces, and the experimenter read the following instructions:

> I am going to read you a list of things that could happen to you and that you would like (dislike) in varying degrees. I want you to judge how much you like (dislike) each of them by giving each item a number. Here is how you assign the numbers. Consider first that you are given a brand-new bicycle (that your brand-new bicycle is stolen) and call the pleasure (displeasure) that gives you *10*. Now if you got something that gave you three times as much pleasure (displeasure), you should call that *30*. If, on the other hand, the next item would be only half as pleasurable (give you only one-half as much displeasure) you would call it *5*. If it were one-tenth, you would call it *1*. If it were one-fiftieth, you would call it *0.2*.
>
> *Notice that you can't run out of numbers in either direction. There are just as many fractions between one and zero as there are numbers between one and infinity. The main point is to assign the numbers in proportion to the degree of pleasure (displeasure) the item would give you using the new bike (stolen bicycle) as your standard called 10.* Think carefully about the gifts (events) before you make your decision, as we want the numbers to reflect as accurately as possible your feelings about these things. Write down the number 1, and then put your numerical judgment beside that for your first item, which is that you are taken to dinner at the Four Seasons (you get a ticket for speeding). Remember if you think that this would give you one and one-half times as much pleasure (displeasure) as a new bike (having your new bike stolen), you would call it *15*. On the other hand, if you think it would be not as good as a new bike (not as bad as a stolen bike) you might call it *8, 5,* or *2*.

RESULTS

Median magnitude estimation values for the eight monetary items of positive utility were used to calculate the slope, which was 0.48 or slightly below one-half, which is consistent with the positive limb of the utility function. The median values of the eight monetary losses give a slope equal to 0.54, slightly greater than one-half.

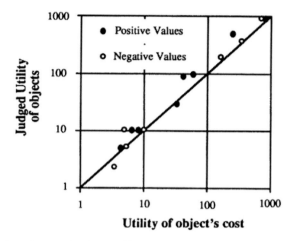

FIGURE 2. Utility of cost and judgment (the abscissa is the logarithm of the utility of the independently estimated cost of positively valued objects [filled circles] and negative valued objects [unfilled circles]; the ordinate is the logarithm of the judged utility of the objects; the linear function line is a visual aid)

This again confirms our findings about the negative limb of the utility function for money—that it is slightly steeper than the positive side.

The central fact that these data reveal concerns the relation between the utility of the nonmonetary events and the utility of the money that would be required either to acquire or avoid them. Figure 2 shows seven of the positive and seven of the negative items for which we could easily estimate, calculate, or otherwise determine their monetary worth. The abscissa represents the utility of the monetary cost of the object, and the ordinate is the judged utility of the object. The diagonal line is a linear function inserted to help see the quality of the comparison.

Notice that both the monetary and the nonmonetary data come from the same subjects. Furthermore, the linearity of the relation between the utilities of the *estimated costs* of the nonmonetary data and the utilities of the nonmonetary data themselves speaks strongly to the consistency between these different kinds of objects.

EXPERIMENT 5

The previous experiments demonstrate within the limits of the magnitude estimation technique that people can judge the utility of nonmonetary events and that there are strong connections between judgments of utility for monetary and nonmonetary objects. This leads to the extended hypothesis that the form and parameters of the utility scale for money can be interchanged with judgments of the utility of nonmonetary events to predict various kinds of utilitarian decisions. Experiment 5 explores this hypothesis.

METHOD

Subjects

The services of a subject recruitment firm in the New York metropolitan area were used in this experiment. The 23 subjects were all women between 18 and 35 years of age. They were all at least second-generation, native English-speaking residents of nearby communities, and all used hair care products, including hair conditioners. They were paid $30 to participate in a 40-min "consumer preference study."

Procedure

College students can estimate fairly easily the utility of familiar objects and events and the utility of monetary gains and losses by magnitude estimation. Getting such magnitude judgments from naive subjects requires additional instruction. Failure to train such subjects carefully may yield data that reflect biases of many kinds (cf. Exp. 1, Results). The consequence is that the methods used here do not permit the analysis of individual subjects. This is not a universal difficulty. Such individual subject analyses are possible when subjects are tested under laboratory conditions using special magnitude estimation methods (Galanter, 1986b). However, the previous data from Experiment 4, Figure 2, attest to the robustness of the relation between the utility judgments of nonmonetary events and the utilities of the money necessary to buy them.

Each subject reporting to the off-campus research facility was greeted and asked to fill in a short biographical inventory to provide demographic data and to ensure payment. The subject then entered the experimental room, which was furnished with a table, a TV set, and a shelf filled with hair care products backed against a one-way mirror through which two television cameras could record the session. The subject engaged in a variety of tasks, one of which was relevant to this report.

After the first 20 min of attitude questions and TV viewing, the subject was given the following verbal instructions:

> We are planning to have a lottery where we will give away hair conditioning products as prizes. You and the other people participating in this study are eligible to win. One of the prizes will be TWO DOZEN BOTTLES OF (PRODUCT NAME). [Show card which contains a graphic representation of the product.] In order to find out how happy you would be to win this prize, we would like you to compare winning this prize to what you would feel like if you won a different prize.

For example, winning a color TV would certainly make you happy [show card], and I'm sure it would make you happier than winning two dozen bottles of

(PRODUCT NAME), Don't you agree?
[Obtain answer.]

How much happier would you be? Two times as happy, three times, ten times or even more?

COLOR TV: (PRODUCT NAME)
[Remove color TV card.]

How would you feel about winning a KEY RING? [Show card.] Wouldn't winning the two dozen bottles of (PRODUCT NAME) make you happier than winning the key ring? How much happier would you say?

(PRODUCT NAME): KEY RING
[Remove key ring card.]

This procedure continued in the same fashion through a set of nine additional comparisons. Among the nine objects there were four that had reference to monetary gains ranging from $1/$2 to $1850/$1900. There were two different sets of nine comparison objects to defend against possible context effects. The eight (four in each set) money amounts were, of course, the items of interest in this experiment.

To validate the utility scale of these items and the money amounts as judged by our consumer sample, we used a control group of 20 Columbia University undergraduates who judged exactly the same items. The only difference was that the Columbia students used a hi-fi cassette system as their modulus item instead of the hair care product. The estimated ratio in monetary value between the cassette and the hair care product was approximately nine.

RESULTS

Figure 3 shows the data points for the utility estimates of the four money values by the hair care group (unfilled circles), and by the Columbia student group (filled circles). The parallel functions for the two groups are clear. The slopes of the functions (ca. 0.62) are steeper than the usual slope for positive monetary gains. This increased slope is probably attributable to the small number of observations. Similar bias in slope appears in sensory scaling when the number of events to be judged is small (Stevens & Galanter, 1957, p. 394). The intercepts of the two functions reflect the approximate difference in the utility of the modulus used by the two groups.

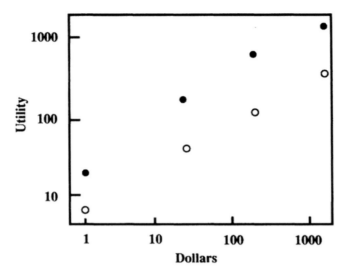

FIGURE 3. Utility functions for four monetary gains based on judgments by female consumers (unfilled circles) and male Columbia University undergraduates (filled circles) (the modulus for the consumers was 24 bottles of a hair care product called "100"; for the students the modulus was a portable cassette player called "100")

EXPERIMENT 6

The data of Experiment 5 were part of a larger market research study that preceded the introduction of a new hair care product into the national market. In addition to the data described above, information from a market test site was available that allowed comparison of the number of sales of the new product with the sales of other similar products at different prices. If the utility values correctly reflect purchasing behavior (i.e., anticipate the price people will pay), the practical value of such utility scales in real economic contexts would be demonstrated.

METHOD

Subjects
   The same subjects described in Experiment 5 also participated in an experiment that affords an opportunity to see the power of these utility measures to assess consumer behavior.

Procedure
   During the experimental session described in the previous experiment, each subject was asked to cross-compare bottles of (PRODUCT NAME) with (COMPETITOR

TABLE 4. Utilities and dollar values of three consumer products (Exp. 6)

Product	Utilities	Equivalent calibrated values	Prices[a]	Utility of prices paid for the products
Test product	1.65	$2.30	$2.19	1.60
Competitor #1	1.54	$2.05	$1.99	1.51
Competitor #2	1.91	$2.95	$2.79	1.85

[a] *Prices represent the average retail prices in a field test that left the consumers indifferent among the products.*

#1) and (COMPETITOR #2). This comparison was accomplished after the ratio estimations had been completed, and after three TV commercials for the three products had been seen. The subject was reminded of the ratio estimation procedure and asked to make similar judgments about the pairwise presentations of the products. After correcting for the modulus shift, the three products yielded utility values that could be translated back into dollars.

RESULTS

The utilities and the dollar values of the three products are shown in Table 4. The dollar values were the posted prices in the test market stores. The utility exponent was chosen to be 0.60, which represents the best guess from these data as the proper figure for expenditures (negative utility increments). The prices of the products shown in the table represent the prices that left consumers indifferent with respect to the products as shown. The third column shows the prices (approximations) reported in the test site markets that generated equivalent sales 3 weeks after product introduction. The fourth column is the utility of the prices. This result shows how the utility scale can be used as a tool for economic analysis.

CONCLUSIONS

These experiments taken together with earlier data lend weight to the view that psychological measures of utility can be constructed for monetary and nonmonetary events. The utilities of both kinds of events can be represented on the same motivational scale, and therefore can be interchanged. This leads to the conclusion that this direct scaling technique, dubbed *utilimetrics*, can refine and enhance those parts of economic decision making that depend on human judgment and choice. People act in a way that can be captured by empirical numerical assignments to objects of desire and aversion. Further, the way these numbers are assigned can be translated directly into monetary terms. Indeed, incremental monetary events can themselves be represented on exactly the same utility scale.

As an example of the advantage of the use of utilimetrics in a practical context, consider the task of setting a dollar value on bonuses for fine-tuning the rate of military reenlistments. The standard economic approach is to calculate a "future value" for each bonus, and then to expect reenlistment behavior to conform linearly to these numbers. If probabilities are introduced into the calculations to "refine" the inadequate correlation coefficients ($r = 0.45$), there is simply more smear and less information (Macpherson, 1979). If, however, the bonus values are converted to utility increments, the enlistment rate correlations swell to $r = 0.80$. In addition to the correlational validation of such models that use nonlinear utility concepts, consider other practical proofs of the reasonableness of this approach. Macpherson (1979) showed that a linear future value model predicted that a pay increase to ca. $350/month during the last year of service before retirement would induce reenlisting. The actual dollar value the retirement benefit required was in fact ca. $500/month. The prediction of $598 by the utilimetric model to induce remaining in the Army is obviously nearer the mark.

The existence of a practical procedure to measure utility does not of itself yield new insights. Rather, these numbers permit us to estimate more accurately which way the cat will jump. Clearly, the use of utility measures as the single representation of value does not provide the necessary apparatus to deal with many topics central to economic behavior. From a theoretical point of view, the most outstanding lack in this concept is, of course, a fine disregard for outcomes that are risky or uncertain, a distinction first proposed by Luce and Raiffa (1957). Most attempts to build a psychology of choice have rested on probabilistic concepts. One reason for this is the belief that behavioral characterizations of utility scales can only be made stronger than ordinal scales by using probabilities as a device to embed choices into a continuum. These ideas stem from the seminal work of Von Neumann and Morgenstern (1951). Utilimetrics may serve a leavening role in just those places where probability must be forced onto what seem to be determinate judgments to make the data tractable.

Within the context of such experiments, the heavy-handed use of probability has made a noisy hash of what appears intuitively determinate. It is just these occasions—the determinate ones, such as the Army reenlistment problem—that occupy the center stage of economics. Of course, we must search for a natural and predictive theory of human choice among risky or uncertain alternatives in order to accommodate situations that are intrinsically probabilistic. But there is no imperative to withhold utility measurement until a suitable interpretation is found for "expected utility." Indeed, if we adopt a simplistic view of the human appreciation of uncertainty as being tripartite—dividing the world into "certain to happen," "certain not to happen," and "uncertain" (cf. Shackle, 1949)—we can with utilimetrics alone account for most if not all of the data from experiments that show departures from normative statistical theories (e.g., Allais, 1953; Ellsberg, 1961).

As a coda to these experiments, let me conclude by a review of the general statements of Kahneman and Tversky (1979) about the form of the utility function. They said, "The value function [our utility function] is (i) defined on deviations from a reference point; (ii) generally concave for gains and commonly convex for losses [i.e., diminishing marginal utility for both gains and losses]; (iii) steeper for losses than for gains" (p. 279). These claims can now be refined into the concrete empirically supported assertions of utilimetrics:

1. Utility is the numerical magnitude of the incremental change from a neutral state in desire or aversion, for the consequence or outcome of a choice or path of action.
2. Utility of monetary increments grows as a power function of money with an exponent of 0.45.
3. Utility of monetary decrements grows as a power function of money with an exponent of 0.55.

To these three assertions we can add the fourth and most important of all:

4. The utility of nonmonetary objects and events can be translated into the utility of equivalent money amounts.

As a rough approximation for practical calculations, gains and losses of money can be treated as the square root of the monetary change. For detailed calculations, the values used for our own analyses are:

$$U = 3.548134\ M^{0.45}\ \text{(increments)}; \quad U = 2.818383\ M^{0.55}\ \text{(decrements)}.$$

Why is so much precision used in our coefficients? The answer is that in some experiments or surveys, for example Macpherson's (1979) study of Army reenlistments, the standard error of estimated present value was 10% of the standard deviation, or less than $4, for a present value of $7,133.75/year.

The coefficients were selected to make $10 equal 10 utiles. Figure 4 is an arithmetic graph of the utility function. Although this figure permits a visualization of the relative growth of the positive and negative limbs, it is impossible on such a graph to extract the utility of an arbitrary money amount. For such purposes a table is more useful.[2]

The obvious applications of utilimetrics for the study of tax rates, wage/price negotiations, income adjustments, and the many other social and political demands

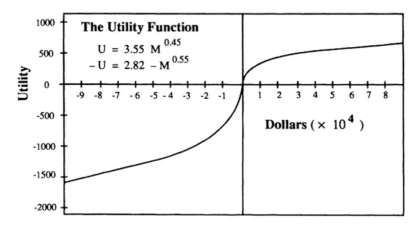

FIGURE 4. An idealized graph of utility as a function of incremental monetary gains and losses in arithmetic coordinates

on economic calculations await attention. When a procedure is at hand that will let our social and political decisions emerge from arbitrary definitions of "rationality" into the realm of empirically supported models, there can be no turning back. We can fold the desires of people into our common purpose, and so expand the principles of social democracy.

NOTES
Experiments 1, 2, and 3 were supported by Office of Naval Research Grant N00014-67-A-0108-0031.

Correspondence concerning this article should be addressed to Eugene Galanter, Columbia University, 460 Riverside Drive, New York, NY 10027.

Received for publication June 28, 1989; revision received November 22, 1989.

1. These items and the questionnaires described below were designed and tested by Gloria Karsten and may be obtained from the author.

2. A table of these utility functions is available from the author.

REFERENCES
Allais, M. (1953). Le comportement de l'homme rationnel devant le risque: Critique des postulates et axiomes de l'Ecole Americain [The behavior of rational man facing risk: Critique of the postulates and axioms of the American School]. *Econometrica, 21,* 503–546.
Bernoulli, D. (1954). A new thoery on the measurement of risk (L. Sommer, Trans.). *Econometrica, 22,* 23–36. (Original work published 1738)
Birnbaum, M. H. (1980). Comparison of two theories of "ratio" and "difference" judgments. *Journal of Experimental Psychology: General, 109,* 304319.

Breault, K. D. (1983). Psychophysical measurement and the validity of the modern economic approach: A presentation of methods and preliminary experiments. *Social Science Research, 12,* 187–203.

Coombs, C., Dawes, R., & Tversky, A. (1970). *Mathematical psychology: An elementary introduction.* Englewood Cliffs, NJ: Prentice-Hall.

Crespi, I. (1977). Attitude measurement, theory, and prediction. *Public Opinion Quarterly, 41,* 286–294.

Curtin, R. T. (1982). Indicators of consumer behavior. *Public Opinion Quarterly, 46,* 340–352.

Davidson, D., Suppes, P., & Siegel, S. (1957). *Decision making: An experimental approach.* Stanford, CA: Stanford University Press.

Ellsberg, D. (1961). Risk, ambiguity and the Savage axioms. *Quarterly Journal of Economics, 75,* 643–669.

Galanter, E. (1962). The direct measurement of utility and subjective probability. *American Journal of Psychology, 75,* 208–220.

Galanter, E. (1986a). Modulus estimation: Quantification of single events. New York: Psychophysics Laboratory, Columbia University.

Galanter, E. (1986b). The shifty modulus: Psychophysical functions for individual subjects. New York: Psychophysics Laboratory, Columbia University.

Galanter, E., Golding, N., & Haber, N. (1978). *A new scaling method to quantify individual attitudes during social surveys.* New York: Psychophysics Laboratory, Columbia University.

Galanter, E., & Holman, G. L. (1967). Some invariances of the isosensitivity function and their implications for the utility function of money. *Journal of Experimental Psychology, 73,* 333–339.

Galanter, E., & Pliner, P. (1974). Cross-modality matching of money against other continua. In H. Moskowitz, B. Sharf, & J. C. Stevens (Eds.), *Sensation and measurement: Papers in honor of S. S. Stevens* (pp. 65–76). Dordrecht, The Netherlands: Reidel.

Galanter, E., Popper, R., & Perera, T. (1977). Annoyance scales for simulated VTOL and CTOL overflights. *Journal of the Acoustical Society of America, 8A*(Suppl.), 1.

Galileo [Galilei, G.]. (1954). *Dialogues concerning two new sciences* (H. Crew & A. de Salvio, Trans.). New York: Dover. (Original work published 1638)

Indow, T. (1961). An example of motivational research applied to product design. *Chosa to Gijutsu, 102,* 45–60.

Kahneman, D., & Tversky, A. (1979). Prospect theory: An analysis of decision under risk. *Econometrica, 47,* 263–291.

Kornbrot, D. E., Donnelly, M., & Galanter, E. (1981). Estimates of utility function parameters from signal detection experiments. *Journal of Experimental Psychology: Human Perception and Performance, 7,* 441–458.

Krueger, L. E. (1989). Reconciling Fechner and Stevens: Toward a unified psychophysical law. *Behavioral and Brain Sciences, 12,* 251–320.

Luce, R. D., & Raiffa, H. (1957). *Games and decisions.* New York: Wiley.

Macpherson, D. (1979). *Analyses of perceptions of compensation and benefits as of 31 October 1978* (MILPERCEN Survey Control No. DAPC-MSF-S-78-26). Bethesda, MD: Army Research Institute.

Mosteller, R., & Nogee, P. (1951). An experimental measurement of utility. *Journal of Political Economy, 59,* 371–404.

Parker, S., & Schneider, B. (1988). Conjoint scaling of the utility of money using paired comparisons. *Social Science Research, 17,* 277-286.

Parker, S., Stein, D., Darte, E., Schneider, B., Popper, R., & Needel, S. (1981). Utility function for money determined using conjoint measurement. *American Journal of Psychology, 94,* 563-573.

Preston, M. G., & Beratta, P. (1948). An experimental study of the auction-value of an uncertain outcome. *American Journal of Psychology, 61,* 183-193.

Ramsey, F. P. (1980). *Truth and probability.* In H. E. Kyburg, Jr., & H. E. Smokler (Eds.), *Studies in subjective probability* (2d ed., pp. 25-52). New York: Krieger. (Original work published 1936)

Schumpeter, J. A. (1954). *History of economic analysis.* New York: Oxford University Press.

Shackle, G. L. S. (1949). *Expectations in economics.* Cambridge, England: Cambridge University Press.

Stevens, S. S., & Galanter, E. (1957). Ratio scales and category scales for a dozen perceptual continua. *Journal of Experimental Psychology, 54,* 377-411.

Tversky, A., & Kahneman, D. (1981). The framing of decisions and the psychology of choice. *Science, 211,* 453-458.

Von Neumann, J., & Morgenstern, O. (1951). *Theory of games and economic behavior* (3d ed.). Princeton, NJ: Princeton University Press.

Weinstein, A. G. (1972). Predicting behavior from attitudes. *Public Opinion Quarterly, 36,* 355-360.

BASE RATES IN BAYESIAN INFERENCE: SIGNAL DETECTION ANALYSIS OF THE CAB PROBLEM

MICHAEL H. BIRNBAUM
University of Illinois at Urbana-Champaign

Several investigators concluded that humans neglect base rate information when asked to solve Bayesian problems intuitively. This conclusion is based on a comparison between normative (calculated) and subjective (responses by naive judges) solutions to problems such as the cab problem. The present article shows that the previous normative analysis was incomplete. In particular, problems of this type require both a signal detection theory and a judgment theory for their proper Bayesian analysis. In Bayes' theorem, posterior odds equals prior odds times the likelihood ratio. Previous solutions have assumed that the likelihood ratio is independent of the base rate, whereas signal detection theory (backed up by data) implies that this ratio depends on base rate. Before the responses of humans are compared with a normative analysis, it seems desirable to be sure that the normative analysis is accurate.

Recent papers contend that humans do not make statistical inferences by means of Bayes' theorem (Hammerton, 1973; Kahneman & Tversky, 1973). In particular, it has been argued that judges neglect base rate information. This conclusion, which is called the "base rate fallacy," is based on the finding that when judges are asked to solve a statistical problem intuitively, the modal response differs from the Bayesian solution. A demonstration, which has already become something of a classic, is the cab problem, variations of which have been investigated by Kahneman and Tversky (1973), Bar-Hillel (1980), Lyon and Slovic (1976), Fischhoff, Slovic, and Lichtenstein (1979), and others. Tversky and Kahneman (1980) state the cab problem as follows:

A cab was involved in a hit-and-run accident at night. Two cab companies, the Green and the Blue, operate in the city. You are given the following data:

(i) 85% of the cabs in the city are Green and 15% are Blue.
(ii) A witness identified the cab as a Blue cab. The court tested his ability to identify cabs under the appropriate visibility conditions. When presented with a sample of cabs (half of which were Blue and half of which were Green)

American Journal of Psychology
Spring 1983, Vol. 96, No. 1, pp. 85–94

the witness made correct identifications in 80% of the cases and erred in 20% of the cases.

Question: What is the probability that the cab involved in the accident was Blue rather than Green?

The modal response by untrained judges is usually observed to be about .8, whereas the so-called "normative" solution is supposed to be .41. The purposes of this article are to question the previous solution and to call attention to the fact that the proper normative solution to the cab problem is a bit more complicated than previously supposed in papers on the "base rate fallacy." In particular, it will be argued that the solution called "normative" in previous papers on this topic makes (implicitly) a very unrealistic assumption. The basic purpose of this paper will be to discuss the implications of signal detection theory for the normative solution.

Bayes' theorem

Bayes' theorem can be written in odds form as follows:

$$\Omega_1 = \Omega_0 \frac{P(\text{"B"}|B)}{P(\text{"B"}|G)} \qquad (1)$$

where Ω_1 = posterior odds $[P(B|\text{"B"})/(1 - P(B|\text{"B"}))]$, Ω_0 is the prior odds of a Blue cab [from the base rate, $P(B)/P(G)$]; $P(\text{"B"}|B)$ is the probability that the witness reports "Blue" given the cab is actually Blue (hit rate); and $P(\text{"B"}|G)$ is the probability the witness reports "Blue" given the cab is actually Green (false alarm rate). The answer to the cab problem, $P(B|\text{"B"})$, is given by the expression $\Omega_1/(1 + \Omega_1)$.

Previous solution

The cab problem is interpreted to imply that when the two colors are presented with equal frequency, the hit rate is .80 and the false alarm rate is .20. Lyon and Slovic (1976) pointed out that early versions of the problem did not clearly identify the hit rates and false alarm rates, giving the reader instead only the percentage of correct identifications. In newer versions of the problem, the judge is informed that the witness made an equal number of errors on each type of cab.[1] The hit and false alarm rates are represented in Figure 1 by the open circle labeled *a*. The problem also states that P(B), the probability of a blue cab, is .15, so the prior odds are .15/.85 = .176.

If it is assumed that the ratio of hit rate to false alarm rate is independent of the proportion of each cab color (dashed straight line in Figure 1), Equation 1 implies that $\Omega_1 = (.176)(.80/.20) = .706$ or $P(B|\text{"B"}) = \Omega_1/(1 + \Omega_1) = .414$, which is the so-called "normative" answer utilized in this work as the number to be compared with the judge's response. Judges often respond ".8" instead of .41, which led experimenters to propose that judges neglect base rate information (Bar-Hillel, 1980; Tversky & Kahneman, 1974, 1980, 1982). However, the previous solution (.41) implicitly assumes that P("B"|B)/P("B"|G) is independent of the base rate, which is inconsistent with theories and experiments in the area of signal detection. It will be shown that the answer .8 is compatible with Equation 1 and signal detection theory.

Signal detection theory

Although it may be reasonable to assume for some sources of information that the ratio of hit rate to false alarm rate is independent of signal probability, this assumption would not be realistic for the human witness[2] (Schum, 1981). A good deal of research has shown that a better approximation to the behavior of witnesses would be the curve shown in Figure 1 (Green & Swets, 1966). The curve in Figure 1 is based on the theory that each color of cab produces a normal distribution on a discriminal continuum, as shown in the inset of Figure 1. The witness responds "Blue" when the value on the Green-Blue continuum exceeds the response criterion, indicated by one of the vertical lines in the inset. For simplicity, the two variances are assumed to be equal and can be set to 1.0.

This signal detection theory can be written:

$$
\begin{aligned}
P(\text{"B"}|B) &= N(b - t) \\
P(\text{"B"}|G) &= N(g - t)
\end{aligned}
\tag{2}
$$

where N represents the cumulative standard normal density function, g is the mean value of Green cabs on the discriminal continuum, b is the corresponding value for Blue cabs, and t is the criterion for responding "Blue" or "Green." It follows that $d' = b - g = N^{-1}[P\text{"B"}|B)] - N^{-1}[P(\text{"B"}|G)]$ where N^{-1} is the inverse cumulative standard normal and d' is discriminability. For hit and false alarm rates of .80 and .20, $d' = 1.68$, which was the value used to derive the curve in Figure 1.[3]

In order to solve the cab problem by means of Equation 1, it is necessary to generalize the hit/false alarm ratio from the court's signal detection experiment, where $P(G) = P(B)$, to the city conditions, where $P(B)$ is only .15. To accomplish this generalization, one needs both signal detection theory (e.g., Equation 2) for the witness and a theory of judgment to predict how the witness will adjust his/her criterion (t in Equation 2) in response to changes in the signal probability (the proportion of Blue cabs). In other words, one needs to know the curve in Figure 1 and also how the point along the curve depends on $P(B)$. Given only the curve, virtually any value from $P(B)$ to 1.0 would be an acceptable solution to the cab problem. To pin down the solution requires a judgment theory, i.e., a theory of t.

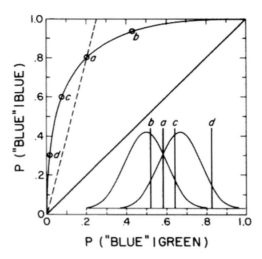

FIGURE 1. Signal detection analysis of the witness in the cab problem. Hit rate [P("B"|B)] plotted against false alarm rate [P("B"|G]. Point *a* shows values specified in the problem. Dashed line shows loci of points for which ratio of hit rate to false alarm rate is constant. The curve was derived from signal detection theory assuming each color of cab produces a normal distribution on a sensory continuum (inset). Point *b* is based on range-frequency theory. Point *c* is based on probability matching. Point *d* is close to a point that maximizes percentage of correct responses. The Bayesian solution to the cab problem changes depending on the theory of the witness. Assuming signal detection theory, virtually any answer from P(B) to 1.0 would be acceptable. The slope of the chord from the origin through the point is the likelihood ratio [P("B"|B)/P("B"|G)]. If point *d* is assumed, then P(B|"B") would be .82, rather than .41.

Unfortunately, competing theories of judgment have received supporting evidence, though under different conditions. Several theories predict that when the signal frequency is increased, the response criterion will move to increase the probability of a correct response (Friedman, Carterette, Nakatani, & Ahumada, 1968; Green & Swets, 1966). Range-frequency theory (Parducci & Sandusky, 1970) predicts that when signal frequency is increased, the criterion will move the *opposite direction,* tending to equalize the two response frequencies.

Range-frequency solution
Range-frequency theory states that judges have a tendency to use response categories with equal frequency. Parducci and Sandusky (1970) have shown that when the witness is not given information about signal probabilities and is not given feedback on each trial, the response probabilities are largely independent of stim-

ulus probabilities. If the witness reports half the cabs are "Blue" and half "Green" and if d' is constant (consistent with the results of Parducci & Sandusky, 1970), then the hit rate and false alarm rate will be .933 and .429, respectively, shown by point b in Figure 1. If such a witness reports "Blue," then by Equation 1, $\Omega_1 = (.176)$ $(.933/.429) = .383$, or $P(B|\text{"B"}) = .28$. Thus, assuming range-frequency theory, the "correct" answer of previous investigators (.41) is too large. The calculations are summarized in Table 1.

Probability matching solution

However, the witness in the street may be aware that only 15% of the cabs are Blue. The witness may have learned this from news reports or from feedback: An observer may judge a cab's color from the distance and then see it up close, see cabs during the day, and/or hear consensus judgments of others concerning color. Should the witness operate according to range-frequency theory, the probability of a correct identification would be only .63. The witness could do better to remain at point a, in which case the witness would be correct 80 % of the time. However, the witness could do still better by *never* saying "Blue," in which case the witness would be right 85% of the time, since 85% of the cabs are Green. Friedman et al. (1968) found that when the observer is given feedback, the response criterion shifts in the opposite direction from that predicted by range-frequency theory.

With feedback therefore, it seems plausible that the witness might match response probabilities to the stimulus probabilities. When $P(\text{"B"}|B) = .599$ and $P(\text{"B"}|G) = .076$, $P(\text{"B"})$ is approximately equal to $P(B)$. This strategy is shown by point c in Figure 1, and row c in Table 1. Assuming constant d' and assuming probability matching, Equation 1 implies that the normative posterior probability $[P(B|\text{"B"})]$ is .58, a normative solution actually greater than .5.

Optimal observer

Given feedback, it is not inconceivable that the witness could adjust the response criterion to maximize the probability of a correct identification, or to minimize some index representing the costs of different types of errors, such as the expected cost (Green & Swets, 1966). The witness could conceivably perform so that $P(\text{"B"}|B) = .302$ and $P(\text{"B"}|G) = .012$, corresponding to point d in Figure 1, giving 89% correct identification, close to the maximal value. In this case, the witness would be highly diagnostic, and if the witness says "Blue," then the probability the cab was actually Blue, by Equation 1, is .82! Thus, it is not necessarily unreasonable for a judge to give .80 as the solution to the cab problem.

Now, suppose the base rate were .50; i.e., $P(B) = P(G)$. Under these conditions, the witness would likely remain at point a, which simultaneously equalizes the two

TABLE 1. Summary of calculations

Limen value	Name	[a]P("B"|B)	[a]P("B"|G)	[b]L	[c]P("B")	[d]p(Correct)	[e,f]P(B|"B")
a	Conditional independence	.800	.200	4.00	.29	.80	.41
b	Equal response frequency	.933	.429	2.17	.50	.63	.28
c	Probability matching	.599	.076	7.88	.15	.88	.58
d	Optimal witness	.302	.012	25.17	.06	.89	.82

[a]P("B"|B) and P("B"|G) are given by Equations 2, with b−g = 1.68.
[b]L = P("B"|B)/P("B"|G) = slope of line from origin to point on ROC curve in Figure 1.
[c]P("B") = P("B"|B) · P(B) + P("B"|G)P(G).
[d]P(Correct) = P("B"|B) · P(B) + (1−P("B"|G))P(G).
[e]P(B) = .15.
[f]P(B|"B") = $\Omega_1/(1 + \Omega_1)$ where $\Omega_1 = \Omega_0 L$; $\Omega_0 = .176$.

response frequencies, matches stimulus and response frequencies, and maximizes the percentage of correct responses. Thus, the Bayesian solution would be .8, virtually the same as for the condition in which the base rate was .15 and the witness was assumed to be an ideal observer. The point is that Bayes' theorem does not necessarily imply an effect of the base rate unless a specific theory of the witness is assumed.

DISCUSSION

Theories of signal detection and judgment are required to generalize from the court's test of the witness to the performance in the street. In many signal detection experiments, data show that L varies as base rate is manipulated. When information concerning base rate is presented or the witness is given feedback, L increases as base rate decreases. When the cab problem is analyzed assuming d' is constant, the "correct" answer would be .28 if one believes the witness will respond "Blue" half the time; it would be .58 if the witness matched the probability of responding "Blue" to the proportion of Blue cabs in the street; it would be .82 if the witness will respond "Blue" less often, in response to the less frequent presence of Blue cabs and/or the possible high cost of a false alarm in the courtroom. In sum, the modal response of .8 by untrained subjects may be closer to the best normative solution than the value of .41 used in previous research. Therefore, there may be no evidence for a base rate fallacy.

The points of this paper may also apply to other problems employed in the literature on the "base rate fallacy" such as the light bulb problem or the engineer vs. lawyer problem (see Kahneman & Tversky, 1973). In the light bulb problem, the judge knows the probability of a defective bulb and the hit and false alarm rates of a mechanical light bulb tester. Suppose that the light bulb tester measures the current in each bulb for a given voltage. Suppose among bulbs that light, the distribution of current readings is normal for both good bulbs and defective bulbs, but the means of the distributions differ. It seems reasonable that any profit-oriented factory would adjust the criterion for deciding "defective" as a function of the costs of false alarms (discarding a good bulb) or misses (replacing a bad one) and the probability of a defective bulb.

In the engineer vs. lawyer problem, the judge is told that there is a group of 30 engineers and 70 lawyers that were tested by psychologists, who then wrote thumbnail sketches. The judges' task is to guess whether a sketch describes a lawyer or engineer. The psychologists gave information such as "he shows no interest in political and social issues … spends most of his free time on … mathematical puzzles." Kahneman and Tversky (1973) found that the judged probability that the sketch described an engineer varied as a function of the proportion of engineers, but the effect of base rate was much less than predicted by Bayes' theorem. However, their calculations assumed that the hit to false alarm ratio for the sketches would be independent of the base rate. The problem is that the probability of a given person *being described* as "interested in mathematical puzzles" would presumably depend on the proportion of engineers and lawyers. For example, if the entire population were engineers, a witness might describe Joe as "weak in mathematics." However, if Joe were the only engineer in a population of lawyers, the same witness would be unlikely to select this description of Joe.

A recent paper by Schum (1981) gives a very thorough analysis of the evidential impact of testimony in Bayesian inference. Schum makes an important distinction between direct testimony concerning the hypothesis and testimony concerning a datum relevant to the hypothesis. Similarly the distinction between the datum and the report of the datum should be maintained. The report may convey more information than the datum itself (Schum, 1981). For example, it may be that interest in mathematical puzzles is not highly diagnostic of being an engineer or lawyer, but the *report* of interest in mathematical puzzles may be highly diagnostic of a rare engineer in a population consisting mostly of lawyers.

The theoretical analysis of this paper shows that many previous investigations of the "base rate fallacy" were based on a normative solution that rested on a shaky and perhaps unrealistic assumption concerning the independence of the hit/false alarm ratio from base rate. It should also be noted that the empirical evidence for neglect of base rate is also inconsistent. When the base rate is manipulated in a within-subjects design, it appears to be utilized by subjects (Birnbaum & Mellers, Note 1; Fischhoff, Slovic, & Lichtenstein, 1979). Birnbaum & Mellers (Note 1) found that the weight of the base rate even exceeds that of highly diagnostic sources. Subjects in within-subjects designs attend to base rate, to source bias, and to source diagnosticity (see also Birnbaum & Stegner, 1979). Tversky and Kahneman (1982) also discuss between-subject results that were interpreted as evidence of subjects attending to base rate information.

CONCLUSION

The moral of this paper is not that subjects are necessarily accurate intuitive statisticians who understand signal detection theory, assume the witness is an ideal observer, and correctly solve the cab problem. Subjects in between-subject studies may indeed neglect the base rate and respond ".8" because this value seems to characterize the believability of the source, as argued by Tversky and Kahneman (1980, 1982), Bar-Hillel (1980), and others. However, this note does call attention to the fact that the normative solution to the cab problem requires the assumption of a theory of the witness, whether by the subject or the experimenter.

NOTES

Thanks are due to Barbara Mellers, David Noreen, Amos Tversky, and Robert Sorkin for comments on an earlier draft.

Requests for offprints should be addressed to Michael H. Birnbaum, Department of Psychology, University of Illinois, 603 East Daniel St., Champaign, IL 61820. Received for publication September 11, 1981; revision received April 28, 1982.

1. Other aspects of the cab problem as stated above are also unclear. For example, the statement that 85% of the cabs in the city are Blue does not necessarily imply that 85% of the cabs involved in hit and run accidents at night are Blue. The decision-maker is presumably supposed to assume that both cab companies operate at night, have drivers with comparable skill, etc., so that the base rate can be interpreted as relevant to the problem. Tversky and Kahneman (1980) discuss effects of variation in the phrasing of the base rate information and contend that if the base rate information seems "causal" then it will be utilized. However, their experiments have not yet unconfounded the so-called "causal" version of the problem from the noncausal but clearly relevant version. Tversky and Kahneman (1982) used a modified form of the cab problem in which the court test is described as being done "under the same circumstances" as existed on the night of the accident, but the base rate and payoff conditions of the test are not explicitly specified.

2. Even mechanical devices such as a light bulb tester may be amenable to the same analysis. Suppose the threshold for the light bulb tester is adjustable, and it is assumed that normal and defective bulbs produce normal distributions of resistance values with different means, the same

analysis would apply as in Figure 1. Thus, the ratio of hit rate to false alarm rate will vary for some mechanical devices as well as for human witnesses.

3. Other signal detection theories assuming unequal variance or using other functions, such as the logistic instead of the normal, would lead to similar conclusions for the present analysis. Empirical curves in signal detection studies with varying base rates typically have a shape similar to the curve in Figure 1 and do not resemble the dashed line in Figure 1 (e.g., Green & Swets, 1966, p. 88, p. 95). However, even very different theories, such as high threshold theory or a linear theory with slope = 1 imply that the ratio of $P(\text{"B"}|B)/P(\text{"B"}|G)$ will change as a function of $P(B)$.

REFERENCE NOTE

1. Birnbaum, M. H., & Mellers, B. A. *Bayseian inference: Combining base rates with opinions of sources who vary in credibility.* Paper presented at the Midwestern Psychological Association, 1978.

REFERENCES

Bar-Hillel, M. The base rate fallacy in probability judgments. *Acta Psychologica,* 1980, *44,* 211–233.

Birnbaum, M. H., & Mellers, B. A. Bayesian inference: Combining base rates with opinions of sources who vary in credibility.

Birnbaum, M. H., & Stegner, S. E. Source credibility: Bias, expertise, and the judge's point of view. *Journal of Personality and Social Psychology,* 1979, *37,* 48–74.

Friedman, M. P., Carterette, E. C, Nakatani, L., & Ahumada, A. Feedback and frequency variables in signal detection. *Perception & Psychophysics,* 1968, *3,* 5–10.

Fischhoff, B., Slovic, P., & Lichtenstein, S. Subjective sensitivity analysis. *Organizational Behavior and Human Performance,* 1979, *23,* 339–359.

Green, D. M., & Swets, J. A. *Signal detection theory and psychophysics.* New York: Wiley, 1966.

Hammerton, M. A. A case of radical probability estimation. *Journal of Experimental Psychology,* 1973, *101,* 252–254.

Kahneman, D., & Tversky, A. On the psychology of prediction. *Psychological Review,* 1973, *80,* 237–351.

Lyon, D., & Slovic, P. Dominance of accuracy information and neglect of base rates in probability estimation. *Acta Psychologica,* 1976, *40,* 287–289.

Parducci, A., & Sandusky, A. Limits on the applicability of signal detection theory. *Perception & Psychophysics,* 1970, *7,* 63–64.

Schum, D. Sorting out the effects of witness sensitivity and response-criterion placement upon the influential value of testimonial evidence. *Organizational Behavior and Human Performance,* 1981, *27,* 153–196.

Tversky, A., & Kahneman, D. Judgment under uncertainty: Heuristics and biases. *Science,* 1974, *185,* 1124–1131.

Tversky, A., & Kahneman, D. Causal schemata in judgments under uncertainty. In M. Fishbein (Ed.), *Progress in Social Psychology.* Hillsdale, N J.: Erlbaum, 1980.

Tversky, A., & Kahneman, D. Evidential impact of base rates. In D. Kahneman, P. Slovic, & A. Tversky (Eds.), *Judgment under uncertainty: Heuristics and biases.* Cambridge University Press, 1982.

PROBLEM SOLVING

AN EXPERIMENTAL INQUIRY INTO THE EXISTENCE AND NATURE OF 'INSIGHT'

MARY ELIZABETH BULBROOK
Cornell University

It was inevitable that the recent occupation with 'learning' should presently lead backward toward the consideration of a rapid, effective and 'intuitional' form of operation. 'Backward' because that had long been a favorite conception of learning, but a conception displaced by the simpler and more manageable forms of the reflex, automatic, psychomotor and ideational varieties which set the experiments of a generation ago. At that time the scientific standards coming into psychology placed a high value upon simple and mechanical concepts and procedures. Sensory processes, simple and direct associations, and the blundering advances of 'trial-and-error' were the popular terms in laboratory studies upon learning in man and in other animals. It was only a matter of time when the limits of these simpler categories of description and explanation should be discovered and when 'higher' processes and modes should be again invoked. Moreover, the recent occupation with the organism, in biology and psychology, as against the analytical inspection of parts, details, and elementary functions, has also contributed to this tendency in the study of learning. Organismal factors, *Gestalten,* the primacy of the general pattern, the influence upon development of the total-body, and the general directiveness of life, have all been facts of this same order tending away from the older and simpler mechanisms. It was natural that 'insight,' 'forecast,' 'purpose,' and even 'intuition' should have been rescued from the commoner and less precise employment of them as dictionary terms and turned to psychological account.

To psychologists familiar with current and recent discussions, it will be unnecessary to dwell upon the revival in periodical and textbook of the term 'insight' and to point out the variety of meaning and the resulting ambiguity in its use.[1] Some of these meanings are perceptive apprehension, acute observation, understanding, foresight and forethought, rapid learning, an intuitive flash, sudden grasp or illumination, intelligence, sophisticated skill, cognized relations, the felt basis of an attitude, experienced determination, a new perception of a goal, and a new configuration.

American Journal of Psychology
July 1932, Vol. 44, No. 3, pp. 409–453

Now there are obvious difficulties in approaching by experiment a topic so uncertain and so variously shaded by theory and point of view. All we have tried to do in this study is to submit to experimental conditions various situations which have been commonly alleged to exhibit experiences and performances characterized by 'insight.' Here it has been our hope that the appearance of a common process, function, or accomplishment might help us to an understanding of this elusive characteristic. In anticipation of our results we may provisionally say that no such common and unique operation of the animal organism has emerged from our quest. Nevertheless, the experiments have thrown considerable light upon a class of performances just now under close scrutiny from many sides.

THE EXPERIMENTS

Most laboratory studies of 'insight' have been of the problem-solving and maze-running kinds and have made use of children, other primates, and white rats. In order to add the very important experimental control which is to be derived from the report of the observer himself, we have used human adults, both individuals trained in psychological reporting and individuals untrained. For both sorts we have added the device of technical *instruction* in order to obtain the actual conditions (commonly left—even in experimental settings—to inference or to speculation) under which the organism is thrown into functional commission. It would seem now to be of less importance to *infer* insight from behavior ('insight' taken, e.g., in one of the above senses) than *to obtain a descriptive account of the actual modes of organic performance* where insight has already been alleged.

We have taken individual observations and also, in the light of results thus derived, have secured observations from small assembled groups. We consider the problems in order, setting down the individual-results first, then the group-results.

Thirteen problems, presently to be given in a natural sequence, were placed before each of 7 *O*s. Five of these *O*s were trained in psychological observation. The other two were without technical training.[2] For the group-presentations, 110 students were used in congregates of 5–8 from an undergraduate course in general psychology.[3] In order to prevent troublesome influences from successive presentations, the following temporal order was adopted: Problems 1, 5, 6, 7, 3, 12, 2, 4, 10, 9, 8, 11, 13. The groups worked through only certain problems.

PROCEDURE

For the individual *O*s, the formal instructions[4] were placed on a large blank sheet of paper which lay on a table immediately before the *O*. The table was in a corner with blank walls in front and to the right, while on *O's* left sat the experimenter. Upon the table were usually scattered various objects, some having little or no relation to the problem, others supplying means for various solutions. The arrangement of these objects remained fixed throughout the experiment.

So far as possible, these arrangements were preserved in the group-presentation. Some changes were necessary. For the groups a large rectangular table was equipped with a single set of the same objects in a similar haphazard arrangement. No less than five and no more than eight Os at a time were seated on three sides, while the fourth was reserved for E. A pencil and mimeographed copies of certain instructions and all questions concerning procedure were placed face downward before each O, to be turned over and read at a signal from E. Other instructions were orally given. All questions were to be answered 'yes' or 'no' except the last one of each set. Emphasis was placed on the fact that the experiment was not an intelligence test of any kind or a competitive trial of capacity. The grouped Os were directed not to handle the experimental objects.

At times during the experiment, however, it was found necessary to assure the grouped Os that a solution was possible, and this assurance sometimes evoked a self-instruction that 'I am being compared with others and must make a good showing.' These by-products of socialization—while they must never be assumed—must always be looked for in group-operations. They frequently determine output and function in the solo experiment as well. Only careful report will turn them up and estimate their influence. As antecedents and determinants of function they can never be behavioristically inferred from mere physical proximity and isolation.

PROBLEM 1

This problem turned on the significant use of materials which might suggest some form of 'insight.' A string of beads was placed directly before O. It consisted of two small white 'pearl' beads alternating with one larger yellow glass bead, except for the middle portion of the string where five white beads separated the yellow. The bore of the white beads was too small to admit of stringing except by a single thread with a moistened and rolled end. The needles supplied were too large.

(A) INDIVIDUAL Os

Two sets of instructions were made, the second for presentation in case an O failed to obtain the solution under the first.

> *Instruction 1:* Make a single regularly repeated pattern without either unstringing or restringing the beads, and without knotting or breaking the thread. Proceed aloud.

Instruction 2: Make a single regularly repeated pattern without either unstringing or restringing the beads, and without knotting or breaking the thread. Use any of the means supplied on the table. Proceed aloud.

Due to the emphasis of the first set of instructions, attention was primarily centered on the experimental object. Each *O* first sought to get the instruction clear and then carefully examine the beads in order to understand fully the conditions and limits of the situation. Twisting the threads together by some means or other and sliding the beads across was one of the most obvious solutions suggested. It never worked, of course; and the *O* soon realized that instructions stood against it. The superfluous beads could not be unstrung.

Four *O*s (*Fe, Si, My,* and *Gl*) went through a process of elimination to arrive at the solution. *Fe* solved by a consideration of various means of eliminating the irregularity, "I see nothing to do but twist the threads together. If they would hold together, the beads could be slipped over." He picked up the beeswax. "It won't do." He picked up the glue. "No, no. That won't do. It is too sticky." He picked up the needle and sought to use it but found that the white beads would not go over it. From the first the various articles and tools available entered into the situation for this *O* as having possible significance. Now he picked up the saw from among the destructive instruments and laughed at using it. But after he had considered all the ways that the superfluous white beads could be eliminated, he suddenly asked, "Can you break the beads? That is the only way of getting them off that I can see," and he picked up the pliers and broke one of them. "Breaking was a last resort. I had tried everything else. I could think of nothing else until that occurred to me as possible."

For *My, Si,* and *Gl* the elimination took place without reference to the objects on the table but from the conditions imposed by the instructions and limitations presented by the object itself. "The beads had to be removed. Since all the natural ways were prohibited, that was the only one left. I tried first to crush them with the fingers but they were too hard. I thought of biting them but that was bad. I looked around and saw the tools and I took the pliers and broke them" (*Gl*). It is obvious here that the instruments played a minor part in the solution. They merely furnished excellent, because stronger, substitutes for hands and teeth. The *O* was set for an instrument to break or crush when he looked at the various materials on the table. "If you cannot move any bead over another bead, you cannot possibly change their relative positions on the string, and they are an uneven number, so they cannot be distributed so as to make a regular pattern. Can the thread be passed through any bead twice? But that would be hard to do. Are you allowed to break the beads?" (*Si*). He then counted the beads and said, "That would do. Why I thought of breaking the beads, I do not know. I just did. It was the only way of doing it." Here again it was only after the correct method of solution was obtained that the instrument for its accomplishment was sought.

My, proceeding step by step, commented clearly and logically, "Two-one, two-one is the pattern. There are five extra white beads. If those five were out, it would be a regular pattern. One might make one by distributing the white beads. How can they be distributed? There are five white beads and twenty-one large ones, therefore they cannot be evenly distributed. The directions say not to unstring or restring, etc.; but those beads cannot be distributed without breaking or knotting the thread. I can try arranging the beads on the paper. Thus far I have been thinking of the pattern on a straight line. I can make a circle or a figure like this, but that won't succeed. Is it permissible to break the beads? The instruction does not say anything about not breaking the beads. I can do that... . That was the only possible solution because, even if you could break the thread or did break the string, you could not make a regular pattern utilizing the beads."

No reference in these two cases was made to the instruments lying on the table. They were as completely extraneous to the solution of the problem as if they were not there. But in the actual breaking the *O* invariably surveyed the outlay and seized the pliers for the purpose. That this instrument easily became a destructive crusher in this situation is not surprising, when one considers its manifold uses in constructive building where it is often used to break or bend.

Three *O*s (*Wi, Je,* and *Mc*) failed to reach the solution. It never occurred to *Je* and *Wi* that the integrity of the beads could be destroyed in any way. The beads were to be removed or redistributed as beads. They never got beyond this assumption, and this assumption was never formally recognized. That all *O*s were inhibited in some measure—although not so completely as with *Je* and *Wi*—against destruction as a means of solution is obvious from the fact that after a consideration of many possible methods of removing or redistributing the intact beads, the *O* either declared it to be impossible or asked if it was not so. At this point he was invariably assured either that "it was not impossible" or that "the irregularity could be eliminated." This is a clear instance where *the occasion* (occasional instruction) stands directly against the carrying out of a formal instruction.

The most interesting case of inhibited action was that of *Mc* who failed to reach a solution under either instruction. Under the first instruction attention was focussed, as in other cases mentioned, on the beads and the limitations imposed by the conditions of the instruction. After various suggestions in attempting to make a uniform pattern, and after having been told that such a thing was possible, he "does not see how it can be done." Under the second instruction, he picked up the saw, "May I use this?" Then he picked up the thread, "This is the only thing that might do." He took up the objects one by one, remarking each time "That won't do" or "This does not seem to be applicable"; but, except for the saw, he never considered the destructive instruments at all. "I'm still utterly baffled by the situation. I see only one way of making it a pattern and that is barred by the instructions."

That *Mc* noticed the instruments was evidenced by his handling the saw; but that they were recognized only in their usual contexts and not in any unusual relation to a delicate string of beads was apparent from his behavior as well as from the above account. This is the opposite of what occurred in the case of *Ke*. The mere presence of the instrument within visual range caused him, intent on some means of removing the superfluous beads, to give consideration to any possible relation it might have to the problem in hand. After examining the string and trying to run another string through the beads with the needle and thread on the table, and after the assurance that the solution was possible, he leaned back, looked at the table, and said, "I might break the beads and take them out.... . The beads could not be moved according to the instructions. The large ones could not be slipped over the small ones. I saw a pair of pliers over here and saw the string of beads over here that could not be moved off. I just re-read the instructions and broke them." The instrument for *Ke*, as for *Fe*, entered into the situation from the first; but for *Fe* 'breaking' suggested the instrument while for *Ke* the instrument suggested 'breaking'.

RESULTS

Acting under occasional and self-instructions and anticipatively apprehending the results *O* eliminated one plan after another until the solution either was reached or was blocked by an interfering occasional instruction or by the failure of comment and imaginative apprehension. The elimination of possibilities may take place either with respect to suitability of means or instruments or with respect to procedure permitted within the limitations imposed by experimental object and formal instruction.

For the *O* there is always a plan or method of approach. When his approaches all fail him, he ceases to try and desires to terminate the experimental period. He never continues, trying at random, in expectation that the solution will simply occur. He always applies a definite method and this method is a contribution of his own under self-instruction. He does not wait for sudden appearance of the solution. He does something that definitely brings about, or causes, or creates that solution. There is always an accompaniment of pleased pride in, and approval of, himself with the accomplishment of the solution. In failure there is frustration combined with impatience and disappointment with himself.

Inability to see an ordinary object in an extraordinary context and a predisposition to respect the integrity of property constituted frustrating moments.

(B) GROUP Os

The instruction was the same as Instruction 1 above, except for the direction "Proceed aloud" which was omitted. The time allotted was 10 minutes. Then the following questions were answered. (The replies are given in percentages.)

		Yes	*No*
1.	Did you look over the table to see what you could use?	14	86
2.	Did you consider the string of beads only and what the instructions did and did not allow you to do to it?	93	7
3.	Did you solve it?	25	75
4.	Did you rearrange the beads to form a different kind of pattern?	42	58
5.	Did you break the beads (imaginatively)?	25	75
6.	Did you think of breaking the beads first and then look for the proper instrument?	12	88
7.	Did the instrument make you think of breaking the beads?	3	97
8.	Comment further upon your procedure, telling any way you went about eliminating the extra beads that is left out in the questions.		

Since a quarter of the group (Question 5) reached the 'breaking' solution and only 15% of them (Q. 6 and 7) considered the instruments, it is obvious that a tenth of them who thus solved did not regard the instrumental means. But then, they were not actually called to smash as the individual *O*s were. This is an interesting difference in solution, which is also supported by Questions 1 and 2 (concentration on the beads). Answers to the last question indicate that practically all the methods employed toward solving by this large number were also employed by the smaller number of individual *O*s. Pattern arrangement, bead counting, and the consequent deduction that redistribution was impossible were means suggested.

In a few cases the solution came immediately. Those who suggested breaking the beads report substantially as follows: "The instruments had nothing to do with it either before or after getting the solution. I took it for granted that the tools on the table were for another experiment." "I thought of breaking them with my teeth or the eversharp in my pocket." "I never thought of the instruments on the table. When I saw the table, it seemed more like a class in vegetable gardening than an experiment"—another good example of apprehension of an object only in its usual context.

Some, after making several tentative and ineffective suggestions, concluded the solution impossible. Most of them, however, failed to get beyond a stage of search or of comment-and-inspection in the time allotted.

These results substantiate those from the individual *O*s. Inhibited solutions are more plentiful, due, perhaps, to the small amount of time; but the initial steps of the solving process—apprehension, inspection-and-comment, search for method, and procedure under self-instruction until that instruction is perceived as inapplicable, re-apprehension and search for another method—are typical here also.

PROBLEM 2

This problem was intended as a parallel to the foregoing. Small white wooden beads were obtained, and some of them were stained black with India ink. They were then strung with the white, the pattern alternating one white with one black, one white with one black, except toward the center where eight whites separated blacks. The solution lay in converting the ink in the bottle on the table to the uses of a dye. No *O* questioned how the black beads were colored but accepted them as given.

> *Instruction 1.* Make a single regularly repeated pattern without either unstringing or restringing the beads, without knotting or breaking the thread, and without destroying the beads. Proceed aloud.

> *Instruction 2.* Make a single regularly repeated pattern without either unstringing or restringing the beads, without knotting or breaking the thread, and without destroying the beads. Use any of the means supplied on the table. Proceed aloud.

If the *O* failed to solve under the first set of instructions, the second was presented.

The solution involved the use of a medium in unusual contextual relations. In some cases it was obtained more easily than in the preceding bead-experiment. The *O* was memorially instructed from cues gained there. "I got the solution of the present string from a cue from the other beads. As soon as I got away from the rearrangement of the beads on the thread, it was easy to think of doing other things" (*Mc*). "I am looking for possible interpretations of your instructions" (*My*).

Je, My, Gl, and *Mc,* as in the preceding experiment, set about seeking the solution, not from a consideration of the whole experimental situation, but from the conditions imposed by the instruction and the experimental object itself. Search for a way of attack, accompanied by a careful inspection and comment upon the situation, was characteristic of the procedure. *Si,* for example, asked about the instructions to make sure he had them accurately and picked up the string and examined it. "There is no catch on the string." He examined the string and beads again carefully. "One thing is obvious; if there are more white than black beads, you must either get rid of some white ones or else get some black ones. There are no black ones. Is this string symmetrically arranged with regard to the center ones? No, it isn't." He read over the instructions again. "For all purposes this is a closed circle and no bead can be moved over another nor can they be broken. Is it unsolvable?" When answered negatively he said: "Well, something must be done to the white beads."

Where the solution was reached, the *O* invariably arrived at it through a consideration of painting the beads. "I did not notice the ink on the table, but I named ink instead of dye or paint because I had had more experience with ink than with either of the other two" (*Mc*). "How about some paint or something? Some black ink if there is any available," he picked up the ink bottle, "Or, better still, the black ink from my fountain pen" (*Si*). "I thought of paint first but then I thought of ink because you would be more liable to have it around" (*My*). Here again the method of solution was obtained before the exact medium for its accomplishment. Since the *O* searched for something he could use in following out his solution, ink easily became, under these circumstances, a dye in spite of the penstaff lying alongside the bottle.

As before, *Fe* and *Ke* derived the solution from the whole experimental situation, taking into account every article on the table and its possible relation to the problem in hand. *Ke* ran his eyes rapidly around the table a few times inspecting and commenting upon all the objects on it. "Suppose I run another string through and pull this one out.... But I guess that is unstringing and restringing. Oh well, I can paint them black," and he seized the ink bottle to do so. *Fe* followed much the same procedure, glancing all around the table and then reaching for the ink bottle. Here there was a very definite instruction resulting from the solution in the former experiment.

Gl and *Je* failed to solve the problem, the case of *Je* exactly paralleling that of *Mc* in the former experiment under both instructions. *Gl*, however, solved it under the second instruction, "It said, 'use any of the means on the table.' I had tried all the arrangements of the beads before and they would not work. I thought there might be some chemical here that you could put on them to change the color. I looked around and saw the ink bottle and thought, 'Aha, that will do it.'"

RESULTS

Here each *O* followed the same general procedure as in the preceding experiment. If he had limited himself before to a consideration of the experimental object and the conditions of the instructions, he did so in this case; but if he had taken the instrumental approach in the first, he followed it now. Only one exception occurred. The change from the first instruction to the second in the case of *Gl* induced a change in the set toward the problem.

In some cases *O*s took cues from the former problem. Practically all of the inspection of the experimental object and weighing of the instructions were absent here from those who approached the solution by an instrumental elimination. Self-instructed, the *O* looked around the table, immediately questioning the suitability of the various objects. Cues were of aid, too, in the other approach, where the *O* paid more careful attention to possible implications in the instructions, and where he took account of and guarded against any inhibiting moments similar to those in the former problem.

But in other cases helpful cues were not carried over. The *O* was as strongly inhibited here as before by his custom of seeing a thing in a useful context from apprehending it in another and a newer one. In one case (*Je*) the cue from the previous problem gave him a set toward destruction as the means of obtaining a single uniform pattern, a set that was useless in the solution. Even under the new instructions, this set was carried over.

The same elimination of one self-instructed plan after another, the same methodical procedure of search accompanied by inspection-and-comment to the formulation of the self-instruction, and, when no other plan could be made, the refusal to continue planless characterized this problem as definitely as the first.

PROBLEM 3

A cork in a large bottle with a very narrow neck was presented to *O*.

> *Instruction.* Remove the cork from the bottle without destroying either the cork or the bottle.

> The situation here differed from the first two in having the solution by instrumental means suggested. A large corkscrew, the usual means of removing a cork from a bottle, lay among the tools, which also included a small flexible wire. While this suggested the use of an instrument, however, it was always that particular instrument. Only one *O* analyzed the situation to the extent of not applying the corkscrew first. *My* sought to gain a thorough comprehension of all the conditions inherent in the experimental object. Inspecting and commenting minutely upon the cork and bottle, suggesting one means after another without reference to the tools, he finally remarked with characteristic acumen, "Judging by the appearance of the cork, I believe mechanical means have been used on this before," and seized the wire, knotted an end which was too small, made a larger knot, caught the cork on it, and pulled it out. *Ke* picked up the wire first but threw it down without trying it, "I must try the corkscrew."

> All the other *O*s, after trying the corkscrew, made a loop of either the wire or the thread, caught the cork at the right angle, and with and without the aid of the corkscrew, pulled the cork out. Here as before a means is employed effectively out of its usual context. No *O* failed in this solution for various reasons; first, because corks inside bottles are a common occurrence, and, secondly, the experimental set-up favored the correct solution. When sharp point and corkscrew were not successful, the *O* invariably seized upon the wire.

RESULTS

When the occasion suggested the correct direction in which solution was brought about, there was a tendency on the part of the *O*s to go in that direction. In most cases, however, the more obvious suggestive factor, the corkscrew, inhibited a consideration of less obvious but equally suggestive factors (*e.g.*, those considered by *My*) until failure brought about a further investigation of the experimental situation with another consequent plan of procedure.

The same inspection-and-comment, the same search with an eye to possible ways of procedure, the same methodical self-instructed plan of procedure and elimination through failure or inapplicability characterized this problem as the others.

PROBLEM 4

This problem consisted of a series of seven cards presented in order bearing seven different arrangements of the line-elements of the letter R lying on its side, but the last arrangement comprising the R as it is ordinarily presented except for its side-wise position (Fig. 1). The principle of this series was suggested by problems in the classification of a new species or variety in taxonomic zoology or botany. The aim was to lead the *O* through a number of steps containing very familiar elements in more or less strange relations to each other to these same elements in their familiar relations. Experimental interest was centered on how soon the *O* saw the familiar relation, and, after seeing it, commented upon the whole series.

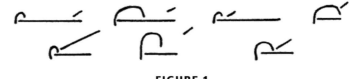

FIGURE 1

Instruction. Identify each member of the series presented to you.

The element of search was quite apparent in most of these observations. "I keep wondering, 'What do you want?'" (*Ke*). "I can name the lines. It seems as if it ought to represent something more definite than that" (*Gl*). "Nothing like sea-lions, is it? Is it a joke or anything of that nature? I try to see something there, but I am not sure of it. It is not supposed to be an ideograph, is it? Is it supposed to be something you can see?" (*Si*).

One thing after another was named by the *O*s as a possible identification; although in practically all of their observations there was an element of uncertainty concerning the object with which it was identified. "It looks like the other figures. It might be two or three objects like tombstones, etc., except for faults" (*Ke*). "It looks like a P on the side with a long vertical part. What the little oblique line is bothers me. It is also a stream of water in a tile" (*Gl*). "It is a railroad track going into a tunnel. I cannot make out the slanting line" (*My*). "It is a mouse that is only partly there. The tail and head are missing" (*Si*).

In every case but one the *O* sought to give a meaning, though often very unsatisfactory, to the figure—to make it a symbol fitting in with known and recognizable phenomena. Only in the excepted case (*Mc*) very little effort was made to name the figure as some familiar object. In this case the object was too uncertain, too unsatisfactory. He comments: "It does not look like anything to me. It looks like a tunnel, a road here, and a soldier." "That is nothing at all." "Nor that. It requires an awful strain to get the soldier and tunnel."

There was a strong tendency on the part of many of the *O*s to analyze the lines before naming the object with which they might be identified. "It is just a curved line, and a straight one, and a short one" (*Ke*). "One is a straight horizontal line, the other a curved one, and the other oblique.... It is again like the other one but this time there is a short horizontal line, with the curved and oblique lines above it" (*Gl*). "I cannot make out the slanting line. The horizontal line is longer" (*My*). "It is a poorly drawn semicircle. It is like the first thing except the curve is longer and the little oblique line higher" (*Fe*). In general, these *O*s, who saw the figure as a group of lines first, tended to make the letter identification long before presentation of the last card; although this identification was, for the most part, as uncertain as the object identifications.

Fe, Gl, Si, and *My* suggested a letter early in the presentation. The first figure for *Fe* is "a sort of P lying on its side with a long stroke," and the second is "like the first except the curve is larger and the little oblique line higher. It suggests an incomplete R." For this second one also *Gl* commented "If I look at it sidewise, it suggests an R with part of it missing." For the fourth, "The curve and the horizontal line suggests an incomplete D," but for the sixth he said, "It looks like an uncompleted R. When I take them (the lines) as water in a tile, the oblique line does not fit. When an R, it does fit." *Si,* in the midst of positing several objects which the lines might represent, said, concerning the third figure, "If I turn it around, I can make an R out of it but I guess I'm supposed to keep it upright." He was self-instructed here to avoid the unusual in position. On the fifth figure *My* commented, "The line is longer, the tunnel is smaller. It looks like the letter R. I turned my head sidewise and looked at it like that. Once before it looked like the letter R rather remotely," and, on the sixth, "It still looks like the letter R."

For *Ke, Mc,* and *Je* the letter appeared only on the presentation of the last figure. Failure to suggest an R earlier was ascribed primarily to the set. "It is an R—a letter. The elements were so scattered in the others that that must be why I never got it before. I never thought of a letter" (*Ke*). He picked up the cards and went through them: "It is easy to see them all as Rs now." "The whole series is composed of various distortions of the R turned sidewise. I was set for a picture. I did not expect anything tipped over" (*Mc*), and for *Je* the set was strong enough to cause him to continue the pictorial identification to the last figure, "The first flash is a rabbit, the semicircular thing representing an ear. I just decided this when I got a very brilliant flash with an incipient shrug of the shoulders, 'Why, of course, that is the letter R.' There never was in any of the earlier figures any suggestion of a letter. I have some suspicion that either the card tipped as you put it down, or my head did. You can see that the same motif was carried out throughout" (*Je*).

Care was taken on the part of *E* to prevent tipping the card. This "kinaesthetic pull toward the left," "tipping or turning the head sidewise" was mentioned frequently in the commentary, not only for a letter, but for objects in motion. "There is a kinaesthetic pull in the shoulders toward the left. I have a visual apprehension of the long angular line travelling toward the left" (*Je*).

From the final reports of the various *O*s it was obvious that every member of the series had taken on the characteristic significance of the R symbol. The purpose of every member now was to represent that letter. "We have our R this time. It is a tied image R, too. The R stands out immediately. There was no regular development in the R, but I can see now that that was what it was all along" (*Gl*). "There is the same general character to the whole series. All of them represent an R quite well, although each of them taken individually could have represented any of the other things equally well. But you can see now that it could not have been anything but an R" (*Si*). *My*, who was sure of the letter on the fifth figure, reported, "I think I noticed the R on the third one. There was not a close enough resemblance. I thought I would see a few more before I committed myself."

For the most part, the same general elements were noted from presentation to presentation, but their direction was undetermined. That "one figure is like the preceding one" or that "there is a certain similarity among them all" was reported time and again; but the significance was never fully determined, except in the case of *My*, until the last and most familiar relationship was presented.

RESULTS

The reports from this problem display every stage of advance toward identification from an almost pure perceptive level, accompanied by the vaguest and most indefinite kind of puzzled search, in some cases, to a more concrete, though tentative, symbolization for some familiarly recognized object or objects, in others.

A uniformity among differences was one of the first general conditions noted, but an uncertainty of its significance accompanied the comment of every observer but one until the last member in the series was presented. Then the significance became certain either immediately or secondarily, depending upon the set of the *O*. After once knowing the correct symbol, a recognition of its appropriateness in comparison with any other identification occurred. This revaluation of the whole series in the light of the last member was characteristic of every *O*.

By a process of finding the most appropriate identification-object, an object which fitted in best with the recognized uniformity, two *O*s named the correct letter midway in the series, the later presentations merely serving to confirm the conjecture.

The disposition on the part of the *O*s to verticality, to apprehending objects in their customary positions, was an inhibiting moment in the identification of the lines as a letter. So also was the predisposition to regard the lines as a picture of something.

Those *Os* who inspected the members as lines first tended to name letters as well as objects for identification early in the presentation. *Ke* was the only exception to this.

PROBLEM 5

This problem was intended to demonstrate a solving procedure combining 'trial and error' with 'insight' (= 'foresight and forethought' or 'new configuration'?). A set of papers, each sheet bearing Fig. 2 (but wanting the dotted diagonal at the centre) was presented to *O*, who was supplied with a red pencil for clear retracing of the lines. Gaps at certain junctions were left to discourage retracing. A clear disjunction of the inscribed figure from the surrounding rectangle was hinted at in the drawing.

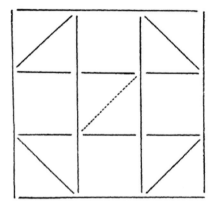

FIGURE 2

Instruction. Here are two figures. Trace continuously (without retracing) every line of both. Use just as small a number of copies as you can. You will be penalized for every wrongly traced set. Comment aloud.

(A) INDIVIDUAL Os

Here as elsewhere conditions were considered and no random stumbling trials were made.

Search for the best way of attacking the figure, and inspection of and comment upon its salient characteristics with reference to the most advisable way of beginning marked the procedure. The *Os* had concerted plans before placing pencil on the figure. "I looked to see how the two could be traced independently. I saw that the square could be gone around simply enough. So could the other figure" (*Ke*). "I did it mostly by means of eye-movements. The solution came practically immediately" (*Mc*).

Some *O*s traced the figure first by moving the eyes over it. Others traced it in the air with the pencil held above the figure. Most of them began the actual tracing on the inside figure; but *Gl* and *Wi* began at points on the outside square. The beginning points were based on occasional instruction *plus* inspection-and-comment. "I saw that I must begin at a point here and I saw that, since the figure is symmetrical, it made no particular difference which of the like points I did begin on" (*Si*). "The outside figure must be begun at a point on the inside one" (*Gl*). "The first glance revealed that a gap would have to be left in the corner of the square which would have to be done at the end. Then the inside figure could be drawn immediately" (*Wi*).

After reading the instructions, one *O* had difficulty in seeing the two figures. "At first the gaps and the two-figure idea bothered me. I saw it first as a square and an octagon with other line-figures" (*Mc*). "I am looking to find the two figures" (*Si*). In general the *O* began by seeking to understand the instructions fully in order not to miss any condition which might be of significance in the given problem.

RESULTS

After a mastery of the instructions and after inspecting and commenting upon the experimental object, the *O* approached the solution by a method of action under self-instruction and perception of its results, that is, of starting from some plausible point and proceeding until balked by an unforeseen condition. Thereupon another point was chosen and the same procedure continued, always, however, with this condition taken into account. This method was followed until the solution was reached.

Owing to the threat of penalization, the figure was concretely traced only after the solution was obtained.

(B) GROUP Os

The same figure under the same instruction, but without the direction "Comment aloud," was presented to the group. Five minutes was allotted for actual tracing.

Questions	Yes	No
1. Did you see the two figures as a square and the figure contained in the square?	92	8
2. Did you begin to trace the figures immediately?	14	86
3. Did the threat of penalization in the instructions keep you from immediately tracing the figure?	44	56
4. Did you look it over before you began to trace it to see first how it should be done?	89	11
5. Did you hold your pencil in the air while you went over it?	56	44

Questions	Yes	No
6. Did you begin on a corner of the inside figure?	52	48
7. Did you begin on the outer corner of the inside figure in order to get from it to the square?	49	51
8. Did you begin on the square?	52	48
9. Did you begin on the square at a point where the inside figure touched it so that when you had finished the square, you could get inside?	41	59
10. If you used more than one copy, did you decide to quit this first one because you could get no further and would have to start over again in a different place?	2	
11. When you began to trace, did you do so deliberately?	87	13
12. Were you looking ahead to see where your movements were leading you?	83	17
13. Did you trace it swiftly?	21	79
14. Had you already determined the correct procedure so that you could trace it swiftly?	17	83
15. Comment further upon the whole of your procedure, filling in details omitted by the questions.		

Eighty-two percent succeeded in tracing the figure correctly. Except for the last four questions, where some confusion seems to exist with regard to the method actually pursued, the procedure parallels to a large extent that of the individual Os. Many Os report in answer to the last request that they were "unable to finish the figure because of the time" or else that they "had not time to consider thoroughly, in order to do it correctly." That most of the tracing (trying out some self-instruction) was done, not on the paper, but above it, is obvious from the answers and from such reports as the following. "I mentally traced it." "After looking it over, its simplicity was evident." "The method of determining the procedure was done in my imagination rather than attempting it on copies."

Action, not a blind headlong sort of action, but from a self-instructed initiation, is characteristic of the procedure. A reason of some kind is reported for every attack. "The square could be traced starting from any point." "I first looked over the whole figure and decided that I should start with the inner figure and then trace the square, which is one continuous line no matter where you start from. I planned how to trace the inside figure and to get from it to the square without retracing. Then I traced it."

The general procedure with individuals and groups alike may be said to have been characterized by a period of search and of inspection-and-comment leading to a self-instruction and action under this instruction, followed by perception of the results.

The figure was repeated on fresh sheets with the dotted diagonal of Fig. 2 now added as an unbroken line. The task was therefore considerably changed.

> *Instruction.* A line has been added. Trace all lines again under the same conditions.

(A) INDIVIDUAL Os

That the added diagonal was a further complication involving more effort for the solution was immediately recognized by most *O*s.

> "This complicates it" (*Si*). "This will take longer" (*My*). "This complicates matters a bit" (*Wi*).
>
> *Gl, My,* and *Si* traced again with the pencil slightly elevated from the sheet, while *Wi* "went over it mentally twice and then drew it."
>
> The reports of no two *O*s were alike and yet a certain uniformity was evident in the procedure leading to the solution. In all cases but one some reason was given for the beginning point and the point of departure from one figure to the other. This one exception reports, "I have decided that I cannot begin where I did before but I will have to begin at the center. The solution seemed to come about naturally" (*Mc*). Most *O*s traced their figures, reporting their procedure afterwards; but one *O* commented while tracing it in air; "If I start on the diagonal, I must take care of the other two lines by crossing. I have to end on one point of the diagonal if I start on the other" (*Si*). Another *O*, who never traced the figure except with his pencil on the sheet, commented: "This has the same figure as the other practically," and, "When I started, I could not swear that the beginning on the middle diagonal would be successful. I knew the square could be traced continuously and that the figure in the previous case could be traced the same way. When I first put the pencil down, I knew that I could get practically all around, but I was doubtful about the corners. When I got to the last corner, I paused and saw that I must do the square and come back to the last line of the inner figure" (*Ke*). "I knew I had to begin on the middle diagonal because I could not reach it without retracing the lines if I began on the outside of the figure. That I would have to leave the inside figure and do the outer one before finishing the inner came because I knew the middle diagonal was substituted for the one I began on in the first sheet" (*My*). "I began at the diagonal because I had just been over the same figure (except for the diagonal), and when the new line was added, the easiest way of getting it in was to begin on it. It was quite obvious that you had to do the square before you finished the middle figure. Otherwise you would never get to the square. If I began on the inside of the middle figure, I would have to end there and there was no way of getting from there to the square" (*Wi*).
>
> The middle diagonal, the new element, commanded primary attention and drew interest away from the outer figure to the inner. Not one *O* attempted to trace the square first, and only one attempted to begin on the inner figure at any point apart from the diagonal. *Gl* held his pencil suspended from the paper, attempting to trace

it, "Go from here to here to here, etc.—That won't do.—The square in the middle puzzles me.—I have decided to start at the same point I did on the former sheet." He was supplied with another sheet which he never traced until he had first gone over it in air, "trying to see the whole figure traced before I start. I got stuck because I kept thinking that I ought to arrive at the starting point. The idea of penalization holds one back." Self-instruction is thus an inhibiting factor in the solution as well as an aid.

RESULTS

Apprehension of the object, search, and inspection-and-comment, leading to action under one self-instruction after another were the essential characteristics of the procedure. The instruction of penalization for every wrongly traced sheet caused most of the trials to be carried out either by eye-movement or by tracing in air. In some cases where the solution was not quickly forthcoming, the figures were so traced again and again. As a result, a sureness and swiftness marked the tracing of those who had solved it to their satisfaction beforehand. Their reasons for this or that movement in order to avoid error were already determined.

On the other hand, those who started to trace before having well in hand the proper way of doing it moved the pencil slowly, glancing ahead to study the whole figure before crossing or turning at some critical point. This looking ahead for possible errors and correct ways of procedure simultaneously with tracing is obvious in the report of *Ke* whose tracing time was 30 seconds,—the longest time except for *Gl*, who, though he traced the figure again and again in air, was still uncertain when he began to trace the actual figure.

(B) GROUPS Os

The same figure was presented to the groups under the same instructions. The time allotted was 7 minutes.

Questions	Yes	No
1. Did you consider this task more difficult and complicated than the preceding?	93	7
2. Did you begin to trace this figure immediately?	14	86
3. Did you run your eyes over these figures before tracing to see how they could best be traced?	93	7
4. Did you go over the sheet holding your pencil suspended until you got the successful way of doing it?	72	28
5. Did you begin on the inside figure?	78	22
6. Did you begin on the middle diagonal of the inside figure?	53	47

Questions	Yes	No
7. Did you begin on one of the outside points of the inside figure?	19	81
8. Did you begin on the square?	26	74
9. Did you begin on the diagonal in order to get it in?	41	59
10. Did you leave the inner figure before finishing it in order to do the square and then come back to the inner figure?	55	45

11. Supply any information that is not covered by the above questions.

Fifty-seven percent succeeded in tracing this second pattern. Of the others, only two Os traced more than one copy. The others either had not time to do so, or else the end of the period found a few of them still searching for a successful way to proceed on the copy first supplied.

The reports in answer to the last request were scanty in this portion of the problem. They were, for the most part, explanations of why the figure was not correctly traced. Too little time given and too much time spent on trying to find the most advantageous starting point are examples. Comments paralleling those in the preceding figure were given. "I did one hurriedly to see how it would work out and I did it wrong. I saw my error and drew the second one correctly by using the lesson I had learned in my first one." "I slowly traced the figure, not having any predetermined course, and was careful not to pass over any intersections that I could not come back to. When about half completed, I saw the way to finish the problem." "I tried it once and got everything but the middle diagonal. It was merely a repetition of the other figure. So I started with the diagonal and got it out of the way."

The results in the main confirm those preceding. That the majority of the Os followed the same procedure as the individuals is evident from the comments and from percentages. Many Os never got beyond the earlier stages of apprehension, search for a procedure, and inspection-and-comment upon the object. Others, going further, acted under one self-instruction after another until the desired result was obtained.

PROBLEM 6

This problem, based on the method of multiple choice, was designed to show 'insight' (= comprehension, sudden grasp, cognized relations?). Fourteen rectangular pill-boxes were glued side by side to a long narrow board. In one box a bit of cotton was hidden. The board was removed from O's sight each time the location of the cotton was changed.

(A) INDIVIDUAL Os

Instruction. There is a bit of cotton in one of the boxes. Find it with the quickest possible dispatch, giving all your procedure aloud.

This problem afforded a very striking example of one self-instruction replacing another after having been upset by the experimental conditions. At no time, not even to begin with, did the *O* open the boxes with no plan. "The best thing is to open the boxes one by one from left to right" (*Mc*). "There is no way but to go through the thing methodically" (*Fe*). Even in the cases of the unsophisticated *O*s, where the formal instruction was obeyed quite literally at first, a definite system of procedure was followed. One *O* (1) opened all the closed boxes beginning at the left; (2) opened with both hands but began at the opposite end. "If this is going to run on for some time, I am going to begin to look for a system. Now that was in the third from the left. There must be some trick about it, so that if I get the right idea, I can go directly to the correct one" (*Si*). This system, self-instructed, varied from time to time as the occasion favored first one and then another. This is better illustrated in a later stage of the comment. (11th trial) "Last time it was third from that end. This time it is third from this one. That doesn't work every time. Maybe there is no regulation." (12) Opened one but it was not the correct one. Opened another and found it. "I am formulating a theory." (13) "It ought to be in this one by the theory, but it is not, and I hereby discard it." This *O* never worked at random although he recognized the uncertainty of his plan. "I may be on a totally wrong track trying to figure these out from the arrangements but I think it is a sensible way of doing it" (*Si*).

The pattern arrangement was the outstanding method of approach to most *O*s. "It occurs to me that I am getting some kind of pattern-test (like the animals') which I am to learn in the course of the presentation" (*Mc*). "I will begin at the left, examining each box as I go. It is in the third I opened next to three empty boxes" (*Ke*).

Any number of cues were tried—the pattern, marks on the boxes, the total number of boxes from one end, either end, and both ends, the number of closed next to empty boxes from either end, the number of boxes moved farther from either end at successive times according to a scheme, the same box every time, etc. The experimental period was marked with pauses while the *O* sat looking at the boxes, noting their position and arrangement, and striving to memorize them.

One *O* remarked that he "must look out for the danger of making it more complicated than it was." Nevertheless he reported at the end, "I made it complicated at first. I thought of all sorts of possible methods" (*Gl*). "I looked for something exceedingly difficult" (*Mc*). Self-instruction toward the difficult was not apparent in any of the other *O*s. *O* merely took advantage of what the occasion had to offer whether difficult or simple. *My*, who was in general the quickest and keenest to take note of all possible relevant conditions, commented, "It must be some simple system because it does not take you long to fix it" (*My*).

The process of elimination of one self-instructed method after another as the conditions changed was most obvious and most logically organized in the case of this same *O*.

1. "There it is." (After opening the boxes systematically from left to right.)
2. "I do not see any sense to it at all. I cannot find any order to it. The first time it was near the three thumb tacks, next it was third from the end. The more boxes I open, the less credit I get, I suppose."
3. "This time there are no threes to go by at all unless I go by the number of closed boxes." (Opened the third closed box from the left and found it.)
4. (Opened them by hunting for the pattern of three. Opened nearly all of them.) "I know that it has some connection with three. It was in the center of the only three closed boxes together."
5. (Opened the one near the group of three open boxes. Opened another and found it.) "I have the wrong pattern." (Examined the thing carefully and made a mark on one end of the board.)
6. "I marked it because I thought it might be in the same box every time, but it was not." (He counted three from the other end and got the cotton.)
7. (Opened from a cue from last time.) "Why do you have more lids on the boxes?" (Opened again and again and found it.)
8. (Opened a wrong box. Opened the right one. Counted the number of boxes.) "I wondered if you had moved it over one, but you had not. This time it was in the center of the pattern as it was two times ago, but that does not hold for all times."
9. (Looked where he did last time.) "Did you move it over three? Would it be a certain number of covered lids from either end? But figures do not prove it." (Then he found it.) "It is in the third from the end."
10. (Looked at the boxes.) "You do not move it over a certain number of times nor does the number three have anything to do with it, nor is it the center of a pattern, nor is it in the same one every time." (Tried the same box, but from the other end this time. It was there.)
11. (Opened the correct box.) "It is the third closed box over."
12. "I thought that when it was five from one end one time, it would be at the other end next time in the fifth box. I have never found it in an end one. I am trying to make sense of the arrangement. This time it is the sixth closed box from one end, and the third closed from the other."
13. "It must be some simple system because it does not take you long to fix it."
14. "Why is it never in the end ones?" (Counted the boxes.) "Next time I shall count the number of open ones."
15. "It certainly is no pattern."
16. "And it is not the same design this time. Apparently you do not have any system, but it has been in this one at other times." (He had opened the third closed one from the end and got it.)
17. "It is the third closed box from the end."
18. (Opened the third closed one from the right.)
19. (Opened the third closed box from the left.) "They alternate." (My).

This protocol is a fine example of the typical procedure in this particular problem. It is rich in illustrations of apprehension of arrangement and place, of search for some plausible ground on which to base a choice, of inspection-and-comment upon the various experimental conditions, of the formulation of the self-instruction dependent upon the occasion (arranged boxes) and action under it, of re-apprehension followed by another self-instruction and action under that, until, all irrelevant plans eliminated, the solving generalization is reached.

RESULTS

The procedure in this problem, as in the others, was marked by a method, a systematic series of interacting self and occasional instructions. A solution was gained through, first, inspection-and-comment upon all conditions possibly relevant to the end sought, and, next, formulation of one self-instruction after another dependent on some occasional instruction until the generalization was reached. Here, again, there was no evidence of any uninstructed and planless activity. Action was always directed, predetermined, relevant to some intention on the part of the O.

(B) GROUP Os

The scheme for group-presentation consisted in placing the cotton always in the second closed box from the right end. It was necessary to make the scheme simpler than the *alternating plan* used above since the number of Os was greater and the presentation-time 10 minutes less.

> *Instruction.* I am going to present to you this series of boxes a number of times in succession. In one of them there is a bit of cotton. On the first presentation, I shall open the box in which the cotton lies. After that you are to write on the paper before you the number of the box in which you think it lies, counting from the right. After you have written down the choice each time, I shall open the correct box.

Questions	Yes	No
1. When the boxes were first presented to you, did you consider that the best way of finding the cotton was to open all the boxes to see where it was?	52	48
2. Did you try to remember which box it had been in from time to time?	74	26
3. Did you try counting the number of boxes from an end?	80	20
4. Did you try to remember the pattern arrangement from time to time?	60	40
5. Did you try counting the number of closed boxes from either end?	42	58

6. In naming the box in which you thought it might lie, was your reason
   for the choice based on some location you had noticed before?   84   16

7. Give any other information which you consider of interest or value
   concerning your solving process.

The percentages and the reports again parallel those of the individual *O*s. "I tried to base my solution on some probable numerical sequence, as some multiple of two. This seemed to work, but failed in the last instance. Hence my solution was incorrect." "First I tried to find a difference from the others in the box containing the cotton. When this proved futile, I tried to notice whether the number of the box had anything to do with the number of empty boxes. At the end I thought it was the number of empty boxes minus one." "When I saw the first time that the right box was the second closed one from the right, I chose that in every succeeding trial, and, finding I was successful, did not try any other method." "My first idea was that there would be a telltale mark on the lid. I found several such marks, but the placement of the cotton did not correspond."

The procedure was obviously the same as above. Self-instructed, the *O* made one choice after another until the instruction was no longer plausible, whereupon another self-instruction dependent upon occasional instruction was formulated. This continued until either the solution was reached or the end of the presentation-period arrived. The results of this group-presentation confirm those obtained from the individual *O*s.

PROBLEM 7

This problem was chosen to show 'insight' (= flash, new configuration?). Six matches were placed on the paper before *O*.

Instruction. You have presented to you six matches. Construct of them four equilateral triangles without breaking the matches. Comment aloud.

All the *O*s went systematically to work on the presentation of the problem constructing plane figures involving triangles. This practice was interspersed with pauses where the *O* was "trying to visualize some large geometrical figure that can be broken up into four equilateral triangles," or "tried to think of all the figures involving four triangles, (some time since my geometry)." Search here was accompanied by inspection-and-comment, "Obviously each match will have to form the side of more than one triangle." "Each side of each triangle must be the length of one match." "The solution seems as if it might lie in utilizing only the half-matches but I can get only three triangles that way."

All the *O*s assumed, without any formal recognition of the fact, that the four triangles were to lie in a plane. Three of them (*Ke, Si,* and *My*) solved it by taking advantage of chance positions in their efforts to lay a plane figure. *Ke* made one triangle. Then he started to lay another match from the apex of it to the base. "As I was laying the match one end down and the other up, I got the idea of not having them in the same plane." *Si,* constructing plane figures, laid out two triangles with a common base so that the figure looked like a diamond with a line across the center. Taking the two matches nearest him, he lifted them, added the other, and constructed the tetrahedron. "I saw all at once that it was a tetrahedron required. Taking two of them up together gave me the notion of getting the third dimension." *My,* also constructing plane figures, started moving the matches around again and then paused with one in his hand. He started laying it down slowly, beginning with one end, "Oh, here it is," and constructed the figure.

The solution followed immediately on the chance occurrence which induced a change in the primary assumption. It undoubtedly was obtained more easily in the cases of *Ke* and *Si,* that of the former because he had taught geometry the year before and that of the latter because he was a physicist and accustomed to deal with mathematical media.

The other *O*s (with one exception) concluded it impossible to construct the required triangles. When no other arrangement could be formed under the self-instruction, the *O* sought to terminate the period. He never continued to move the matches aimlessly. On the second and third presentations he acted under a self-instructed plan; but when the instruction ceased his action ceased.

Mc never realized the impossibility of constructing the figure according to his plan. Even when shown the solution, he never saw it as a three-dimensional figure of planes in various relations to each other, but as a solid. "The idea of a solid never struck me at all. Triangle means to me something in a plane."

RESULTS

The solution here consisted in a recognition of the three-dimensional alternative. Perceptive apprehension of a significant condition was prevented by a predisposition to lay figures in a plane. For some this set was so strong as to inhibit a recognition of the implications attendant upon lifting the matches from their two-dimensional arrangement to place them again in another plane arrangement, while for others a self-instruction that there must be something tricky or catchy about the problem created an attitude of search and uncertainty in the attempts to lay a plane figure satisfying the conditions. For these the re-apprehension of the type of figure required entailed a recognition of the predisposition to lay plane figures with the resulting formulation of another self-instruction.

Action under self-instruction, accompanied by search for a method of solution and inspection-and-comment upon the situation characterized the procedure. For those who solved the problem, the occasion brought about a re-apprehension with a consequent recasting of the instruction.

PROBLEM 8

This problem also was intended to show alleged 'insight' (of the same sort.) The experimental object consisted of a flat steel rectangle with a slot of definite pattern cut in it. The right-left slotted groove was long and had annexed to it above and below 2 shorter T-shaped prolongations. Ten steel buttons, which could be turned or slid in any direction, were permanently fastened in the slot. Each bore a letter of the word 'perplexity,' the letters arranged in haphazard order. Because of the arrangement of the slot, the letter 'p' could not be moved from its position at the right of all the others. The solution lay in turning the puzzle and the letters on the buttons upside down with reference to the obvious top of the puzzle, which was indicated by the imposed name "The perplexing puzzle."

> *Instruction.* Solve this puzzle, commenting aloud.

In every case the *O*s assumed at first that the word was to be spelled according to the words lying above the slot. Under self and occasional instructions, *O* shifted the buttons in every imaginable way. "It is just a matter of moving them around" (*My*).

Search and inspection-and-comment under a misleading occasional instruction characterized the early stages of the solving process. "Where has it got to be when I spell it? Where is the trouble? How do you get the Y over there? The Y is stuck" (*My*). "This takes three, and this takes three, and four have to go there, but they won't" (*Ke*). "You have to get the Y out of there first. You cannot do it. I wonder if any of these are uneven? They are all eccentric; they all roll round" (*Si*). "The Y should go to the end. I see that it is going to be the whole difficulty to get the Y out of there. The P won't let the others pass. There is something fishy here. Is there any possible way of getting them past each other? There are too many letters for this. Now what am I going to do?" (*Gl*).

At times throughout the experimental period the *O*, with an abstracted look on his face, would cease to move the buttons around, or else do so in an aimless, desultory way; but, when asked what he was doing, he reported, "I am trying to see what I can do." "I have got all but one letter in the correct positions, but I do not see how the P can be got in" (*Fe*).

Marking the later stages of the solving process were action under self and occasional instructions and elimination of one plan of action after another, shifting the buttons around until the realization was reached that the letter P could not be moved from its end position. At this point two *O*s declared its solution impossible. "I still have that P down there, and there is no way of getting it out. There must be some way for P to pass some of the others but I cannot see it" (*Ke*). "It is no use forcing the metal; that would not do any good. I cannot get that Y out of there to save me" (*Gl*). One *O* never realized this impossibility because he failed to notice the relative positions of the letters at the beginning of the observational period. "I did not remember whether the P was in that position to begin with or not. I might have got it in that place by moving the buttons around" (*Fe*).

For the others, the impossibility of the removal of the P from the end suggested utilizing that letter as the beginning of the word. "Perplexity is presumably to be spelled in this direction, but I can spell it in the other direction. May I? I can turn it upside down which is not against the directions" (*Mc*). "When I picked it up, I realized that the P was still on the end and there was no way of getting it on the other side. I must be able to spell it with P on that end, then. And it occurred to me that I could turn it upside down, twist the buttons around, and spell it forward" (*Gl*). *My* spelled it backward and turned it bottomside up. "It was the only way it could be done. I had tried every other way of doing it and was bound to get this way sooner or later" (*My*). "The labelling would indicate that it was to be spelled like it but the P cannot be shifted" (*Si*). He spelled it backwards and then turned the puzzle upside down. "Ho, ho, wait a minute!" and he turned the buttons so that they spelled it forward, and laughed, "I turned it upside down to read it backwards, then I thought of using a mirror, and then I saw the letters could be turned around."

RESULTS

The procedure in this problem, as in others, consisted in apprehension of the object, search for a method by which to spell the word, inspection-and-comment upon the conditions of the situation, action under self and occasional instructions, and re-apprehension due to a further realization of the limiting conditions of the experimental object.

The assumption that the word was to be spelled according to the one paralleling the slot was a misleading instruction from the occasion. Failure to arrive at the solution was due either to no change in this assumption, or to an imperfect apprehension of the experimental material, as in the case of *Fe*.

PROBLEM 9

The following word-series were designed to bring out 'insight' of some kind. The approximate sounds of two famous Shakespearean passages—Macbeth's tragic soliloquy from the Fifth Act and the soliloquy from *Hamlet*—were presented in serial form. The Macbeth was given first because it was the less familiar.

Macbeth's Soliloquy

tomb	this	bull	lie
arrow	pet	of	Ted
and	tee	record	fools
tumor	pays	dead	the

row	from	thyme	weight
in	data	an	too
Tom	day	awl	does
are	tooth	hour	tea
oh	he	yes	death
crypt	lass	todays	
e'en	silly	have	

Hamlet's Soliloquy

two	weather	sling	oar
beer	'tis	sand	toot
knot	know	air	ache
tube	blur	row	arm
bee	inn	sough	sag
thought	them	out	ens
is	end	ray	tea
thick	twos	just	sift
west	offer	four	rub
shun	this	tune	bulls

(A) INDIVIDUAL Os

One of the above series was placed on a sheet of paper without the title.

Instruction. Read aloud.

The Os began by reading the list once. Then they invariably paused, running their eyes up and down the list while commenting. "It is a group of disconnected words. I did not think of the meanings of the words at all. Several of them are rather unusual" (*Mc*). "I noticed that there were some nicknames and a few words together tended to make sense, and some I sought to pronounce in a different way like 'row'" (*Gl*). "I looked over it and thought of some catch in pronunciation. I thought only of each separate word. Then I started reading down fairly rapidly for myself. The 'petty pace' part gave me the first inkling" (*Si*). "I thought it might be like James's 'Pas de lieu Rhône que nous.' Then I saw 'tube' and 'bee' which looked like 'to be.' I suspected what it was then and went to reading it systematically" (*Fe*). "These words, 'tomb, arrow, and tumor,' fell together as I read them. I thought the list might be only scattered phrases, therefore I took them separately" (*Ke*). "When I read it, I knew it sounded like something faintly familiar and the first phrase and the last one made sense right off. The rest of it is this" (*My*).

The solution was dependent mainly upon the occasional instruction and only in part on self-instruction. Search is evident in the report where the Os ask themselves "what it can be for" or wonder "what you want done with this," or an O wishes that he "knew what he was to get out of it;" but in any case the *O*s knew that there was something there, not apparent but to be found.

For *Mc,* who failed to recognize the passages after several readings, the formal instruction was changed twice; first to "Read until learned," and then "Read through quickly." Under the first he got slower and slower in his reading. "They are disconnected words for groups of which I have to manufacture connections to help me learn ... . When I tried to learn it, the slower I went, the more disjointed it became." On reading it quickly he "noticed this last time 'weather 'tis nobler.' I am beginning to get a glimmer that this is a meaningful sentence of some sort."

Gl's complete ignorance of one of the passages in question and his very imperfect acquaintance with the other prevented his getting the meaning. Time and again he struck a leading note: "A few words tended to make sense," and "I wonder if I could make sentences out of it. No, they are too disconnected." Even when the instruction was changed to "Read aloud as quickly as possible" and the report reads, "I could not help noticing the rhythm—there are places in it where a number of words almost make sense," he made no attempt to work it out as had *Ke,* (who was very unfamiliar with the passage first given him), but remained doubtful concerning it. The meaningful phrases suggested by the words were never like those in the original passage, but were like the words of the lists, *e.g.,* 'to be thought,' 'offer this sling.'

Ke, starting from the first phrase which "fell together," methodically worked out the remainder of the passage on paper, repeating phrases aloud and going back to change those already done to fit the meaning. "Two or three of these could be 'tomorrow,' and then there is 'pays from day to day to the last syllable of recorded time.' And 'whole hour yesterday.' He went over it slowly, writing down these phrases. 'Have lighted fools the way to dusty death. Tomorrow and tomorrow and tomorrow,' I see that all right." He looked at the list awhile. 'Creeps—creeps in this petty pace.' He read on slowly, 'and all our yesterdays.' Then he read from the paper the whole passage correctly.

RESULTS

When one passage was identified, the *O* was instructed by the occasion that the other was similar. Therefore the stage of undefined search was absent in the second procedure. In general, the *O* who recognized the first passage also recognized the other; while for the one who did not recognize the first, the second also was hard of recognition.

The disconnected and strange series of visual words tended to inhibit the recognition of the rhythmical and familiar sequence of verbal sounds.

The procedure was characterized first as perceptive and comprehensive, accompanied by a vague and diffused form of search. Occasional instruction tended to objectify concretely this element and to lead to verbal recognition. Auditory cues from a swift reading aloud led in some cases to identification with the familiar literary passage. Where the passage was not so familiar, the *O* worked out under self-instruction the meaning of the whole in a methodical way.

(B) GROUP Os

The series of words simulating Hamlet's soliloquy was arranged on a white cardboard 3 ft. x 2½ ft. The other series was omitted because of the lesser familiarity of the quotation.

> *Instruction.* I have here a chart on which there is a series of words. I shall present them to you and we shall read them aloud in unison three times, increasing the speed with each reading. After the last reading you may immediately turn over your questions and answer them. Here are the words. Let's begin.

Questions	*Yes*	*No*
1. Did you wonder what it was all about when you were asked to read these words?	88	12
2. Did these words remain a group of disjointed words without any connected meaning?	53	47
3. Did you think that they might make sense before you read them?	37	63
4. Did any of the words fall together to make sense as you read them?	77	23
5. Did the whole series make sense only after the second or third reading?	27	73
6. Tell anything about your procedure that these questions have left out.		

> From the percentages it is evident that about three-fourths of the *O*s failed to recognize the passage. The causes of this failure may have been either lack of familiarity with the passage or the dominance of the visual over the auditory stimuli.
>
> The reports run parallel to those of the individual *O*s. "The increased speed in reading seemed to make them more meaningful and I left the visual words for the audible." "The unfamiliar word 'sough' was the most definite cue to me that this series was not disconnected." "There seemed enough verbs, nouns, and adjectives to make complete sentences, but there was not time enough." "I thought it was an association-experiment and I tried to memorize the words but only a few of the unusual ones stayed." "Certain words went together like 'thick, west, shun,' and 'toot ache' that could have been 'toothache.' The whole did not make sense."

The dependence of the solution on occasional instruction is quite obvious from these reports where occasional instruction (*e.g.* that it was an association-experiment) often inhibited useful cues. This may be added to those given above as another cause for failure to apprehend the words as familiar and well-known.

PROBLEM 10

This problem was designed to show whether some form of 'insight' was concerned in applying a physical principle to a problematical situation. A deflated toy balloon, a 75-cc. flask, penstaff, pencils, and file were presented to the *O*.

(A) INDIVIDUALS

Instruction. Blow up this balloon and tie it inside the bottle.

Here the simplest and most obvious performance was to place the balloon in the bottle and blow on it. That was the procedure invariably followed, by all *O*s,—even by *Si*, a physicist. Failure led to the question, Why? "Now, why the deuce won't that blow up in the bottle?" (*Si*).

In the majority of cases the *O* quickly recognized the cause as air-pressure and lack of an escape for it. "I must have something to let the air out" (*Ke*). "I just thought of letting the air escape as I put the balloon in" (*Mc*). "All the air is in there and I have to get it out or the balloon won't blow up" (*Gl*). "I saw that it was air-pressure keeping it from blowing up" (*Si*). *My*, the logician, was the only one to make a correct scientific analysis. "To blow it up would have required compressing the air in the bottle but lungs are not strong enough to do that." An excellent example of employing an object as instrument out of its usual context occurred in this case. After finding that the balloon did not expand, he asked, "Can I use anything else?" He looked over the table and said, "I haven't the right machinery. Oh, yes; I am going to show you something now." He quickly unscrewed his pipe-stem from the bowl, inserted it by the side of the balloon and inflated the balloon, the air escaping through the pipe stem. He reported, "Therefore I put a tube in the neck of the bottle and then the air in the bottle escaped through the tube." The pipe-stem was apprehended no longer as a pipe-stem with its specific application but was generalized into a tube.

Fe, who never solved the difficulty, reported that "the problem never announced itself to me as physical. I knew the air had to get out but I never thought of it as a physical problem." To what extent that prevented a solution on his part is doubtful. In the commentary he formulated the question, "How do you get the air out of the bottle?" and he "does not see how the air can escape." Here is a definite recognition of the difficulty but no instrumental solution is suggested.

The other *O*s used the penstaff and pencil indiscriminately. *Ke* picked up the file and inserted it but decided it might break the balloon.

RESULTS

The procedure consisted of action under self-instruction followed first by a period of search for the cause for failure under the first trial and then by a re-apprehension of the experimental conditions with a consequent new self-instruction followed by action. As a general rule, when the cause for failure to inflate the balloon on the first trial was comprehended as due to air-pressure, the solution by instrumental application followed immediately.

Except for one case, *Fe,* formulation of the difficulty led to a consideration of the means of solution. In this case, however, imperfect comprehension of the laws of air-pressure inhibited the apprehension of a means of solution.

(B) GROUP Os

> *Instruction.* If I place this balloon in this bottle and blow, thus, no matter how hard I, or anyone else, blows, the balloon will not go up. Nevertheless, there is a way by which the balloon can be blown up in this bottle under these present conditions. If I gave you the balloon and asked you to blow it up in the bottle, how would you do it?

Questions	Yes	No
1. Did you find a way of blowing up the balloon in the bottle?	73	27
2. Did you decide that the air in the bottle prevented the balloon from blowing up?	72	28
3. Did you search for some means of allowing the air to escape?	61	39
4. Did you consider any of the objects lying on the table?	69	31
5. Did you think of some absent object as a means?	83	17
6. Did your solution consist in holding some object in the mouth of the bottle parallel to the neck in order to allow the air to escape?	47	53
7. Give any of your attempts at solving which are not covered by these questions.		

> Various methods of obtaining the desired result in addition to the one in the sixth question were reported in the answers to the last question. "I thought of pushing the balloon in the bottle, thus allowing the air to escape as the balloon blew up. Of course, this entailed having a tube fastened to the neck of the balloon through which one could blow. I could not find the instrument on the table so considered the problem unsolved." "Wire wrapped round the neck of the balloon (in the neck of the bottle) to keep it smaller than the neck space and allow the air to escape as the balloon got larger." All sorts of other means were offered as impractical as, or more impracticable than, those quoted.
>
> Others reported concerning the sixth question. "The object I should use is a corkscrew with the point away from the balloon because then the balloon could not expand around the object to shut off egress of air." This was another example of an instrument, not only used out of its usual context but assumed to have the generalized character of a tube. "I solved it nearly instantaneously due to my knowledge of

physics and air-pressure." "Because of the question in the bead problem, I definitely started by looking over the table." The *O* was self-instructed here from a cue from a preceding experiment.

RESULTS

Great variety in type of solution is evident in the results. Those *O*s who never apprehended the cause of the difficulty naturally failed entirely to reach any solution. Others, self-instructed from past experience, suggested various methods for the most part entirely unsuited to the experimental conditions. Others apprehended the correct cause of the difficulty but spent the allotted time in search for a method of solution; while still others, apprehending the difficulty, had no trouble in immediately apprehending the best and simplest means of solution under the conditions given.

Inhibiting factors were, first, failure to apprehend the cause of the difficulty due to an imperfect acquaintance with the behavior of gases, and, secondly, self-instruction from past instrumental applications combined with failure to apprehend limiting conditions in the instruction and the experimental situation.

PROBLEM 11

This problem was chosen as parallel to the foregoing. The *O* was presented with a bit of wood about 2 in. long, beveled convexly below and so rocking easily from end to end. The top was channeled out longitudinally with a concave bottom. Two small shot were placed in the groove which was then transparently covered. As the piece sat on its rocking bottom, the shot lay together at the centre, but separated by a wire partition. Small pockets were dug out at the outer ends of the groove. The problem was to cause the two shot to go right and left at the same time and so ride up to the two pockets. The solution consisted in twirling the piece suddenly, thus sending the shot centrifugally to the two pockets.

> *Instruction.* Place a ball in each pocket simultaneously. Comment aloud.

> All the *O*s began with the self-instruction that it was a matter of manual dexterity or skill. When that principle failed them, some assumed it a mere matter of chance, which was denied by the experimenter. As a result of that self-instruction the *O* tended to cease in his efforts at solution. "I do not see that there is anything to it but manual dexterity. I do not see anything but that it must go in by chance." (*Fe*). "I think it is a mere matter of skill. . . . It will just be chance if it falls in" (*Ke*). "Is it a trick of dexterity or is it a matter of luck?" (*My*).

> Every method that might lead toward a solution was tried with the object in every possible position. Only in extreme impatience did the *O* violently and aimlessly shake

the object. Every way of holding the box, of sudden striking and jerking, was tried,—a methodical procedure with a definite basis. "The best bet is to get one in a hole and hold it there while rolling the other along the glass top, but I have not succeeded in doing it yet" (*Mc*). "I am trying to keep one ball in the hole while I quietly and diligently get the other in, but I get it nearly there when the other one moves out" (*Gl*). "I have a better idea, I will put one in and then put another one in by striking the bottom sharply" (*My*).

Gl and *My* noticed the structure of the puzzle. *My,* who solved it, said emphatically, early in the experimental period, "One thing is certain, I suppose that wire in the center (partition) has something to do with it.... Why is it made in a rolling fashion like that? There are no grooves in it any place, it is just semicircular. That wire must mean something—that one is to be on either side of it." *Gl,* who did not solve it, commented in the interrogative, "Why was it made like this? That wire down there is kind of funny. Why do you suppose it is there?"

That there might be some mechanical principle whereby it could be solved occurred to most *O*s. "One could set up an oscillatory motion so that the balls go up and down in opposite directions, I suppose" (*Mc*). "I do not know any principle of mechanics whereby both could be put in together" (*Gl*). *Fe,* when told that the puzzle was obtained from a physicist, commented interrogatively, "I wonder if the inclined plane has anything to do with it?" *My,* who solved the problem, reported that, "If I had a magnet, I believe I could do it. ... I wonder if it depends on any scientific law. It looks as if the wire should keep them apart. You have to get them in a place where a single motion would put them both in at once.... What kind of motion would drive them in? The only thing left after thinking of all possible forces was centrifugal."

When those who desired to cease trying for the solution were told that the secret of it was centrifugal force, various comments were obtained showing that, though centrifugal force as a name was familiar, not one *O* had a clear notion of the significance of the concept. "I have heard of it but it means nothing to me" (*Fe*). "Centrifugal force—force toward the outside? I never would have thought of spinning it. I thought it was a mere matter of skill" (*Ke*). "Centrifugal force? I know what that is" (*Gl*). He got up and whirled around holding the puzzle in his outstretched hand. "All it ever meant to me was a whirling pail of water" (*Gl*). "When you spin a thing around?" (*Mc*). He took it in hand and tried to go around with it as one whirls round with a bucket of water. Even though these latter two now knew the principle of the solution, they never tried the correct way of spinning the object.

RESULTS

The characteristic procedure here for those who came nearest the solution and for the one who attained it was action under self-instruction accompanied by search for a different and possibly more relevant method of solving, and by inspection-and-comment upon the experimental object.

In three cases the first self-instruction of manual dexterity was never changed—a self-instruction inhibiting the apprehension of relevant conditions which would necessitate a reformulation of the plan of procedure. When *O* found that skill of manipulation did not obtain the desired result, he ceased to attempt the solution. When he had no other feasible plan, he never continued to try aimlessly.

In other cases failure to solve could be attributed to the inhibiting effect of a vague and imperfect knowledge of the controlling physical principle.

PROBLEM 12

This problem was designed to examine an 'insight' which might divine the suitable. Two series of numbers were composed. The pattern of the one first presented was as follows. To all odd numbers additions were made; from all even ones, subtractions. The numbers so added and subtracted ranged from 1 to 14. After 12 first appeared, it then appeared in every 4th place. The pattern for the second was a subtraction-and-addition pattern; thus, $-3+2-1$, $+6-5+4...$.

First Pattern		Second Pattern	
13	13	24	26
14	22	21	25
12	12	23	31
9	1	22	26
13	13	28	30
18	26	23	27
12	—	27	—
5		24	

Instruction. Here is a series of numbers with the last one lacking. Supply the correct number. Comment aloud.

The interesting thing about the first series for the *O*s was its pattern arrangement. All gave 12 as the number, basing their choice on this arrangement. The formal instruction was as meager as possible, leaving wide range for self- and occasional instructions. Not one *O* made any initial assumption that the other numbers followed necessarily from the first according to some ruling principle. All read the series first, inspecting its characteristics and generally seizing on what the occasion had to offer.

Various patterns were described but the one leading to the right number was the most obvious and the most generally found. "Beginning with the third number, every fourth number of the series is 12. Therefore the last one would be 12 to fit in the rule. I saw it was a pattern 13, 12—13, 12 all the way" (*Fe*). "I happened to notice that the numbers occurred in groups of four—that the first number of each group was 13, and the third (?) was 12" (*Ke*). "There are three groups with smaller ones separating them. I would say it was 12, just to keep up that sequence" (*Si*). *Mc* read the series and was struck by the regular rhythmical recurrence of certain numbers. "Without analyzing, one would say that 12 is the number because every fourth time it comes in. Just the fact of the rhythm alone would make one think that 12 was the number" (*Mc*).

My was partially self-instructed in the search for the number, "Do they go in pairs, I wonder?" He tried various schemes of adding and multiplying. After finding himself wrong, he re-read the whole series and announced, "According to the pattern the number should be 12." Occasional instruction, here as in the above cases, led to the correct number.

Gl, under self-instruction, commented, "I went through the series getting the difference between 13 and the other numbers. I found a constant relation between it and the third (?) number from it. I therefore judged it to be 12. I simply took 13 as a standard and worked from it."

Greater variety was shown in the second series. Two *O*s obtained the number by working out the scheme according to which it was composed, one because he had inquired as to the way in which the former group was constructed, "Is that the same business of adding and subtracting?" (*Fe*); the other because systems of additions and subtractions were the simplest and most often used means of forming a series, "I read through the numbers and did not see anything. Then I began by taking the differences. I tried to see if that were the thing here, since most series are made up in that manner" (*Si*). Here the *O* was self-instructed to search for *E*'s method in constructing the series.

The occasion, however, furnished the basis for the other solutions. Self-instruction was less useful. "I have already decided that you are not going to use the same method you used before" (*Ke*). "I suppose you start with a number and the rest follow by rule" (*My*). Such self-instructions were wholly abortive. The pattern gave the correct number except in the case of *Mc*, who, by two pattern schemes, obtained the incorrect number 35, and in the case of *My*, who obtained the correct number but not through working out a pattern. By a process of elimination, counting the numbers and the number of times each occurred, he inferred that the only number in the twenties not occurring at all (*i.e.* 29) was correct.

RESULTS

The progress toward solution consisted in, first, apprehension accompanied by inspection-and-comment upon the series and by a search for any cues likely to be of aid in obtaining the desired number, and, secondly, occasional instruction (in most cases), a self-instruction (in a few), under which the number was supplied.

Strong occasional instruction suppressed the formulation of self-instruction in the majority of cases.

PROBLEM 13

This problem also was designed to explore for 'insight' discerning the suitable. The following stanzas with one word lacking were presented in succession. Care was taken that only one word, and that the author's, could be supplied. The five examples were chosen to bring out differences in literary perception of form and in available vocabulary.

(1) Yea, in the valley of Death I awoke,
   Pallid and strange as a vision.
   All of my sorrow is vanished as smoke—
   These are the valleys............

(2) Once where the unentered temple stood, at noon
   No sun-ray pierced the dim unwindowed aisle,
   And all the flooding whiteness of the moon
   Could only bathe the outer............

(3) Let us go hence; the night is now at hand;
   The day is overworn, the birds all flown;
   And we have reaped the crops the gods have sown;
   Despair and death; deep darkness o'er the land
   Broods like an owl; we cannot understand
   Laughter or tears, for we have only known
   Surpassing vanity: vain things alone
   Have driven our perverse and aimless ....
   Let us go hence, somewhither strange and cold,
   To Hollow Lands where just men and unjust
   Find end of labor, where's rest for the old,
   Freedom to all from love and fear and lust.
   Twine our torn hands! O pray the earth enfold
   Our life-sick hearts and turn them into dust.

(4) The skies, they are not always raining
   Nor grey the twelvemonth through;
   And I shall meet good days and mirth,
   And range the lovely lands of earth
   With friends no worse than............

(5) Well! wind-dispersed and vain the words will be,
   Yet, Thyrsis, let me give my grief its hour
   In the old haunt, and find our tree-topp'd hill!
   Who, if not I, for questing here hath power?
   I know the wood which hides the daffodil,
   I know the Fyfield tree,
   I know what white, what purple fritillaries

The grassy harvest of the river-fields,
Above by Ensham, down by Sanford, yields,
And what sedged brooks are Thames's............

(A) INDIVIDUAL Os

Instruction. Here is a verse with one word lacking. Supply the correct word, doing so aloud.

The first verse is composed of four alternately rhyming lines, one of the most common of rhyme schemes, the last rhyme lacking. A word of three syllables, the word 'Elysian,' which is fairly familiar, was to be supplied. All *Os* followed more or less the same procedure in attempting to supply the word. Some trusted to the feel they had for what was required. "One word to rhyme with 'vision.' 'Elision,' 'provision,' 'incision,' 'ambition.' All right, 'Elysian.' That is the correct word" (*My*). "It seems as if there should be more than one word, 'valleys of something.' I am trying to find something to rhyme with 'vision' " (*Gl*). *Fi* read it again rhythmically, beating her foot to keep time, and supplying 'dum dee dum' in place of the word.

Other *Os* analyzed in greater detail with regard to metre, rhyme, and part of speech. "It needs three syllables, accent on the second to rhyme with 'vision' ... I thought, 'Why should not an adjective do?' " (*Fe*). "The name may be some foreign proper name. This notion was strengthened by the fact that it goes with a plural noun with only three syllables to supply. There is a posture that it must be an adjective that is needed as I recall the poetic formula of modifier after noun" (*Je*). "The word has three syllables, the last part of a dactyl, and a trochee. 'Decision' fits the rhyme but makes no sense" (*Mc*).

One *O* (*Ke*) read the word immediately into the blank. Otherwise an attitude of search occurred. The others (whether or not the right word was obtained) invariably substituted other rhyming words which had no connection with the sense in attempting to get the correct rhyming word. 'Derision,' 'division,' 'decision,' 'incision,' 'elision,' 'collision,' 'oblivion,' 'provision,' 'ambition,' were variously employed. *Je* was prevented from supplying the correct word obviously because he continually assumed the word to end in 'ision,' identical with the ending of the word 'vision.'

Those to whom the word 'Elysian' occurred were convinced that it was correct if familiar to them. To *Si* the word occurred immediately, " 'Elysian valleys,' something like that is used in classical poetry. I am not sure of the word and I cannot spell it. It begins with a capital E, but I am not sure of the rest. I guess that would be right.... . Yes, wasn't it the Elysian fields that Greek heroes went to after death?" To *Mc* and *Gl* the word was none too familiar. *Mc* reported, "I knew the word. 'Elysium' was the only thing that meant anything here, however. The adjectives from it simply did not emerge;" and *Gl* reported, "I knew it but I never thought of it. I never use it ordinarily, anyway."

The second verse is also a 4-line alternately rhyming verse with the last word lacking. This last word, 'peristyle,' is semi-technical and ordinarily absent from the vocabulary of common usage.

The search for the word ran parallel to that of the other verse. Words like 'domicile,' 'campanile,' 'mile,' etc., were supplied. Only in one case was this absent. *Ke* read 'peristyle' into it immediately. That the metre was harder here was indicated by the large number of one-syllable words supplied. *My* and *Gl* never realized the fact that more than one syllable was required. "It might be any noun that rhymes with 'aisle'—'style,' 'file,' 'defile,' 'mile,' 'Nile,' etc. The rhythm is so irregular that it might be any syllabled word. It ought to be 'pile,' a one-syllable word. A two-syllable word would be awful" (*My*).

Without formally stating it, *Mc* assumed that the word was at least of more than one syllable. He read 'domicile' into it. "Words like 'pile' spring up but they are too short." *Si* methodically attempted to get the metre, "I do not know whether it would be one syllable or three. I think it could get away with one. I will try 'domicile,' which is not the word for the metre. Three syllables sound better."

Mc, Gl, and *Si* tried to obtain the word from the meaning as well as from the rhyme. "It looks as though it would refer to the vestibule or something like that. Is this a technical word connected with a church? I am now visualizing a cathedral with various parts that might be illuminated by the sun. This term might apply to the roof or walls, or to the general outer part of the church" (*Mc*). "It would not be good poetry but you could say the 'outer tile' if it were made of tile" (*Gl*). "What is outer that is bathed by moonlight? So many words have three syllables but that is all. Minaret is not right, of course" (*Si*).

Only one *O (Mc)* had no acquaintance with the word. *Gl* and *Si* had heard of it but had no knowledge of its meaning. *Ke* had heard the word until it was familiar enough to read directly into the verse, but he was not clear as to its meaning. "What does 'peristyle' mean? It fits according to the rhyme and metre but I do not know what it means."

The third verse, the Italian sonnet, was selected for its definite and unchangeable rhyme-scheme and metre. Anyone knowing the sonnet form would have no trouble in analyzing the rhyme-ending and the exact number of syllables required. As a matter of fact, no one of the *O*s analyzed the metre to determine the number of syllables lacking. In reading the verse there seemed to be a feel for the correctly syllabled word, probably due to the familiarity, formally recognized or otherwise, of all *O*s, with the sonnet form.

Two *O*s, *Mc* and *My*, inferred the rhyme from the form. "Oh it is 'band.' I have written too many sonnets not to get that, a b b a, a b b a, c d, c d, c d" (*My*). *Mc* supplied 'band' and said, "It is the sonnet form and I knew it would have one of the 'and' endings," but added that the rhythm or metre puzzled him at first. 'The rhythm does not seem to be any good. This tended to upset the rhyme-scheme."

The others without recognizing the sonnet form gave some reason for their choice of a rhyme. "I knew it had to rhyme with 'understand' because before it had been 'hand,' 'flown,' 'sown,' 'land,' and 'understand,' 'known,' 'alone;' must be 'band.' It naturally falls into first and last, second and third rhymes. I divided the thing into quatrains, and 'band' just came like that" (*Ke*).

Ke and *My* supplied the proper word from the requirements of the rhyme and metre. The sense was not considered except in so far as it did not contradict the word supplied. The others obtained the word through a consideration of the meaning. "I looked then at the sense and 'band' came" (*Mc*). "Oh, 'us,' that makes it plural. 'Have driven our perverse and aimless band' " (*Gl*). " 'Band' is the most reasonable word. 'Land' and 'hand' do not fit so well. A land is not driven generally. The 'us' is not just an editorial 'us' because it says 'our life' and 'sick hearts' " (*Si*).

The fourth verse was chosen for its irregularity of rhyme-scheme. All *O*s read the word 'you' into it, more from a sense of the demands of the verse as a whole than from any one variable, such as the meaning, the determination of the metre, or the feel for the rhyme. This was obvious in the comment of *Ke*, "I do not know why I rhymed it with 'through.' 'You' just came like that and it just happened to rhyme with 'through.' I did not definitely try to rhyme it with anything." "It is the sort of poem addressed to someone, 'friends no worse than some person' and it has to rhyme with 'through' " (*Si*). "It would not look well rhyming with 'earth;' besides, this is the usual way it rhymes. It means something to rhyme it with 'through' and it did not mean anything when I sought for a rhyme for 'raining' " (*My*).

The rhyme played a major part in the search of *Mc* for the correct word. "When I came to the third line I noticed 'mirth' and thought of 'birth' but when I met 'earth' I knew it would not do. It was a closed couplet. Also it would not rhyme with 'raining.' 'You' came and fitted in the sense." Here a very cogent reason was given for not having a consecutive three-line rhyme, but no reason at all was set forth for choosing a rhyme for the second line rather than the first. An aesthetic element, a feeling for what is most pleasing, seemed to enter here; for instance, "I do not know why I think it has to rhyme with 'through,' but it sounds better and brings the poem to a close" (*Si*).

In the last verse the meaning played the leading rôle in obtaining the absent word. "The sense decided me in favor of the 'fritillaries' rhyme" (*Ke*). "The brooks suggested Thames's 'tributaries' " (*Gl*). "I tried to do it by the sound but could not do so. Then I took the sense and sought for the relation of brooks to the Thames" (*Si*). "It filled up the sense of the sentence and rhymed with the unusual word 'fritillaries' " (*My*).

Although the meaning was the surest means of obtaining the correct word, the rhyme was given a fair amount of attention. There was very little uniformity among *O*s on this score, although all of them supplied the correct word. Two of them attempted to rhyme the word otherwise than with 'fritillaries.' "I did not know when I first read it whether the word to supply would rhyme with 'trees' or with 'fritillaries.' … I knew it rhymed with that word because no one would use a word like that unless he were using it for a rhyme" (*My*).

Mc was the only one to differ markedly from the other *O*s. Whereas they laid the major emphasis on meaning and only minor emphasis on the rhyme, with none whatsoever on metre, he gave prime importance to the consideration of rhyme-scheme, secondarily considering the metre, and, as a last resort, the meaning. "As I read it, it flashed through that it might be a sonnet. Then the line ending with 'tree' showed it not to be that. 'Tree' rhymed with 'be.' All the other lines are complete couplets and 'fritillaries' stood out alone without a partner." Then he read the line ending in 'fritillaries,' rhythmically beating his fingers on the table. " 'Fritillaries,' two trochees." He read the last line also moving his fingers to the rhythm, "Two trochees there, too. 'Tributaries.' I was not sure of the exact word required. What could the Thames have that I might know? 'Capillaries' came but it was not the right one. Then 'tributaries' came in with a click, not logically. I was too much concerned about the structure of the word and too little about the meaning."

RESULTS

Apprehension of the material was followed by a period of search which varied from a general diffused type, where the feeling for what was suitable to the verse as a whole was considered, to a more concretely objectified search as requirements relative to rhyme-scheme, metre, meaning, and part of speech were analyzed and commented upon. Inspection-and-comment was a function much used.

Lack of vocabulary or a faulty apprehension of the literary form were inhibiting factors.

(B) GROUP Os

Copies of the first and fourth examples were presented to members of the groups.

Instruction. Here is a verse with one word lacking. Supply the correct word.

Questions (1st selection)	Yes	No
1. Are you familiar with the word 'Elysian'?	47	53
2. Did you read the verse as if you were scanning it?	69	31
3. Did you count the number of syllables required?	45	55
4. Did you try to rhyme the word with 'vision'?	96	4
5. Did you try to rhyme it with any other word?	15	85
6. Did the meaning suggest the word?	35	65
7. Did you supply the word and then test it by the meaning?	24	76
8. Did you name words ending in the 'ision' sound which fitted the rhyme but not the meaning in your search for the proper word?	80	20

	Yes	*No*
9. Were you sure of the word which you supplied?	29	
10. Was this certainty due to the fitness or suitability of the word?	28	
11. Make other comments on how you went about supplying the word.		

Twenty-nine percent of the *O*s supplied the correct word, 38% left it blank, while 43% supplied various words with a more or less correct rhyme but, for the most part, lacking in meaning. These words were identical to a great extent with the words named over in the search for the proper word by the individual *O*s; for example 'decision,' 'oblivion,' 'elision.' On the other hand, some of the words supplied were imperfect as to rhyme, but the meaning suited the context. Such were 'Stygian,' 'Elysium,' 'eternal,' 'arisen.' The *O*, when he did supply a word, based it on his apprehension of what was required and his inspection of the conditions. It is interesting to note that, whereas 72% of them supplied a word, only the 29% who gave 'Elysian' reported a certainty concerning the word supplied.

The reports from the last question parallel reports from the individual *O*s. "Meaning, rhyme, and number of syllables left no doubt in my mind that 'Elysian' was the correct word." "I could think only of 'eternal,' but I knew it would not fit. I tried to get a rhyme with 'vision.'" "I finally tried 'Stygian' from the river Styx. I did not like it, but could think of no other." "I took all the letters of the alphabet and tried putting them in front of 'ision'." "I knew it needed an adjective, but I could not think of any that fitted. I did not know the word anyway."

Questions (4th selection)

	Yes	*No*
1. Did you read 'you' into the blank immediately?	78	22
2. Did you try to rhyme the word with any other line than the one ending in 'through'?	26	74
3. In trying to get the word, did you name over other words with the dipthhong 'oo' sound?	25	75
4. Did you determine the number of syllables required?	47	53
5. Did the meaning suggest the word?	74	26
6. Did you supply the word and test it by the meaning?	17	83
7. Were you sure of the word you supplied?	71	29
8. Was this sureness due to the suitability of the word as regards rhyme and meaning?	72	28
9. Report anything about your solving process that these questions have omitted.		

Ninety-one percent of the *O*s supplied the word 'you' in the blank; 2% supplied other words obviously unsuited to anything except, perhaps, the rhyme; and 7% left it blank.

It is evident from the reports that the *O*s were self-instructed from cues gleaned from the first verse and the questions concerning it (occasion). "My first step was to look for the rhyme-scheme. There were three possibilities, though only two (rhyme with first or second line) were likely. Then I read the verse for the meaning and 'you' came at once. It was unnecessary to count the syllables. The metre was too obvious." "The solution was very simple. After reading the verse, the word 'you' followed immediately to complete the meaning. Then I tested it for metre and found that it fitted."

The majority read the word directly into the blank. "There was no conscious effort to think about what word was necessary. There was no recognition of the rhyme. It merely was the immediate cognizance that 'you' would rhyme and fit without any other qualification." "I tried to supply a word that coincided with the spirit of the lines." "A decided sense of satisfaction prevailed throughout the process because of the felt fitness of the word immediately supplied at the first reading."

The uncertainty attendant upon some who supplied the correct word was explained as follows: "The word 'you' did not seem to fit my idea of the sense I would like the verse to have, so I was not sure of it." " 'No worse than you' sounds quite sarcastic. The word was evidently 'you.' However, I could not see the meaning when used with 'worse'."

The procedure here consisted in an apprehension of the meaning of the verses accompanied by search for the word most suitable to the rhyme and meaning or to the stanza as a whole. Individual variations occurred in the bases given for supplying the word Some, sought for a word to fit the meaning first, others to fit the. rhyme while still others supplied it from both rhyme and meaning, or from a sense of fitness to the whole. Lack of an apprehension of the poetic form was an inhibiting factor. To some the occasion was a poetic construction; to others, a non-aesthetic verbal exercise. A wide range of occasional instructions appeared.

INTERPRETATIONS AND CONCLUSIONS

Throughout the course of the experiments we have constantly looked for 'insight' under its various alleged forms. In the first three problems, which encouraged 'insightful' discernment and recognition of available materials (beads and cork-in-bottle), we turned up various forms of the apprehensive functions operating to recognize tools and instruments in an unusual setting. There occurred two approaches toward solution, one involving the perceived applicability of the available instruments to the occasion offered, and the other the applicability of an instrument after reaching an imaginative solution of the problem set by the formal instruction. The first approach involved search together with perceptive apprehension, both extended by inspection-and-comment. All these psychological functions were induced and guided by occasional and self-imposed instructions as well as by a rehearsal of the problem as formally proposed. In those instances (both individual *O*s and group *O*s) where search led to an imaginative apprehension which devised promising instrumental means of solution, the actual application of these means was either itself imaginational (as in the non-executing groups) or actional (as when the individual, having once conjured up means, turned to the table and demonstrated his solution). In both cases, the protocols instanced under Problems 1, 2 and 3 will reveal the very large part usually played by verbal comment in *O*'s progress toward the solution. Just what takes the place of this comment where children, apes, and rats are wanting in linguistic resources is too often covered up by the ambiguous term 'insight.'

These first three problems also reveal some special procedures which are likewise often disposed of in the same way. We may cite the *O* who, after handling the beads of Problem 1, laid them down, leaned back, thus bringing the pliers within his range of vision, and apprehended them as means of solution. If there was 'insight' here, it was obviously an extension of the apprehensive functions *plus* inspection-and-comment. We may approach more closely the actual organic resources of solution in such a case when we observe that the enrichment of the apprehension was obviously due to the preceding search and comment, under appropriate instructions of all our three kinds, formal, self, and occasional. Having determined these essential conditions, the addition of an alleged act of 'insight' would seem to be superfluous.

In Problem 4 were the mutilated and displaced Rs, with a gradual approach from nonsense-forms to the standard letter. The formal instruction to identify each form as it came tended toward configuration, taken in the non-technical sense. The initial perception together with this instruction set up a puzzled search which led first to a family likeness among the forms as they came along, secondly to the perception of figures, animals, and the like, and finally (usually at the seventh and last member) to the symbol R. Thereupon, in retrospect, all the members had become (imperfect) Rs. The successive appearances (which were at times 'sudden') might be called 'insights'; but, more descriptively, perceptive changes under formal and occasional instructions and a puzzling search, the search gradually becoming informed and directed as the series progressed. One moment in the occasion (the prone letter) tended to block understanding (the symbol R) until the letter was practically complete in linear form. The occasional flashing out of the R would be called by some an insight; but with as little justification as the earlier perceptions.

Problem 5 called for the tracing of the rectangle and inscribed figure, with and without a central diagonal (see Fig. 2). *E* had meant to invent a problem in which trial-and-error should be supplemented by something which might be called 'insight.' As a matter of fact, the combination of occasional and formal instruction led chiefly to inspection-and-comment instead of to a headlong tracing of the lines with the red pencil. Our *O*s proved to be neither Thorndikean cats nor *Köhlersche Affen*. Upon comprehending the instructions and perceiving the figure, they set about, under inspection-and-comment, to solve the problem. Imaginational apprehension played its part and so did search and various simple forms of action. At times a failure to solve led to a new direction of search and to a new plan. As the tracing (actual or imagined lines) proceeded, the occasion was modified, and in turn modified—by its new instructions to the organism—further procedures. This may be called trial-and-error; but it is certainly not the blundering and blind 'mechanics' of the older maze-experiments. The addition of the diagonal made the task more difficult and called out more verbal comment and self-instruction; but the general procedure was the same both with individual *O*s and in the groups. The added line decidedly changed the occasion which faced the organism and made new demands upon resources and functional expedients. Where there is an occasional 'aha!' in the protocols, it may be set down among many comments upon the course and terminus of a search. It should be noted that the 'aha!' and the 'flash' (dear to the champions of *closure)* were no more in evidence at the final solution than at various steps along the way. Here that form of the behaviorist's fallacy which interprets performance out of the experimenter's own thoughts and fancies is obviously to be discouraged.

In Problem 6 were the pill-boxes and the hidden cotton. The intent of the arrangement was to induce a situation where many possibilities offered. This intent was realized. *O* devised a plan when the boxes were presented and the formal instruction read. Upon the formulation of the plan ("I shall begin from the left," "I'll try even numbers," "I must find hidden markings," and the like), the search changed from an indefinite thrust "to solve" to "this is my way of hunting." Failure to find led to comment, to imaginative forecast, and to a new plan. As the cotton was found and replaced, the specification of method made memorial use of past success. The occasion changed, the self-instruction changed, inspection-and-comment grew; but the search went on. It is a good instance in little of scientific observation and the gradual elaboration and correction of a theory. Our commentaries throw much light upon this complex functional procedure. While many functional resources of the organism were called forth by the problem, the most notable and outstanding was comprehension, in the sense of understanding or grasping-the-significance-of. Surrogative means doubtless exist in various animals for problem-solving where plural choices offer without perceptive cues, but our commentaries make it abundantly evident that comprehension was the central resource in all our human *O*s.

The three-dimensional construction with the matches was called for in Problem 7 and the spelling of "perplexity" in Problem 8. Both exercises are of the 'puzzling' kind. Both involve a certain spatial arrangement where something bars the way to solution. In the first it is the lay-out on the plane surface: in the second, it is the ordinary left-to-right set-up of letters in a word. Under this handicap to success, search and inspection-and-comment go on. The outcome is a manual construction. Where O succeeded (there were many failures), some chance change in the situation led to the match-solution, and the discovery that the initial "P" (in "perplexity") could not be moved from the right end of the slot led to the word-solution. Free trials were abundant in these puzzles; but *free trials under comment,* which tended to advance the problem toward solution. This is rather 'trial-and-advance' than 'trial-and-error.' There is nothing new here to suggest a unique operation of 'insight.' It is informing to observe how easily wont, habit, or the accustomed prevents those functional accomplishments which would lead on to invention and discovery. It appears that man's functional resources are much greater than his actual accomplishments.

In Problem 9 again (the burlesqued soliloquies) the organism was misled so far as verbal understanding was concerned. Understanding there was, from the outset, but of individual verbal symbols which did not integrate into a linguistic and aesthetic whole. If the ultimate emergence of such a whole, in a strange context, demands 'insight,' then our Os showed that they possessed that gift. Flashes and illuminations were absent, however; and our theories did not lead us toward 'closures.' What little clear perception there was was chiefly buried under a constantly shifted comprehension which first integrated small groups of words, then larger, and finally (in many cases), the entire Shakespearean text. Underlying these progressive comprehensions were self-instructions constantly warring with the occasional instructions and fed by a search which changed its direction when inspection-and-comment brought the hint 'this is a significant passage.' It is a fine case of two conflicting comprehensive functions, one sustained by visual receptors and the other by auditory. The visual is at first dominant; but the auditory gradually gains the ascendency by virtue of formal and self-instructions which promote and direct search. The partial successes and the failures (in E's sense!) are quite as instructive as the reports of those Os who read in the soliloquies. Here the groups were very informing. They reveal the organism working away under the lead of the various instructions and using one device after another. Especially do they show the effectiveness of the function *search,* a describable operation distantly related to the mechanician's 'drive.'

Problem 10 presented the flask-balloon, and Problem 11 the centrifuged shot in the rocker. Both suggested the initial comment 'puzzle to work!' which set off a fairly simple action-train (inserting the balloon, tipping and rocking the shot). Failure to carry out the formal instruction usually led to long inspection-and-comment with interspersed actions. The special resource demanded by the occasion and the formal instruction was a formulated principle or 'natural law' (air pressure, 'centrifugal force') and the comment 'This is a case of ...' This is commonly called 'the applying of physical knowledge.' 'Knowledge' in this situation involves the *inclusion* in comprehension of a generalized rule and the *comment* that the rule applies here. The mere grasp of the principle is not enough. Understanding must fit it to the occasion. Occasional and formal instruction are not sufficient for a solution. Our commentaries and our group-question-aries show in a very striking way the functional modes involved in the solution, wherever the solution actually took place. These problems are probably more difficult for our *O*s than any preceding, in the sense that more functional devices and resources of the organism, combined in more subtle combinations, were called out. We might ignore the whole procedure and simply label the means 'insight'; but that would be to give up the central psychological problem. It is obvious that our problems of this sort only touch the surface of these important human procedures, which call loudly for searching experimental study.

In our last two problems, Problem 12 (discovering and completing a number-pattern) and Problem 13 (completing a poetic stanza), the presented occasion *contains within itself* the means for completion (*i.e.* omitted final number, omitted final word). It contains it, however, only when the occasion is *for the solving observer* a number-pattern (first problem) or a poetic structure (second problem). Here appreciation of pattern or form takes the place of outside physical principle and application in the two problems just now reviewed (10 and 11). Our commentaries and the replies to the group-questions throw a good deal of light upon the means (occasional and self-instructions, search, comment, understanding and imaginational apprehension) which supply—and also fail to supply—the required solution. Search (for a pattern) and occasional instruction leading to comment were the chief means used in Problem 10. It is obvious that the discovery of pattern in the first series helped to define search in the second series and so led toward the goal.

In Problem 13 the temper and training of *O* were important. Without an appreciation of metrical form and of poetic phantasy, the *O*s usually found it impossible to secure the correct final word. Here we come upon the important distinction between occasion-for-the-observer and the 'stimulus' as set up or assumed by the experimenter. It is only the former, that-which-is-present-for-the-organism, that is of primary significance to the psychologist. Where the *O* poetically understood, the formal instruction set a definite search and led (through the intervention of self and occasional instruction, inspection-and-comment, and imaginational apprehension) to the missing word. A limited vocabulary sometimes defeated the search. Our group-results are of especial importance in this problem because they have helped us to discover by inquisition the relative uses of rhyme, metre, rhythm, vocabulary, poetic appreciation, and other factors, in attempting to solve the problem. Less than one-in-three of the group-members found the missing word 'Elysian' under the restrictions imposed. The fourth selection profited (91% of the group *O*s supplied 'you') from the earlier solutions, and it was also simpler and less dependent upon the appreciative abilities of the individual. Again, this experimental fragment only touches the surface of a large problem, the discovery of the psychological means resorted to by the adult and literate organism in selecting and verifying 'the suitable' in a poetic sense.

We began by listing various ways and contexts in which the term 'insight' has been recently used. Were we to review our own commentaries and the answers to our group-inquiries, we could easily find instances of the following sorts to which we might apply the word without very greatly extending it beyond its present uses. The instances are: (1) perceptive apprehension extended on the side of use and means, (2) perceptive apprehension accompanied by imaginative revaluation, (3) anticipative imagination, (4) comprehension of a solving generalization, (5) sudden drop in learning-time, (6) re-apprehension of experimental material under occasional instruction, (7) comprehension of a general principle and its applicability in a specific instance, (8) apprehension of a total pattern-arrangement or of particular relevant features in the pattern, and (9) comprehension of a constructive scheme, of the rules or canons of an art, or of the natural relation between presented objects.

The fact is that the further experimental description and functional analysis go in the directions taken, the looser, the more ambiguous, and the less satisfactory the term 'insight' becomes. Its recent revival in psychology has been natural if not inevitable—as we saw in the beginning of our study—; but there would seem to be no longer any sanction for its varied and uncritical connotations. Under arbitrary definition it may serve for some time as a label for certain behaviors in rat-running, primate-manipulation, and school-accomplishment. As a cause and explanation of these behaviors, insight will probably be less and less appealed to in factual and experimental contexts.

Our own procedure in the problematical situation used has been (1) to present a definite and solvable problem, (2) to provide a brief, unambiguous, and constant formal instruction, (3) to employ trained and untrained observers, individually and in groups, (4) to determine by report and interrogatory[5] a descriptive account of the psychological functions brought into play, together with the instructions (formal, occasional and self) and other antecedents which threw the functions into commission.

The functions most frequently and effectively found in our solutions have been search, the three forms of apprehension (perceptive, memorial and imaginational), inspection-and-comment, and comprehension. In the examination of our descriptive material we have found no characteristic process, operation, form of conditioning or mode of discovery, which we could with propriety distinguish as 'insight.'

NOTES

Accepted for publication May 1, 1931. From the Psychological Laboratory of Cornell University. The research was directed by Professor Bentley.

1. Only here and there has a critical voice been raised. Examples are G. W. Hartmann, The concept and criteria of insight, *Psychol. Rev.*, 38, 1931, 242–253, and S. C. Fisher, A critique of insight in Köhler's 'Gestalt Psychology,' this JOURNAL, 43, 1931, 131–136.

2. *Observers.* The trained *O*s were Dr. S. Feldman (*Fe*), Dr. J. G. Jenkins (*Je*), R. B. MacLeod (*Mc*), members of the staff; E. H. Kemp (*Ke*), A. D. Glanville (*Gl*), graduate students in Psychology. The untrained *O*s were H. A. Myers (*My*), and K. M. Simpson (*Si*), graduate students in Philosophy and Physics respectively. C. M. Wiltse (*Wi*), and R. G. Fisher (*Fi*) were occasional observers.

3. For the group-presentations, 110 observers from the undergraduate classes in Psychology volunteered. This number observed in all problems presented to the groups except problems 5, 6, and 10, which had 63, 50, and 64 observers respectively. Since the experimental period of each group was limited, it was found necessary to alternate problem 5 with problems 6 and 10.

4. For the three main forms of *instruction* (formal, occasional and self) see O. F. Weber and M. Bentley, The relation of instruction to the psychosomatic functions, *Psychol. Monog.*, 35, 1926 (no. 163), 1–15; M. Bentley, *The Field of Psychology*, 1924, 389–396.

5. The groups were always formed and interrogated after a given problem had been studied through the elaborate reports of trained individual observers. Only in this order could the groups be sensibly and usefully questioned, and only so could the individual and the grouped results be reasonably compared. We found this form of group-observation extremely informing.

RETENTION OF PROBLEM SOLUTIONS: THE RE-SOLUTION EFFECT

ROGER L. DOMINOWSKI
University of Illinois at Chicago

LINDA S. BUYER
Governors State University

Four experiments compared the re-solution performance of prior solvers with that of prior nonsolvers given the correct solutions. Experiments 1 and 2 challenged Weisberg and Alba's (1981) contention that solving a problem and being shown the solution yield equivalent problem knowledge. In both experiments, students who initially solved problems showed near-perfect recall of the solutions after a 1-week delay, far superior to recall by students who had been shown the correct answers. In Experiment 3, solvers showed poor solution retention when the connection between the problem and the solution was not meaningful. Experiment 4 showed that with meaningful problems, solvers and those merely provided with solutions have qualitatively different problem representations. The findings can be explained in terms of differential understanding of problems and their solutions.

The bulk of problem-solving research has focused on the initial discovery of solutions, with little attention paid to how well solutions are remembered. The scarcity of research on solution memory is surprising because the topic involves important theoretical issues. Historically, a contrast existed between associative and Gestalt approaches to problem solving. Associative theorists (e.g., Thorndike, 1911) viewed problem solving as the acquisition and elicitation of associative bonds. From a Gestalt perspective (Kohler, 1925/1976; Maier, 1940; Wertheimer, 1945/1982), it was accepted that problems could be solved by direct application of past experience, but emphasis was given to another form of problem solving that involves the reorganization or restructuring of experience and knowledge (Ohlsson, 1984).

Insight refers to the new knowledge of problem structure that follows reorganization. It was held that solutions involving restructuring and insight would be remembered well (Osgood, 1953; Woodworth & Schlosberg, 1954). Indeed, in Kohler's studies with apes, skillful solutions often were observed when a problem

American Journal of Psychology
Summer 2000, Vol. 113, No. 2, pp. 249–274

was presented a second time, which implies excellent solution memory. In contrast, in Thorndike's puzzle box experiments with cats, many trials were required before efficient solutions occurred, which implies that little was learned or remembered from solving a problem once and led to the view of problem solving as a gradual, trial-and-error acquisition process. Although both associative and Gestalt approaches were later applied to human problem solving, researchers did not explore the differential expectations regarding solution memory. In a general discussion of human and animal problem solving, Scheerer (1963) repeated the Gestalt position, asserting that solutions accompanied by insight will be easily retained.

In a complete rejection of Gestalt views of problem solving, Weisberg and Alba (1981) specifically questioned the validity of Scheerer's assertion, stating that he presented no supporting data. More importantly, Weisberg and Alba reported that after a 1-week interval, only 65% of their subjects solved the nine-dot problem when it was presented a second time. They concluded that their data contradicted the Gestalt prediction and that solution memory showed quite ordinary forgetting, consistent with their overall position that problem solving involves primarily retrieval of information from long-term memory, with no role for insight. The adequacy of Weisberg and Alba's retention finding may be questioned. Their subjects, rather than having solved the problem on its first presentation, had failed to solve and been given the solution. The solution had been acquired not via problem solving but in a manner similar to a standard memory task. Consequently, the appropriateness of their data for characterizing retention after successful problem solving is at best unclear (Dominowski, 1981).

Selected aspects of work on the generation effect are potentially relevant. The basic generation effect is illustrated by Jacoby's (1978) study. He gave subjects simple associative puzzles (e.g., "given *foot* s _ _ e, complete the second word") and found that recall of the solution words was better when subjects had generated them than when subjects had read the solution words (e.g., *shoe*) immediately before puzzle presentation. Jacoby's results show that generating an answer leads to better recall than reading an answer, but his results may not be directly relevant to Weisberg and Alba's (1981) finding. Weisberg and Alba's subjects had tried unsuccessfully to solve the nine-dot problem before receiving the solution, a condition that Jacoby did not explore. This condition was studied by Slamecka and Fevreiski (1983), using materials similar to Jacoby's (e.g., "find the opposite of *pursue*, given *av _ _ d*"). They found that, compared to a condition in which answers were read, recall of solution words was better when subjects attempted to generate answers, whether or not they were successful. For present purposes, the most important finding was that there was no recall difference following successful versus unsuccessful generation attempts. That finding supports Weisberg and Alba's contention that whether a subject solves, or fails to solve but is given the solution, is of no consequence. Several accounts of the generation effect, although differing about details, agree that the effect depends on the item being represented in memory as a familiar unit (Slamecka & Fevreiski, 1983; Gardner & Hampton, 1985). Therefore, they are compatible with the view that problem solving is nothing more than cued retrieval of information from memory (Weisberg & Alba, 1981). The view just outlined stands in clear contrast to that of the Gestalt psychologists. Their emphasis on restructuring differentiates problem solving from ordinary memory. Wertheimer (1945/1982) commented on the difference between solving a problem via restructuring and being shown a solution after failing to solve. He downgraded the latter as unlikely to result in recreating the process of restructuring necessary for real understanding. Recently, Metcalfe (1986a, 1986b) found differences between problem solving and memory, with her results generally supporting a restructuring process in problem solving. From this perspective, one would expect solvers to differ from nonsolvers who are given solutions.

Buyer and Dominowski (1989) found a retention difference favoring solvers of number-phrase riddles. In that experiment, subjects had to complete phrases referring to "facts" about numbers (e.g., "64 = Squares on a Checkerboard") from partial cues (e.g., "64 = S on a C"). Successful generation led to far better retention than unsuccessful generation (with solution feedback), which was no better than mere reading of the items. Although subjects had to already know the relevant number facts in order to complete the phrases, it is clear that the phrases as items of general knowledge are more complex, less familiar, and less well integrated than the words used by Slamecka and Fevreiski (1983). The solutions to the nine-dot problem and other problems are still more complex, do not exist in subjects' semantic memories before problem presentation, and gain meaning only in the context of the problem situation. A plausible inference is that for such problems, solvers' retention will be decidedly superior to that of nonsolvers who are given the solution. The present studies provide the data necessary to evaluate this expectation.

To summarize the issues, from a memory retrieval viewpoint, performance when problems are presented a second time should be the same for prior solvers as it is for nonsolvers who have been given solutions, and both groups should show less-than-perfect performance. From a restructuring viewpoint, solvers should be near-perfect and better than nonsolvers who have received solutions. To make the data of this study comparable to those of Weisberg and Alba (1981), a 1-week retention interval was used. To provide some generality to the results, several problems were used, including the nine-dot problem used by Weisberg and Alba.

EXPERIMENT 1

METHOD

Subjects and Design

The subjects were 50 students from an introductory psychology class at the University of Illinois at Chicago (UIC) who participated in partial fulfillment of a course requirement. Each subject participated in two sessions separated by a 1-week interval; subjects attempted seven problems in Session 1 and were given the same seven problems in Session 2. Session 1 performance was used to identify solvers and nonsolvers separately for each problem; comparison of Session 2 (retention) performance by the two groups was the primary contrast.

Materials

Seven problems were selected from published reports; they were chosen to provide some variety, to be amenable to paper-and-pencil presentation, and to yield a reasonable number of initial solutions within a few minutes' working time. The problems were the prisoner, horse trade, nine dot, train, and farmer problems (Maier & Casselman, 1970), the card problem (Davis, 1964), and the "gold dust" version of a water jars problem (Restle & Davis, 1962). Each problem was presented on a single sheet of paper that included space for recording solutions. Three of the problems required drawing line patterns to meet problem constraints (prisoner, nine-dot, and farmer problems). The horse trade and train problems require interpreting a paragraph of information to arrive at a correct numerical answer (amount of money made, number of trains seen on a trip); for the answer to be counted as correct, subjects had to provide an adequate explanation of how they arrived at their numerical answers. The card problem requires interpretation of a series of sentences (e.g., "To the right of a king there is a queen or two") to determine the identities of three playing cards aligned in a row. The water jars problem requires finding a series of "transfers" between jars having stated capacities to arrive at a designated amount.

Procedure

Subjects signed up for two sessions. At the beginning of Session 1, they were told that the research project required giving each person a number of problems, some of which they would receive in this session and some during Session 2 a week later. They were not told that the Session 1 problems would be repeated in Session 2.

Session 1 data were collected using small groups. For each problem, worksheets were distributed face down (these sheets contained complete instructions and workspace); a start signal was given, and subjects were given 3–5 min to reach a solution (working time varied across problems). When time was up, a stop signal was given, worksheets were collected, and the solution to the problem was shown via overhead projector. Solution feedback remained in view as long as at least one subject indicated a desire to study it further. This procedure was followed for each of the seven problems.

Subjects were seen individually for Session 2. They were given the same seven problems, using the same problem order and time limits as in Session 1. Solution feedback was given if subjects failed to solve a problem. After the seventh problem, subjects were told the purpose of the study and were asked to assist further with the research by refraining from discussing the experiment with other students.

RESULTS AND DISCUSSION

The prisoner problem and the train problem yielded one and two initial solutions, respectively; these problems will not be considered further, and the results concern performance on the other five problems. The data of primary interest concern performance by prior solvers versus prior nonsolvers when problems were presented a second time after a 1-week delay. Solver and nonsolver groups were defined separately for each problem. Figure 1 shows the overall performance levels in Session 2 for the two groups. Figure 1a shows that prior solvers showed near-perfect retention, re-solving problems at a 98% rate, which was much higher than the percentage of solutions by prior nonsolvers (61%), $z = 6.27$, $p < .001$. Across problems, prior solvers were uniformly successful in reproducing solutions, whereas success rates for prior nonsolvers varied. The solver–nonsolver difference in solution rate was statistically significant for the horse trade, card, water jars, and nine-dot problems ($p < .05$). The one exception was the farmer problem, which was solved in Session

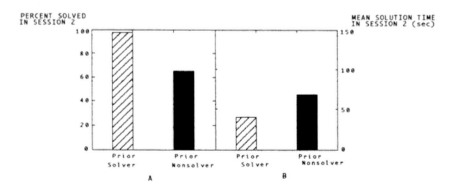

FIGURE 1. Performance of prior solvers and prior nonsolvers in Session 2, Experiment 1: (a) percentages of problems solved; (b) mean solution times, based only on problems actually solved

2 by 95% of prior nonsolvers. It should be noted that for the nine-dot problem used by Weisberg and Alba (1981), Session 2 performance by prior solvers (100%) was far superior to that by prior nonsolvers (38%), $z = 2.66, p < .01$.

As shown in Figure 1b, when prior nonsolvers did succeed in Session 2, they were slower than prior solvers in producing solutions, $t(48) = 3.63, p < .001$.[1] Figure 2 shows mean solution times for the two groups for each of the five problems. Prior solvers were faster for every problem, and solution times varied across problems; the solution time difference between groups was statistically significant for all but the nine-dot problem. These solution times, because they concern only solutions actually produced, do not completely represent performance differences between groups across problems. If minimum solution times (time limit + 1 s) were added for all those failing to solve in Session 2, the gap between prior solvers and nonsolvers would increase substantially. For the farmer problem, which nearly all subjects in both groups solved in Session 2, the data in Figure 2 show that prior solvers (mean = 13.8 s) were decidedly faster than prior nonsolvers (mean = 32.1 s), $t(46) = 2.54, p < .02$. Application of a two-factor ANOVA to the solution time data gave no suggestion of a problem-by-group interaction.

Success or failure on any particular problem was independent of performance on other problems. Phi coefficients varied from −0.14 to +0.43, with a median value

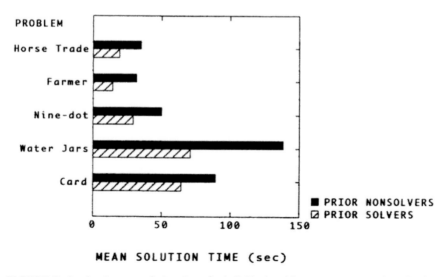

FIGURE 2. Session 2 mean solution times for individual problems, Experiment 1, based only on problems actually solved

of + 0.06. Therefore, solver and nonsolver groups did not differ systematically in any general problem-solving abilities.

The results are clear with respect to the main issues: In terms of solution probability, prior solvers showed virtually no forgetting over a 1-week period. In addition, prior solvers were faster than prior nonsolvers who had been given the solution. The findings support Wertheimer's proposal that reorganization of problem information leads to excellent memory for the solutions. They indicate that Weisberg and Alba (1981) overestimated the amount of solution forgetting by people who have solved a problem and contradict their proposal that generating a solution and being given a solution are equivalent. But they do agree with Buyer and Dominowski's (1989) findings that self-generation produces superior recall.

Experiment 2 was a constructive replication of Experiment 1, addressing some procedural issues that concerned primarily the poor Session 2 performance by prior nonsolvers. Because Session 1 data were collected in group sessions, it was possible that some nonsolvers paid inadequate attention to the solution feedback. In addition, for two of the problems, the feedback might have been technically incomplete. For both the prisoner and nine-dot problems, the completed solution consists of a pattern of lines; subjects were shown the completed pattern but not how it is drawn, so it might be argued that they had not been given all of the solution. Regarding prior solvers, the first experiment did not, strictly speaking, provide data showing that they had learned and remembered anything from their initial solutions to the problems. Although this notion seems unlikely to be correct, Session 1 solution times are needed for comparison with Session 2 re-solution times; a reduction in solution times for prior solvers would unambiguously demonstrate that they had learned and remembered useful information from their first solutions. In the second experiment, therefore, individual Sessions 1 and 2 were used, with a comparison of two types of feedback given to nonsolvers of the prisoner and nine-dot problems in Session 1.

EXPERIMENT 2

METHOD

Subjects and Design

Fifty UIC students in an introductory psychology class participated in partial fulfillment of a course requirement. Each subject participated in two sessions held 1 week apart, attempting seven problems in Session 1 and the same problems in Session 2. For two problems (prisoner and nine-dot), two forms of solution feedback (static vs. dynamic) were used in Session 1, with approximately half of the nonsolving subjects receiving each form.

The seven problems and the procedures used in Experiment 1 were again used, with the following changes. Individual first sessions were conducted, with solution times recorded for solvers and with nonsolvers receiving solution feedback on a sheet of paper to be examined for as long as they desired. For the prisoner and nine-dot problems, a schedule was created to randomly assign subjects to receive either static or dynamic solution feedback in Session 1. Static feedback consisted of the predrawn solution (as in Experiment 1), whereas for dynamic feedback the experimenter drew the solution lines in full view of the subject (and repeated doing so if requested). Because some subjects solved these problems and thus did not require feedback, each form of feedback was received by approximately half of the nonsolving subjects. In Session 2, half the subjects were asked whether they had worked on any of the problems during the week between sessions and, if so, to describe what they had done.

RESULTS AND DISCUSSION

As in Experiment 1, the data are based on five problems (excluding the prisoner and train problems, which had a total of three initial solutions), with solvers and nonsolvers defined separately for each problem. The overall results replicated the findings of Experiment 1. As shown in Figure 3a, prior solvers were 99% successful in re-solving problems presented in Session 2, compared to only 55% solutions for prior nonsolvers, $z = 6.77$, $p < .001$. The difference between groups was statistically

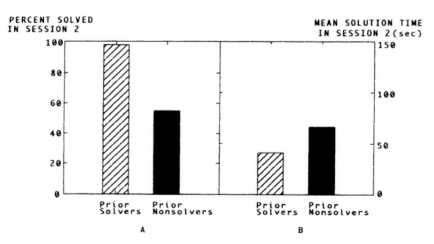

FIGURE 3. Performance of prior solvers and prior nonsolvers in Session 2, Experiment 2: (a) percentages of problems solved; (b) mean solution times, based only on problems actually solved

significant for the card, water jars, and nine-dot problems (p <.05, one-tailed). For the farmer and horse trade problems, prior solvers were 100% successful, but prior nonsolvers did only slightly worse in Session 2 (96% solutions for the farmer problem, 94% for the horse trade problem). As in Experiment 1, Session 2 performance by prior solvers of the nine-dot problem (100%) was much higher than that by prior nonsolvers (46%), z = 2.66, p < .01.

Replicating a finding in Experiment 1, success on any one problem was independent of success on other problems, with phi coefficients ranging from +0.01 to +0.28, with a median value of +0.05. This finding indicates that solver and nonsolver groups did not differ in general problem-solving abilities. Rather, the act of solving a problem has important consequences for later performance.

Figure 3b shows that when Session 2 solutions were achieved, prior nonsolvers were generally slower than prior solvers in producing them, $t(48)$ = 3.05, p< .01. Figure 4 presents solvers' and nonsolvers' mean solution times for the individual problems; as in Experiment 1, solvers were faster on all problems. The solution time difference between groups reached statistical significance for the card and farmer problems. These data reflect only solutions actually produced; inclusion of minimum solution times for those who failed to solve would yield huge differences between prior solvers and nonsolvers for the card, water jar, and nine-dot problems.

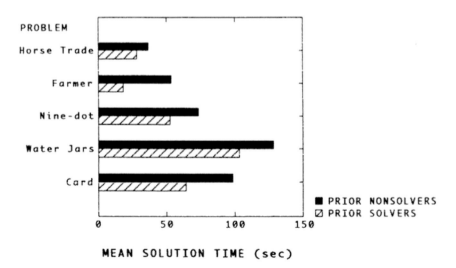

FIGURE 4. Session 2 mean solution times for individual problems, Experiment 2, based only on problems actually solved

For the farmer problem, which was solved in Session 2 by nearly all prior nonsolvers, solvers (mean = 17.5 s) were nonetheless markedly faster than nonsolvers (mean = 53.3 s) in producing solutions, $t(47) = 3.29$, $p < .01$. Application of a two-factor ANOVA did not suggest a problem-by-group interaction.

One purpose of Experiment 2 was to determine whether solvers learned anything from their initial solutions. On average, solvers' Session 2 solution times were more than 80 s faster than their first solutions. Re-solution times were faster in 96% of the cases, confirming the expectation that solvers would acquire useful information from their initial solutions. Across problems, there was some variation in the size of the reduction (52–139 s), which reflected differences in initial solution times (i.e., problems with longer initial solution times tended to have larger time reductions in Session 2). Within problems, first solution times were poor predictors of second solution times; correlations ranged from −0.17 (card) to +0.44 (horse trade), with a median value of + 0.22.

Two problems had sufficient numbers of initial solvers to allow a comparison of fast versus slow Session 1 solvers (using median splits) with respect to changes in solution times between sessions. For the horse trade problem, fast and slow solvers' ($n = 9$ each) initial solution times were vastly different (38.3 and 121.1 s, respectively), but their re-solution times were systematically shorter and differed only slightly (19.6 and 36.1 s, respectively). For the farmer problem ($n = 18$ per subgroup), fast (68.6 s) and slow (143.6 s) solvers' initial times were quite different, whereas their re-solution times were much shorter and more similar (11.5 and 23.6 s, respectively). These data suggest that reaching a solution is more important with respect to later performance on a problem than how long one took to find the solution. Experiment 4 allowed us to examine this phenomenon in greater depth because we collected data on the students' problem representations. Thus, we were able to explore both the relationship of solving/not solving in Session 1 to the characteristics of the problem representations and the relationship of the representations' characteristics to Session 2 performance.

The type of solution feedback given to nonsolvers of the prisoner and nine-dot problems in Session 1 had no effect on Session 2 performance. Static and dynamic feedback led to Session 2 solution rates of 42% and 46% for the prisoner problem and 50% and 43% for the nine-dot problem, respectively. Thus, allowing nonsolvers to observe the drawing of solution lines did not improve Session 2 performance. Also, providing solution feedback on an individual basis in Experiment 2 did not benefit nonsolvers, compared to Experiment 1, where group feedback was used. In Experiment 2, the nonsolvers' Session 2 performance was slightly poorer and the solver–nonsolver difference was slightly larger than in Experiment 1.

Subjects reported thinking about or attempting to work on a small minority of problems (15%) during the 1-week interval between sessions. No subject reported directing any attention to a solved problem during the interval. In Session 2, the solution rate for worked-on problems (43%) was equivalent to the overall solution rate for prior nonsolvers (48%). Efforts to work on unsolved problems during the interval generally were not beneficial; less than one third of the reported attempts were described as successful (subjects sometimes could not reproduce enough of the details of a problem to make a meaningful attempt). When attempts were described as successful, the problem was always solved in Session 2. Consequently, a minority (about 15%) of the Session 2 solutions produced by prior nonsolvers actually represented re-solution of a problem solved during the interval between sessions. The results replicate the findings of Experiment 1 in regard to the near-perfect retention shown by prior solvers, the large differences between prior solvers and prior nonsolvers, and differences across problems. The data also showed that re-solutions by prior solvers are substantially faster than their original solutions, indicating considerable learning and retention. Varying solution feedback procedures did not lead to improved subsequent performance by nonsolvers, suggesting that neither inattention to feedback nor static solution feedback is responsible for failures by prior nonsolvers when problems are presented again.

Experiment 3 was designed to extend these findings by exploring the consequences of having subjects solve problems in which the relationship between the problem and the solution was arbitrary. We hypothesized that if Wertheimer (1945/1982) was correct in asserting that restructuring plays a critical role in the retention and application of problem solutions, then there should be no memorial benefits derived from correctly solving problems that have arbitrary solutions. On the other hand, if Weisberg and Alba (1981) are correct in their assertion that restructuring is irrelevant to the retention of problem solutions, then we should find that memory for previously solved problems is nearly perfect (as we found in Experiments 1 and 2) even when no restructuring is possible.

EXPERIMENT 3

Contrary to the predictions of Weisberg and Alba (1981), the data from Experiments 1 and 2 support the Gestalt position regarding the role of restructuring as a causal factor in solution retention and ease of application (Kohler, 1925/1976; Maier, 1940; Wertheimer, 1945/1982). Experiment 3 was intended to extend these findings by showing that the re-solution effect disappears when there is no meaningful relationship between the problem and its solution. Thus, for this experiment the problems and their solutions were paired randomly.

METHOD

Subjects

Thirty UIC students participated in the experiment for credit in an introductory psychology class. They were told that the experiment was about extra-sensory perception (ESP).

Materials

Forty-eight randomly selected, concrete words (taken from Paivio, Smythe, & Yuille, 1968) were divided randomly into two sets of 24 words each. One of the sets was designated as the cue words. The other was designated as the response words. Then one response word was randomly designated as the correct associate for each of the cue words. The 48 words were presented to subjects on a single sheet of paper with the 24 cue words arrayed in a column on the left side of the page. There was a blank next to each cue word. The column was divided into eight groups of three words each. For each group of three cue words, the three correct response words were randomly arrayed in a row on the right side of the page. This arrangement was used so that subjects would average about one-third correct responses.

Procedure

Subjects were told that word pairs had been formed by randomly pairing words together. The subjects were then instructed to use their ESP to select the correct associate from among the response terms for each set of three cue words (and write it in the blank next to the cue word). Subjects were next shown a list of the correct word pairs and asked to estimate the percentage of people who would guess that those two words would be paired. The subjects were asked to estimate the percentages to make sure that they actually processed each of the correct word pairings (Stage 1). Subjects returned 1 week later and were asked first to recall (Stage 2) and then to recognize (Stage 3) the correct response terms. In Stage 2, students were first presented with a sheet of paper containing the cue words in a column on the right side of the page and asked to write the correct response terms in blanks next to the cue words. The cue words were listed in the same order they had appeared in Session 1. Subjects were told to leave a blank empty only if they were absolutely certain that they could not recall the correct response word. In Stage 3, subjects were presented with a sheet of paper that differed from that used in Stage 2 by the inclusion of an alphabetical list of response words in a column on the left side of the page. Subjects were told to match the correct cue–response word pairs by using all of the response words only once and filling in all of the blanks.

RESULTS AND DISCUSSION

We first checked to make certain that all subjects had correctly paired at least some of the cue–response word pairs presented in Session 1. In Stage 1, subjects correctly guessed approximately one third of the correct response terms (mean = 29.9%, SD = 9.4%) and no subject guessed fewer than 12.5% of the correct responses. Thus, for each subject we obtained Session 2 data on both solved and unsolved problems.

Recall performance in Session 2 of this experiment was nothing like the recall performance in Session 2 of Experiments 1 and 2. The recall rates (10% for correctly guessed items, 3.5% for incorrectly guessed items) are substantially worse than the recall rates found in the first two experiments (99% and 98% for correctly solved problems and 55% and 61% for incorrectly solved problems), although we again found that self-generated correct responses were better recalled than responses that had merely been provided, $t(29) = 2.49, p < .05$. In fact, in this experiment the probability of guessing the correct response term in Stage 1 was greater than the probability of correctly recalling a guessed item in Stage 2, $t(29) = 6.1, p < .01$, or of recognizing it in Stage 3, $t(29) = 1.973, p = .058$.

Stage 3 data again produced results similar to those found in the standard generation effect paradigm (Buyer & Dominowski, 1989; Slamecka & Fevreiski, 1983; Gardner & Hampton, 1985); that is, 22% of the response terms that had been correctly identified in Stage 1 were recognized, whereas only 11.9% of the response terms not correctly identified in Stage 1 were recognized, $t(29) = 3.51$, $p < .01$. However, the recognition rates from this experiment (22% and 11.9%) are extremely low when considered in light of the recall rates from Experiments 1 and 2. This is especially true because, other things being equal, one usually expects better recognition than recall performance.

The hypothesis we derived from Gestalt theory was that if we eliminated meaningful relationships between problems and their solutions we would dramatically reduce memory for solutions to correctly solved problems. The enormous difference in recall rates between Experiment and Experiments 1 and 2 suggests that when no restructuring is possible (e.g., when the relationship between a problem and its solution is arbitrary) there is virtually no retention benefit to having previously solved a problem. Thus, these results again support the Gestalt position that restructuring plays an important role in retaining and applying problem solutions and contradict Weisberg and Alba's (1981) contention that restructuring is an irrelevant component of solution memory.

EXPERIMENT 4

The data from Experiments 1–3 can be summarized as follows: When a problem solution is not arbitrary, Session 2 performance is virtually perfect following success in Session 1, and prior solvers outperform prior nonsolvers. When a problem solution is arbitrary (and there is nothing to understand about it, as in Experiment

3), Session 2 performance is abysmal even by those who earlier correctly solved the problems. A remaining question involves the nature of the difference between those who have and those who have not successfully solved a meaningful problem. Experiment 4 was conducted to address this question.

In Experiment 4, both written and verbal protocols were collected so that we could explore any differences in problem representations between solvers and nonsolvers. Based on both Gestalt and information processing theories, we expected to find that the representations by solvers were structurally different than those constructed by nonsolvers. Specifically, we expected to find that the problem representations constructed by solvers reflected the inherent structure of the problems, that they were well organized, that they accurately encoded the objectively defined problems, and that they were connected to related knowledge already present in the subjects' memories.

To examine a broad range of problems, problems representing Greeno's (1978; Greeno & Simon, 1988) problem typology were used. Greeno defines problem types according to the cognitive abilities required to solve the problems. The three basic problem types are: problems of inducing structure (e.g., analogies), which require identifying relationships among components and fitting relationships into patterns; transformation problems (e.g., water jars), which require planning skill based on a means–end strategy; and arrangement problems (e.g., cryptarithmetic), which require composition skills and constructive search. In the current experiment, subjects were presented with one of each of Greeno's three problem types in Session 1. Subjects were asked to solve the identical problems again in a second session 1 week later.

METHOD

Subjects

Subjects were 54 UIC undergraduates who participated in the experiment for credit in an introductory psychology class.

Materials

Each of the three problem types Greeno (1978) identified was represented by two isomorphic exemplars of each type. (Problems that are isomorphic are structurally identical to one another.) Katona's (1940) card trick problem was used as an arrangement exemplar, Luchins's (1942) water jars problem was used as a transformation exemplar, and inducing structure problems were represented by the Bourne, Dominowski, and Loftus (1979) matching problem. A coin was flipped to assign each of the pairs of isomorphic problems to a set of problems (one each of arrangement, transformation, and induction) to be given to subjects to work on in Session 1. In Session 1, approximately 50% of the subjects received one of the sets and the remainder received the other set.

Subjects were asked to think aloud while they were working. A tape recorder was used to collect the verbal protocols. (Concurrent verbal protocols are verbalizations during problem solving; retrospective protocols are postproblem verbalizations.) The concurrent verbal protocols were collected for a purpose unrelated to the present experiments and will not be mentioned further. The verbal protocols from three subjects were lost through mechanical failure of the tape recorder used to collect the data. Subjects were provided with the problems on separate sheets of paper and asked to show their work. Each sheet had room on it for the solution.

Procedure

Subjects in this experiment were run individually in both sessions. To acquaint subjects with the thinking-aloud procedure, each subject was first asked to count the number of windows in his or her house (Ericsson & Simon, 1993). No subjects expressed discomfort with this procedure. Any time a subject was silent for more than 10 s, he or she was told to keep talking.

In Session 1, each subject was asked to solve one each of the induction, transformation, and arrangement problems. Each problem was presented with a time limit. A pilot study was performed to find time limits for each problem such that 50% of the subjects could solve the problem within the limit. Time limits ranged from 3.5 to 13 min. When subjects solved each problem or the time allotted for the problem ran out, the problem sheet was removed, the subjects were shown the correct solution (if necessary), and subjects were asked the following questions about the problem.

In your own words, would you please describe this problem to me (that is, what are the instructions)?

Would you describe, in detail, what steps you took to solve the problem? (If the problem was not solved, the question was rephrased as "what steps were you taking to try to solve the problem?")

Does this problem seem at all similar, in any way, to any other problem or situation you've ever encountered?

The answers to these questions constituted the retrospective verbal protocols. Two graduate students rated these protocols for correspondence to the objectively defined problem (based on the answers to the first question), coherence of the subject's internal representation (based on the second question), and the number of connections between knowledge of the current problem and other knowledge (based on the third); the same two students independently rated the written protocols (the subjects' worksheets) for the presence or absence of structural understanding (Wertheimer, 1945/1982). These measures are detailed in Appendix A.

Two subjects never wrote anything while working on any of the three problems. Four additional subjects failed to show their work for one of the three problems. If subjects failed to solve a problem within the time limits, they were allowed to view the correct answer until they indicated that they were satisfied.

Subjects were asked to return 1 week later and asked to solve the same problems, in the same order, again. In Session 1 the need for Session 2 was explained by saying that there were too many problems to do in a single session and that more problems (with no specification as to their nature) would be presented the next week.

RESULTS AND DISCUSSION

In Session 1, the arrangement, transformation, and inducing structure problems were solved by, respectively, 32, 38, and 37 of the 54 subjects. As we found in Experiments 1 and 2, students were much more likely to solve a problem in Session 2 if they had successfully solved it in Session 1. Of the prior solvers, 94%, 97%, and 100% re-solved, respectively, the arrangement, transformation, and inducing structure problems. Only 67% (arrangement), 71% (transformation), and 69% (inducing structure) of those who initially failed to solve succeeded in Session 2. These percentages are approximately the same as the comparable initial solution percentages (59%, 70%, and 68.5%). Separate analyses of variance for each problem type using success in Session 1 as a predictor of solving in Session 2 were all significant, smallest $F(1, 52) = 7.58$, $MSE = .13$, $p \leq .01$.

As in Experiments 1 and 2, solvers were faster at producing solutions in Session 2 than were initial nonsolvers (mean difference for the arrangement problems = 79.37 s, mean difference for the transformation problems = 30.3 s, mean difference for the inducing structure problems = 29.5 s). Only the t test for the transformation problems reached significance, $t(46) = 3.7$, $p < .01$. However, the other t tests approached significance: for arrangement problems, $t(43) = 1.85$, $p = .07$; for inducing structure problems, $t(46) = 1.93$, $p = .06$. Re-solutions in Session 2 were all substantially faster than the initial solution times in Session 1 (mean difference in first and second solution times for the arrangement problems = 225 s, mean difference for the transformation problems = 67.2 s, mean difference for the inducing structure problems = 48.5 s), smallest $t(36) = 4.99$, $p < .01$.

Although solvers and nonsolvers in Experiments 1 and 2 did not appear to differ in general problem-solving ability, different problems were used in Experiment 4, and it is possible that Session 1 solvers are good problem solvers and Session 1 nonsolvers are poor problem solvers. Total number of problems solved in Session 1 and speed of initial solutions both seemed to be reasonable indicators of general ability and were used as predictors. To adjust for differences in problem difficulty, solution speeds were indexed by the mean of the proportions of the maximum allowed time that was used to solve a problem. Because solving only one Session 1 problem, however quickly, might reflect a different caliber of problem solver than does solving all three Session 1 problems quickly, the interaction was included in the analysis as a third predictor. The criterion variables were solution speeds in Session 2. Because this is a repeated-measures analysis, only subjects who solved all three problems in Session 2 are included ($n = 39$). The univariate between-group analyses indicated that none of the three measures of problem solving ability predicted speed of Session 2 solutions, largest $F(1, 35) < 1$, all ps ns). None of the multivariate within-group analyses revealed any interaction effect of the problem types with general ability on Session 2 solution speed, smallest Wilks's $\lambda(2, 34) = .9$, all ps ns.

Analysis of Experiment 2 data indicated that Session 1 solution times were poor predictors of Session 2 solution times. Because the majority of the subjects in Experiment 4 solved all of the problems in Session 2 (39 of 54), it was possible to relate initial solution speed for each problem to Session 2 solution speed on all problems. Separately for each of the three problem types, Session 1 solution times were divided at the median into faster and slower groups. Thus, for each problem, we identified the solvers as faster or slower problem solvers. We then used the Session 1 faster/slower designations of performance to predict speed of Session 2 performance. None of the three repeated-measures ANOVAS showed that being a faster or slower problem solver in Session 1 was predictive of Session 2 solution times, largest $F(1, 27) < 1$, smallest Wilks's $\lambda(2, 26) = .815$, all ps ns. Differences in Session 2 solution percentages and solution times between solvers and nonsolvers cannot be accounted for by differences in the solvers' general abilities.

Additional analyses were conducted to determine whether solving is associated with different problem representations than is nonsolving. Retrospective verbal protocols were analyzed because they best reflect the subjects' knowledge state after either solving or being shown a solution. Because the maximum values of the correspondence and coherence measures computed from the verbal protocols vary widely from problem to problem, they are discussed in terms of percentages of the maximum for the remainder of this article. Using solving in Session 1 as the predictor variable and the four measures of understanding (correspondence, coherence, connection to other knowledge, and structural understanding) as dependent measures, repeated-measures ANOVAS were computed (separately for each of the three problem types) to determine whether the nature of their problem representations would differentiate the solvers from the nonsolvers. All three repeated-measures analyses showed that success in Session 1 was significantly related to the understanding measures, smallest $F(1, 48) = 4.85$, $MSE = .17$, $p < .05$. The understanding measures for solvers and nonsolvers are shown in Table 1. Post hoc single-degree-of-freedom contrasts showed that for all three problem types, solvers were able to summarize the solutions more coherently than were the nonsolvers, smallest $F(1, 48) = 5.38$, $MSE = .04$, $p < .05$. In addition, the inducing structure and transformation solvers exhibited greater structural understanding than did their nonsolving counterparts, smallest $F(1, 48) = 9.26$, $MSE = .19$, $p < .01$, whereas the arrangement solvers were marginally better able to enumerate the problem's components (thus indicating greater correspondence) than were the nonsolvers, $F(1, 49) = 3.98$, $MSE = .03$, $p = .05$. Thus, it is clear that solvers and nonsolvers differ primarily in terms of the degree of integration (as measured by structural understanding and coherence) of their stored representations.

Finally, an ANOVA with the Session 1 understanding measures and problem type as predictors and the proportion of time required to solve a problem in Session 2 as the dependent variable was computed. This analysis was conducted to

TABLE 1. Understanding measures derived from the written and verbal protocols

Understanding measures	Status in first session	
	Solver	Nonsolver
	Arrangement problems	
	Mean (*SD*)	Mean (*SD*)
Corrected[a] correspondence rating	.96 (.07)	.87 (.26)
Corrected coherence rating	.52 (.38)	.18 (.23)
Connection to other knowledge	.34 (.47)	.29 (.45)
Structural understanding	.56 (.47)	.42 (.48)
	Transformation problems	
Corrected correspondence rating	.87 (.16)	.93 (.10)
Corrected coherence rating	.80 (.31)	.15 (.31)
Connection to other knowledge	. 74 (.59)	.67 (.49)
Structural understanding	.88 (.28)	.17(.36)
	Inducing structure problems	
Corrected correspondence rating	.59 (.22)	.53 (.25)
Corrected coherence rating	.30 (.21)	.16 (.15)
Connection to other knowledge	.71 (.52)	.75 (.48)
Structural understanding	.53 (.48)	.13 (.34)

a Corrected *means that the raw rating for each problem was divided by the maximum rating possible for that problem (i.e., it is a proportion of the total possible).*

determine whether the problem representations constructed by students as a result of their Session 1 experiences would predict speed of Session 2 solutions. The analysis indicated that all of the predictors, with the exception of the binary-coded structural understanding measure, account for variance in the Session 2 solution times: correspondence, $F(1, 55) = 3.8$, $MSE = .05$, $p = .056$; coherence, $F(1, 55) = 5.04$, $MSE = .05$, $p < .05$; connection to other knowledge, $F(1, 55) = 3.46$, $MSE = .05$, $p = .068$; problem type, $F(1, 55) = 5.56$, $MSE = .05$, $p < .01$. Pearson correlations indicate that the relationship of each of the understanding measures to Session 2 solution times is in the expected direction. Greater correspondence, $r = -.25$, $p \leq .05$, more coherence $r = -.47$, $p < .01$, and structural understanding, $r = -.33$, $p \leq .01$ are all associated with faster Session 2 solution times.

In summary, as in Experiments 1 and 2, those who succeeded in solving a problem in Session 1 showed near-perfect retention of the solution after a 1-week interval. Not only did prior solvers remember the solutions, but they produced them much more quickly in Session 2 than they did in Session 1. Again, as in Experiments 1 and 2, they were also faster than those who had been shown the correct solutions after an unsuccessful solution attempt.

The analysis of the protocols indicated that solvers and nonsolvers have distinctly different problem representations after their initial experiences with the problems. The primary difference appears to be related to the coherence of the subjects' internal representations. This finding offers an explanation of the mechanisms accounting for the near-perfect solution retention for the prior solvers. It also provides strong support for Wertheimer's (1945/1982) contention that solving a problem produces an understanding that is different from that of someone merely shown the solution.

Further analysis of the protocols indicated that the quality of students' problem representations was predictive of Session 2 solution times. Students were more efficient problem solvers in Session 2 if they had constructed representations in Session 1 that reflected the inherent structure of the problems, that were well organized, that accurately encoded the objectively defined problems, and that were connected to related knowledge already present in memory. Thus, solving in Session 1 is positively associated with the quality of the Session 1 understanding measures, and these measures, in turn, are negatively associated with Session 2 solution times. This finding provides further support for the contention that solving a problem and being shown a solution are qualitatively different experiences.

Recent work by Berardi-Coletta, Buyer, Dominowski, and Rellinger (1995) and Chi, de Leeuw, Chiu, and LaVancher (1994) has shown that eliciting self-explanations produces differences between those who provide self-explanation and those who do not that mirror the observed difference between solvers and nonsolvers. Students who produce self-explanations produce better-integrated, more accurate mental models than control students. Thus, metacognitive prompting creates mental representations similar to those created by solvers. This suggests that the metacognitive activity implicit in self-explanation may cause the restructuring to which Wertheimer attributes the near-perfect recall.

GENERAL DISCUSSION

In Experiments 1, 2, and 4, solvers showed virtually perfect performance after a 1-week retention interval and were decidedly superior to prior nonsolvers who had been given a solution. The findings are consistent with expectations based on Gestalt theory and contradict Weisberg and Alba's (1981) proposal that generating a solution and being given a solution should lead to equivalent subsequent performance. The contrast in retention rates between Experiments 1, 2, and 4 versus Experiment 3 supports Metcalfe's (1986a, 1986b) distinction between problem solving and simple memory retrieval and is compatible with the idea that at least some problem solving involves a restructuring process.

Slamecka and Fevreiski (1983) found no retention difference after successful versus unsuccessful attempts to generate target words. In contrast, we found large differences between solvers and nonsolvers in Session 2 performance. However, this distinction between solvers and nonsolvers is in complete agreement with the results of Buyer and Dominowski's (1989) study using number-word phrases. Successful generation of the phrases led to far better retention than unsuccessful generation (with feedback), which was no better than mere reading of the items. Note that the problems and their solutions used by Buyer and Dominowski were more complex, less familiar, and less well integrated than the words used by Slamecka and Fevreiski. The problem solutions of the present study are still more complex, do not exist in subjects' semantic memories before problem presentation, and gain meaning only in the context of the problem situation. The pattern of results suggests that with solutions of even modest complexity, actual production of solutions will yield better subsequent performance than being given the solutions. Put differently, a positive effect from unsuccessful generation attempts might occur only with familiar words. It is worth noting that in Experiments 1, 2, and 4, producing solutions led to much higher performance levels and a greater advantage than has typically been found in studies using word lists or similar verbal materials (as in Experiment 3). Indeed, questions have been raised about the robustness of the generation effect with word lists (Begg & Snyder, 1987; Sutherland, Krug, & Glover, 1988). Subjects in Experiments 1, 2, and 4 were not simply trying to remember words; rather, they were attempting to produce more elaborate behavior that would meet stated criteria within the constraints of a particular problem. Therefore, one might reasonably expect results different from those observed with simple word recall (as in Experiment 3).

Perfetto, Bransford, and Franks (1983) found that access to potentially useful information could be inhibited by prior learning of interfering material. Applying the interference notion in the present context, it is possible that prior nonsolvers performed poorly when given problems a second time because of interference from incorrect solutions they had produced during Session 1. The data do not support this idea, however. Examination of double failures for Experiments 1 and 2 showed 9% repetitions of the same error, 49% different errors, and 43% cases to which the notion did not apply (e.g., no solution was offered on the initial failure). The improbability that interference was a major factor in prior nonsolvers' performance is further demonstrated by an examination of their performance on the horse trade and train problems. For both problems, nonsolution virtually always involved offering an incorrect solution. Across the two experiments, only 37% of prior nonsolvers solved the train problem in Session 2, but 91% of prior nonsolvers solved the horse trade problem when it was repeated. This massive difference in performance cannot be explained in terms of interference, which was presumably maximal for both problems. Overall, the data imply that interference from earlier incorrect solutions was not an important influence on prior nonsolvers' Session 2 performance.

Metcalfe and Wiebe (1987) used patterns of "warmth ratings" to separate insight from noninsight problems. For insight problems, subjects' feelings of nearness to solution ("warmth") showed abrupt transitions from low values to the maximum value at the point of solution. In contrast, warmth ratings exhibited a gradual increase over the course of work on noninsight or incremental problems. It was also found that subjects were less able to predict their performance on insight problems than on incremental problems. Both the difficulty of predicting success and the sharp changes in warmth are consistent with the idea that a process of restructuring takes place in solving insight problems. Three problems used in Experiments 1 and 2 were also used by Metcalfe and Wiebe (1987). The horse trade and farmer problems were classed as insight problems, whereas the water jars problem was categorized as an incremental problem. One aspect of the present findings showed marked differences among these problems. Re-solution times for prior solvers were the shortest for the horse trade and farmer problems, whereas those for the water jars problem were the longest. The partitioning of these problems in terms of re-solution times replicated the categorization reported by Metcalfe and Wiebe.

Variation in re-solution times might reflect the kinds of differences in processing proposed by Metcalfe and Wiebe (1987). Rereading the problem statement and literally executing the solution would require small and roughly constant amounts of time across problems. If so, then re-solution times would depend on the form of solution knowledge possessed by prior solvers. Greeno (1977, 1978) suggested that problems differ in the likelihood and form of understanding that might be acquired when solving them, and Sweller and Levine (1982) demonstrated that successful problem solvers can differ in the amount of knowledge about problem structure they acquire. The data from our experiments suggest that if the components of a solution can be organized coherently, as when a key idea or insight is involved, then re-solutions might be expected to occur rather quickly when the problem is presented again (as in Experiments 1, 2, and 4). On the other hand, if a problem lacks overall structure, if its solution consists of a number of weakly integrated steps, then solvers' knowledge would be less organized and quick re-solutions seem less likely (as in Experiment 3).

In summary, our data indicate that there are meaningful relationships between problem-solving processes and subsequent retention phenomena. The findings for nonsolvers (Experiments 1, 2, and 4) support the argument that providing solutions is not likely to yield understanding. Whereas solvers generate solutions from the features of the problem situation, relationships between solutions and problem features may not be grasped when solutions are provided. Furthermore, the data from Experiment 3 support the idea that meaningful problem–solution relationships are very important for good solution retention. This interpretation of our findings provides a link between research on the generation effect and research into the consequences of self-explanation by providing a single explanation for all of the sets of findings.

Research on the generation effect has shown that the effect depends on the degree of self-generation (Buyer & Dominowski, 1989; Fiedler, Lachnit, Fay, & Krug, 1992). Research into self-explanations has shown that greater amounts of self-explanation produce better understanding of textual material (Chi et al., 1994), that self-explanation produces more efficient problem learning and better ability to transfer solution knowledge (Berardi-Coletta et al., 1995; Buyer, Walsh, & Russell, 1997), and that it produces positive changes in problem conceptualization (de Grave, Boshuizen, & Schmidt, 1996). We believe that the positive effects associated with self-generation and self-explanation result from the construction of complete, well-integrated, meaningful mental representations of the to-be-understood material. Whether externally provided solution feedback can be augmented to be equally effective is a matter for further research.

APPENDIX A. PROTOCOL ANALYSES

MEASURE OF CORRESPONDENCE

Correspondence between the subjects' representations and the problems was coded by counting the number of basic problem facts included in their retrospective descriptions of each problem. Subjects were assigned 1 point for each basic fact mentioned in their problem descriptions. Then the points were totaled to obtain a correspondence score.

Pearson product–moment correlation coefficients were computed for each problem type to assess the interrater reliability of the correspondence ratings. For the arrangement problems, $r = +.838$; for the transformation problems, $r = +.712$; and for the inducing structure problems, $r = +.752$. The variable representing correspondence was constructed by computing the average of the two sets of ratings.

MEASURE OF COHERENCE

Coherence was coded by counting the number of required solution steps mentioned by the subjects when retrospectively describing their solutions. Subjects were assigned 1 point for each step mentioned. They were also assigned 1 point for each time a solution step was mentioned immediately before or after the "next" solution step. Thus, a subject who mentioned two steps in the correct sequence received a total of 3 points for those two solution steps.

Pearson product–moment correlation coefficients between raters were computed for arrangement problems, $r = +.858$; for the transformation problems, $r = +.810$; and for the inducing structure problems, $r = +.883$. The variable representing coherence was constructed by averaging the two sets of ratings.

MEASURE OF CONNECTION TO OTHER KNOWLEDGE

Connection to other knowledge was coded by counting the number of different problems or situations that subjects said were similar to the current problem. Subjects received 1 point for each similarity mentioned.

Pearson product–moment correlation coefficients were computed for each problem type to assess interrater reliability of the connection to other knowledge ratings. For the arrangement problems, $r = +.866$; for the transformation problems, $r = +.811$; and for the inducing structure problems, $r = +.860$. The variable representing connection to other knowledge was also constructed by averaging the independent ratings together.

MEASURE OF STRUCTURAL UNDERSTANDING

The written protocols provided by subjects as they worked on the problems (their worksheets) were binary coded as reflecting the presence or absence of structural understanding. Good structural understanding was defined as evidence that the subjects grasped the principle underlying the solution to a problem; the structure of the relationship between the problem and its solution had to be evident from the worksheet.

Interrater reliability was assessed by computing the percentage agreement between the raters. For the arrangement problems, the raters had 84.3% agreement (43/51); for the transformation problems, the raters had 92.2% agreement (47/51); and for the inducing structure problems, the raters had 84% agreement (42/50). The variable representing structural understanding was constructed by averaging the ratings assigned by each of the coders.

NOTES

This research was supported in part by a grant from the University of Illinois Research Board. Appreciation is expressed to Anders Ericsson and an anonymous reviewer for their comments on an earlier version of this article. Correspondence concerning this article should be addressed to Roger L. Dominowski, Psychology Department (m/c 285), University of Illinois at Chicago, 1007 W. Harrison St., Chicago, IL 60607 (e-mail: rdomin@uic.edu). Received for publication February 17, 1998; revision received December 8, 1998.

1. For the overall comparison of prior solvers and nonsolvers, the mean solution time for the appropriate problem was subtracted from each individual solution time, producing adjusted times that were independent of problem differences. The statistical test was performed on the adjusted times, with degrees of freedom conservatively based on the number of subjects rather than the number of entries (Myers, 1966).

REFERENCES

Begg, I., & Snyder, A. (1987). The generation effect: Evidence for generalized inhibition. *Journal of Experimental Psychology: Learning, Memory, and Cognition, 13,* 553–563.

Berardi-Coletta, B., Buyer, L. S., Dominowski, R. L., & Rellinger, E. R. (1995). Metacognition and problem transfer: A process-oriented approach. *Journal of Experimental Psychology: Learning, Memory, and Cognition, 21,* 205–223.

Bourne, L. E., Dominowski, R. L., & Loftus, E. F. (1979). Problem solving. In *Cognitive processes* (pp. 231–268). Englewood Cliffs, NJ: Prentice Hall.

Buyer, L. S., & Dominowski, R. L. (1989). Retention of solutions: It's better to give than to receive. *American Journal of Psychology, 102,* 353–363.

Buyer, L. S., Walsh, S., & Russell, T. A. (1997, May). *Metacognitive training produces transfer across problem types.* Poster session presented at the 1997 American Psychological Society Convention, Washington, DC.

Chi, M. T. H., de Leeuw, N., Chiu, M.-H., & LaVancher, C. (1994). Eliciting self-explanations improves understanding. *Cognitive Science, 18*, 439–477.

Davis, J. H. (1964). The solution of simple and compound word problems. *Behavioral Science, 9*, 359–370.

de Grave, W. S., Boshuizen, H. P. A., & Schmidt, H. G. (1996). Problem based learning: Cognitive and metacognitive problems during problem analysis. *Instructional Science, 24*, 321–341.

Dominowski, R. L. (1981). Comment on "An examination of the alleged role of 'fixation' in the solution of several 'insight' problems" by Weisberg and Alba. *Journal of Experimental Psychology: General, 110*, 193–198.

Ericsson, K. A., & Simon, H. A. (1993). *Protocol analysis: Verbal reports as data* (rev. ed.). Cambridge, MA: MIT Press.

Fiedler, K., Lachnit, H., Fay, D., & Krug, C. (1992). Mobilization of cognitive resources and the generation effect. *Quarterly Journal of Experimental Psychology, 45A*, 149–171.

Gardner, J. M., & Hampton, J. A. (1985). Semantic memory and the generation effect: Some tests of the lexical activation hypothesis. *Journal of Experimental Psychology: Learning, Memory, and Cognition, 11*, 732–741.

Greeno, J. G. (1977). Process of understanding in problem solving. In N. J. Castellan, D. B. Pisoni, & G. R. Potts (Eds.), *Cognitive theory.* Mahwah, NJ: Erlbaum.

Greeno, J. G. (1978). Natures of problem-solving abilities. In W. K. Estes (Ed.), *Handbook of learning and cognitive processes.* Mahwah, NJ: Erlbaum.

Greeno, J. G., & Simon, H. A. (1988). Problem solving and reasoning. In R. C. Atkinson, R. J. Hernstein, G. Lindzey, & R. D. Luce (Eds.), *Stevens' handbook of experimental psychology.* New York: Wiley.

Jacoby, L. L. (1978). On interpreting the effects of repetition: Solving a problem versus remembering a solution. *Journal of Verbal Learning and Verbal Behavior, 17*, 649–667.

Katona, G. (1940). *Organizing and memorizing.* New York: Columbia University Press.

Kohler, W. (1976). *The mentality of apes.* New York: Liveright. (Original work published 1925)

Luchins, A. S. (1942). Mechanization in problem solving: The effect of *einstellung Psychological Monographs, 248.*

Maier, N. R. F. (1940). The behavior mechanisms concerned with problem solving. *Psychological Review, 47*, 43–53.

Maier, N. R. F., & Casselman, G. C. (1970). Locating the difficulty in insight problems: Individual and sex differences. *Psychological Reports, 26*, 103–117.

Metcalfe, J. (1986a). Feeling of knowing in memory and problem solving. *Journal of Experimental Psychology: Learning, Memory, and Cognition, 12*, 288–294.

Metcalfe, J. (1986b). Premonitions of insight predict impending error. *Journal of Experimental Psychology: Learning, Memory, and Cognition, 12*, 623–634.

Metcalfe, J., & Wiebe, D. (1987). Intuition in insight and noninsight problem solving. *Memory & Cognition, 15*, 238–246.

Myers, J. L. (1966). *Fundamentals of experimental design.* Boston: Allyn & Bacon.

Ohlsson, S. (1984). Restructuring revisited: I. Summary and critique of the Gestalt theory of problem solving. *Scandinavian Journal of Psychology, 25*, 6578.

Osgood, C. E. (1953). *Method and theory in experimental psychology.* New York: Oxford University Press.

Paivio, A., Smythe, P. E., & Yuille, J. C. (1968). Imagery versus meaningfulness of nouns in paired-associate learning. *Canadian Journal of Psychology, 22,* 427–441.

Perfetto, G. A., Bransford, J. D., & Franks, J. J. (1983). Constraints on access in a problem solving context. *Memory & Cognition, 11,* 24–31.

Restle, F., & Davis, J. H. (1962). Success and speed of problem solving by individuals and groups. *Psychological Review, 69,* 520–536.

Scheerer, M. (1963). Problem-solving. *Scientific American, 208,* 118–128.

Slamecka, N. J., & Fevreiski, J. (1983). The generation effect when generation fails. *Journal of Verbal Learning and Verbal Behavior, 22,* 153–163.

Sutherland, J. A., Krug, D., & Glover, J. A. (1988). The selective displaced rehearsal hypothesis and failure to obtain the generation effect. *Bulletin of the Psychonomic Society, 26,* 413–415.

Sweller, J., & Levine, M. (1982). Effects of goal specificity on means–end analysis and learning. *Journal of Experimental Psychology: Learning, Memory, and Cognition, 8,* 463–474.

Thorndike, E. L. (1911). *Animal intelligence.* New York: Macmillan.

Weisberg, R. W., & Alba, J. W. (1981). An examination of the alleged role of "fixation" in the solution of several "insight" problems. *Journal of Experimental Psychology: General, 110,* 169–192.

Wertheimer, M. (1982). *Productive thinking.* Chicago: University of Chicago Press. (Original work published 1945)

Woodworth, R. S., & Schlosberg, H. (1954). *Experimental psychology* (rev. ed.). New York: Holt.

THE PSYCHOLOGY OF CHESS
AND OF LEARNING TO PLAY IT

ALFRED A. CLEVELAND

In this study an attempt is made to sketch the psychology of the game of chess, to trace the stages in the development of a chess player, and to interpret this progress in psychological terms. That the task, owing to the complexity of the processes involved and the impossibility of applying anything like satisfactory objective tests, is a difficult one, is obvious, but it is one that seems to the writer worth attempting.[1]

I. THE PSYCHOLOGY OF THE GAME

Chess is, as every one knows, a mimic battle fought upon a field of sixty-four squares with pieces moved according to an elaborate system and having powers suggestive of a variety of fighting units. The purpose of each player is to checkmate his opponent, that is, to hem in and threaten the latter's king in such a fashion that he is subject to capture at the next move. In our discussion of the psychology of the game it will be convenient to consider it first as a form of human play and then to take up more particularly the mental powers involved.

1. CHESS AS A FORM OF HUMAN PLAY

Forms and Varieties of the Game
The game of chess has not been confined to any particular age, race, country, or class. It is without doubt one of the oldest, if not the oldest, of the intellectual pastimes, and it is the game of skill *par excellence.* Its origin is not definitely known and there have been many claimants for the honor of its invention.[2]

Especially in its later history the game has developed a number of off-shoots in specialties which for many people share the interest of play across the board. The chief of these is the composition and solving of chess problems, which now has quite a literature and many devotees. Another is correspondence play, in which the strict rules of the typical game are somewhat relaxed on account of the peculiar

American Journal of Psychology
July 1907, Vol. 18, No. 3 pp. 269–308

conditions of play. Others, practiced as feats, but of especial psychological interest, are blindfold playing, to which Binet has devoted a special research,[3] and the playing of many games at once (either blindfolded or with sight of the board). To some of these special forms we shall return later.

Instinctive Factors in Chess Playing

Chess is, as we have said, a game of wide distribution and popularity. Dr. Emanuel Lasker states that over one million English speaking people know the game, that there are in the United States, England and Canada between seven and eight hundred good sized chess clubs, many of which have over one hundred members each, and that the City of London Club has over four hundred members;[4] and judging from the number of chess clubs, chess periodicals and players of high rank in Germany, France, Russia, Austria, and Poland chess is no less popular in those countries. If one were asked what class or classes of people play chess one might truthfully reply that all classes play it.

The question then arises: Why has chess proved so widely popular at all times and in all places? How has it been possible for a game making severe intellectual demands to hold a place historically and in geographical distribution beside such universal forms of human play as gambling, horse-racing, athletics, and hunting, and to claim devotees, if less numerous, at any rate as loyal as any of these? The answer is, of course, that, in common with a multitude of other games and sports, it appeals to the fundamental instinct of combat, in a way that is direct and at the same time exempt from the anti-social features that are inherent in actual physical combat. Here lies a large share of its attractiveness, and its capacity for stiring emotion. It takes hold upon those suppressed survivals of savage impulse (if we are to credit the savage alone with a first hand liking for a contest) which in their modified exercise have been shown to be so large a factor in adult sport.[5]

In this, however, it shows but the typical qualities of the genus to which it belongs—that it is one of the strongly competitive games.[6] Its own specific attractiveness lies in the fact that it is a competitive game of *skill,* more particularly of intellectual skill as opposed to merely manual or bodily dexterity; it is a contest of scheme against scheme; it is a game of generalship.[7] Each particular situation appeals to the player, not only as an occasion for attack or defense, but also as a situation to be met by taking thought, a difficulty to be seen through and overcome, a problem to be solved. There is, therefore, in chess playing all the challenge that lies in baffling but fascinating problems and much of that which lies in the solution of puzzles. That the interest in this aspect of chess is real and important is abundantly evidenced by the growth of the chess "problem," of which we shall have more to say presently. Lindley in his "Study of Puzzles"[8] holds it likely that in the puzzle solving passion we have a form of the preparatory play impulse to which Groos rightly attributes so much of both animal and human play.[9]

Still another factor of interest in chess is the pleasure of invention and origination, the pleasure of being a cause.[10] In the returns of my correspondents a decided preference is expressed for original plans of attack and defense.[11] Most say that they get away from the standard book plays as soon as possible after the first few moves. Some say that they play from book not from choice, but from necessity; but most say that while they follow the book openings for a few moves, they prefer to get away from them as soon as they possibly can without detriment to their game. They prefer their own game because it is more real, and is a better representative of their own ideas. As one player puts it, " There is little satisfaction in catching your opponent on a line of play that you have simply memorized." There are, also, of course, various practical reasons for this preference. An original plan throws both players on their merits and removes the game at once, so far as possible, from a mere memory exercise, thus depriving a player of the advantage which a superior memory or a better knowledge of book games might give. There is an advantage to the player himself in an original plan in that his game is more likely to be a unit and consequently more consistently played than one partly remembered and partly originated. While the inability to remember particular lines of play is undoubtedly a determining factor in the choice between an original plan and what is known as book play, nevertheless, there is something attractive about a game which one feels to be his own, especially if it is successful.

In summary we may say of chess as a form of human play that in the first place it is a contest, and, as such, it appeals to the fundamental fighting instinct, the instinct which in every normal individual impels him to measure his skill with that of others. In the second place chess offers its devotees opportunity to exercise their ingenuity in the solution of problems and puzzles, a form of pleasure that may well rest upon that general interest in the unknown which at one time must have had the greatest survival value. It would seem further, that intellectual activity is indulged in for the pleasure which such activity gives in itself, and sport of this kind is, perhaps, an expression of the general play instinct. "Intelligence," as Lindley holds, "is no exception to the law of exercise. Just as those animals, which by fortunate variation were born with a tendency to indulge in preliminary exercise of those activities which were to serve the serious ends of adult life, were favored by natural selection, and were able to transmit such advantages in the form of general play instincts, so in a more special way those creatures, endowed with the strongest tendencies to exploit the intelligence, may have perpetuated this superiority as a general intellectual play instinct."[12] Again, the chess strategy of an individual is largely the product of his own brain; it is his own, and merely as such is interesting to him. No matter where or how he got his knowledge of the game, if he is anything of a player, he has assimilated it and made it a part of his mental self, and his game, in turn, reflects something of his personality. There is also what might be termed a secondary, derived or æsthetic interest in chess, namely, in the finer and subtler points of the game, in what the chess world calls its "brilliancies." Appreciation of and consequent admiration for the skill of others is a contributory element in this pleasure. And finally it is, notwithstanding its own exacting demands, a means of mental relaxation and as such is attractive to the mental worker.

2. GENERAL FEATURES OF CHESS FROM A PSYCHOLOGICAL POINT OF VIEW

The Emotional Effects of Play

We have already alluded incidentally to the emotions which may be stirred by the chess combat. The desire to win is fundamentally connected with the fighting instinct.[13] Young and ardent players especially find the elation of victory and the bitterness of defeat by no means small; they work hard at the game and feel the outcome in proportion to their efforts. The chess manuals and magazines repeat suggestions as to how one should wear his laurels or accept defeat, but in spite of this well intended advice every chess club has its members who invariably make excuses for every lost game. A good many players, however, have the sportsman's feeling strongly developed and are not unpleasantly affected if they are conscious of having played well. They do not enjoy winning if their victory is the result of a "fluke" on their own part or of a palpable oversight on the part of their opponent.

Personal and Temperamental Differences of Players

The opinion is general among chess players that a man's temperament enters into his play and determines its style. Many of my correspondents state that they have recognized and often utilized this factor in actual play by forcing an opponent to adopt a line of play for which he was unfitted by temperament. For example, a slow, careful game is played against the aggressive and daring player, who is often provoked by these Fabian tactics into recklessness and loss.

Chess players are also very firm in the belief that one's game is an index of his character in a wider sense, and no one will be likely to deny that the fundamental traits of character are revealed in unimportant matters especially when one becomes so deeply absorbed that he forgets all else. Chess offers just such an opportunity for deep absorption, and it is not unreasonable to suppose that one's real rather than his conventional character will reveal itself.

3. ATTAINMENTS OF PLAYERS OF AVERAGE EXPERIENCE

In order to form some conception of the skill and knowledge which a chess player of average experience possesses, let us consider (a) his ability to plan moves ahead and to anticipate those of his opponent; (b) to disentangle a complicated situation; (c) to reconstruct the status of an unfinished game from memory; and lastly, (d) his "position sense." For information on these points I shall, of course, have to depend almost wholly on the replies of my correspondents.

Ability to Plan Moves Ahead

It is evident from the variety of answers to the questions on these points and the qualifications attached to many of them that the questions were interpreted in a variety of ways. Some points seem clear, however. The number varies from position to position, is dependent upon the number and positions of the pieces and the player's physical and mental condition at the time. Very few stated any definite number of moves which they thought they usually planned ahead, but allowed a considerable margin. The following are typical of the answers received:—"five to ten," "two to six," "two to ten," "six to ten," "three to seven." Very few state that they are unable to plan at least three moves ahead in a complicated situation. Four, five, and six are favorite numbers.

Most state that they can anticipate as many of their opponent's moves as they plan for themselves, and that they do so habitually. A few state, on the other hand, that they can anticipate only a much smaller number of their opponent's moves.

Almost without exception my correspondents write that practice has greatly increased both numbers, but especially the number of the opponent's moves that can be foreseen. A few who have played a great many years or who seldom play now, say that the number has decreased. While with most players the increase in number has been considerable, the increase in accuracy has been the main gain. The beginner, owing to the great number of possibilities, is not able to plan far ahead and scarcely thinks of his opponent's plans at all. A little later he plans two, three, and four moves, but he overlooks so many possibilities that his plans are practically worthless. Progress in this regard consists first in the increasing ability to perceive the most likely and feasible continuations both on his own part and that of his opponent; second, in refusing to reconsider lines of play after going over them carefully once and discarding them; and third in increased ease, rapidity and accuracy in calculation.

Visual Imagination

It was asked "Can you imagine, pictorially, what difference in the position a move would make, or are you absolutely without such an image, relying wholly on successive associations of one move with another?" The answers seem to indicate that there are three classes of players in this regard. There are, first, those who have a clear visual picture of the situation as it will appear after a series of moves; secondly, those who have some visual picture, but rely also on successive associations, in verbal or possibly motor terms, of one move with another, that is, they are unable to picture a resulting situation, but must build it up move by move by means of visual and other kinds of imagery. With these players the final term is probably held in verbal terms. The last class of players are those who are without a visual image of any sort. The first class is perhaps the smallest. The players in this group state that the presence of the pieces is not only not an aid in planning combinations, but that it is a positive hindrance. They have difficulty in imagining a piece in a changed situation or on a square which is at that time occupied by another piece when the pieces are on the board before them.[14] Billet quotes Selkirk approvingly as saying that in working out a plan one is obliged to represent to himself the position of the pieces after each supposed move and that the sight of the board only confuses. Dr. Tarrasch, the German master, holds that all games are played in part without sight of the board and that consequently visual imagery is an essential factor in planning moves ahead, especially in far reaching combinations.[15] This statement, it seems to the writer, is valid only for players of the first class mentioned above. The players of the second group have some picture but find the presence of the pieces indispensable; while those of the third group rely wholly on the presence of the pieces. In some cases this dependence on the pieces is largely a matter of habit, since the players state that while they rely almost exclusively on successive associations, nevertheless, they can often discover errors in their games when the board is not before them.

Ability to take in Large Sections of the Board

Most of the players state that when getting ready to move they can readily take in the whole disposition of their men, or, in other words, they can comprehend the board as a whole. This ability to take in readily the whole disposition of the men is generally regarded as one of the signs of a considerable degree of chess skill. Ability in this regard varies with the physical and mental condition of the player and with the complexity of the situation. The explanation of the gain in skill of this sort seems to be that, as a player progresses in skill, the game takes on more and more meaning and that the individual moves become more and more a part of a definite series or of a number of series each with some particular end in view. The different moves and situations, also, as they are handled in larger masses, are dealt with in an increasingly symbolic manner. A more detailed consideration of this will be taken up in another section.

Reconstruction of the Status of an Unfinished Game

Little or no trouble is experienced by most players in setting up an unfinished game from memory, provided the game itself was interesting and too great a time had not elapsed. The number of pieces on the board is also a factor, though it would appear that it is not of very great importance. A very few state that they can do this only when they are playing regularly. One player reports that he retains a position in correspondence play for a month without difficulty, and another that he is engaged at present in eleven correspondence games and that he retains the positions in all of them without reference to his record.

Different methods are employed in the reconstruction, but all are reducible to two types, namely, setting up the final position, and replaying the game from the start. Some are able to do either. There are different varieties of the first method. Some seem to have a mental picture of the whole board and to arrange their pieces accordingly. They have photographed the situation as a whole and the eye tells them if anything is out of order or missing. Analogous to this in a small way is the ability to see a misspelled word in proof-reading. Others also reconstruct the final position as a whole, but do it by remembering crucial situations and building around them. This memory may be in terms of almost any sort of imagery, but it is most likely to be in visual terms. Verbal imagery also plays an important part. The plan of attack or a certain situation in that attack, is very often the central point from which the position is built up. This would mean that the steps which had been planned ahead were also factors in the recall. Sometimes it is necessary to begin back of the final position at some important place and to build up to it. The second method, that of replaying the game from the beginning, means the running over of a series of successive associations aided and guided by the critical points and by the general plan of the whole game which gives a meaning to the individual moves. The reconstruction from memory of a position involving any considerable number of pieces is not possible to most beginners. If they are of the photographic mental type they get lost in the mass of impressions which the situation involves, and if of the verbal or some other type the situation has not sufficient meaning to give definite place and order to so many pieces.

"Position Sense"

Among chess players and writers on chess great stress is laid on what is called "position sense," that is, the knack of knowing in an intricate situation how to place the men to the best advantage. It is a common observation that many chess players are able to tell at a glance which player has the better position without being able to give offhand any reason for the opinion. It is even stated that many players are able to give a correct judgment at times without being able to carry out the analysis necessary to prove its correctness. Bird, the well known English player, used often, in consultation play, to point out the move with the remark that the others might analyze as much as they liked, but that he felt and knew that it was the right move, and it is said that he was generally right. With scarcely an exception all who answered the question stated that they have noted a considerable improvement in "position sense." Many state that improvement in the sense of position and chess improvement are one and the same thing. This latter statement is a little too sweeping, however, since it does not necessarily follow that the mere knowledge of the strength or weakness of a position will enable one to choose the best of the infinite possibilities which arise at every step. Experience is the blanket term which most use in the attempt to explain the development of "position sense." The player is said to "feel" the position or the proper move. Some interesting reasons are given, however, to account for the ability to judge a position at a glance. In brief they are somewhat as follows: The mind has been drilled to feel any deviation from principles ; it is due to a vague idea of similar situations leading to success or failure; it is the recognition of several fundamental points of strength or weakness ; and lastly, it is a symbolic shortening, a dropping out of intermediate processes of inference. Perhaps we should not be wrong in saying that it is all of these. It is undoubtedly the product of experience and involves the same sorts of psychic processes that are employed in the formation of general ideas—abstraction and generalization. Players of equal experience differ so widely in "position sense" that it seems reasonable to suppose that there is a difference in their native endowment in this capacity, just as, according to Professor James, people are differently endowed with the capacity for memorizing. "Position sense" is, however, not dependent on memory alone.

Different Grades of Chess Players

Certain mental qualities are essential to the chess player who attains any degree of proficiency whatever, and players differ both in their relative and their absolute endowment of these qualities. Master players combine to a marked degree an accurate and persistent chess memory, quickness of perception, strong constructive imagination, power of accurate analysis and a far seeing power of combination. It is impossible to say just what the proper proportion of these qualities should be, and to be ideal it would have to be modified to meet each new opponent. When these various qualities are combined in something like the proper proportion we have what is generally designated as a separate quality, namely, "judgment." But when we say that a player has good judgment in chess do we mean more than that he combines in something like the proper proportions the qualities which make up the uniformly consistent and successful chess player?

4. ATTAINMENTS OF THE CHESS MASTERS

We have attempted to give some idea of the endowment of the chess player of fair ability and have avoided all reference to the remarkable achievements of the chess masters. The feats of some of these are certainly marvellous, and one is apt to think that genius alone can account for them. The chess expert displays his skill under one or all of four forms, namely, Simultaneous Play, in which several games are played at the same time against as many opponents; Blindfold Play; Recapitulation of Games played by himself or others; and, in actual play, by the Announcement of the End of the Game several moves before that event.

Simultaneous Play
In simultaneous play the lone player, of course, never plays against those of his own rank, but usually against strong local players who are able to take advantage of any oversight. As examples of what can be done, the following, recorded in the different chess magazines, may be cited:—Gunsberg played eighteen games simultaneously against as many opponents, winning fourteen, losing three and drawing one; Bird played nineteen, winning fifteen, losing one and drawing one; Herr Schallop in four and one-half hours played forty simultaneous games, winning thirty-three, losing five, and drawing two; Lasker played twenty-two games, winning nineteen, losing two and drawing one. Since that time he has often played thirty games simultaneously. As an example of the rapidity of moves made in simultaneous play Napier's twenty-one games should be cited. During the first hour he made four hundred and fifty moves, an average of nearly eight per minute. Of the twenty-one games he won eighteen, lost two and drew one. Evidently simultaneous play requires the ability to focus the attention strongly on a single game, to banish for the time being every other game from the mind, to call up instantly at the sight of any board just what combinations it had been planned to carry out there, and finally to recognize and meet a situation promptly. In all such feats experience is an indispensable factor. The player who plays several games at the same time relies on his knowledge of position, gained through long practice, to give him a quick grasp of the essential situations as he passes from board to board.[16] This factor and the power of concentration seem to account for the distinctive features of simultaneous play.

Recapitulation of Games and Other Feats of Pure Memory
The recapitulation of games is a feat of memory pure and simple. The player simply plays over, or dictates from memory games which he himself or which others have played. The games thus enumerated may consist of fifty or even more moves

on each side making sometimes a total of one hundred or more individual moves. Morphy, the next morning after his blindfold contest against eight other players at Paris, dictated to his secretary all of the moves in each of the eight games. Morphy's secretary, in his book entitled "Exploits and Triumphs in Europe of Paul Morphy," gives the following account of the performance:—"Next morning Morphy actually awakened me at seven o'clock and told me if I would get up he would dictate to me the moves of yesterday's games. I never saw him in better spirits nor less fatigued than on that occasion, as he showed me for two long hours the hundreds of variations depending upon the play of the previous day, with such rapidity that I found it hard work to follow the thread of his combinations."[17] In speaking of Morphy's knowledge of games played by Anderson, he writes: "With his astonishing memory he gave me battle after battle with different adversaries, variations and all."[18] And in another place, "What wonderment he has caused with his omnipotent memory. I have seen him sit for hours at the Divan or the Regents, playing over, not merely his own battles, but the contests of others, till the spectators could not believe their senses."[19] Morphy himself made the statement that he had never forgotten a game that he had played after his chess powers were mature. Blackburne likewise has a tenacious memory for his past games. In 1899 he recalled any number of games which he had played in 1862, pointing out with the utmost precision the flaw or the beauty in each.[20]

In regard to the recapitulation of games it should be noted that the player is recalling a number of known situations each the result of a well known series of moves, and that each game as a whole is constituted of, and characterized by, a number of situations joined together by distinctive features which may consist either of individual moves or of combinations of them. The case is similar to that of a remembered conversation; the one who recalls it does not recall each word separately but rather the *meaning* of each remark and its connection with what preceded or followed.

Other Feats of Memory

Blackburne, without sight of the board, is able to *give* the moves known as the knight's tour, which consists in placing the knight on any designated square and making it strike in succession every square on the board. This is by no means an easy task with the board in sight, a fact of which any one may easily convince himself. Aside from chess Pillsbury performed some rather difficult memory feats. If any portion of a deck of playing cards was called off to him, he was able to name the cards remaining in the deck. On one occasion, after playing blindfold games for two and one half hours, during the intermission, a list of thirty words, numbered from one to thirty, was read to him. He memorized the words in groups of five taking ten minutes in which to complete the task. Then he was able to give the word corresponding to any given number or the number corresponding to any given word and to repeat the whole list either forward or backward.[21] He made use, of course, of some mnemonic device and the case is interesting only as showing what can be accomplished in that way.

Announcement of Mate in Advance

The announcement of mate several moves ahead means, in case it is not merely a remembered position, that the player has looked ahead of the actual play and is able to say the precise number of moves necessary to bring about the end of the game. It is a common thing for players of the first rank to announce mate five or six moves in advance and their combinations in the middle game often reach beyond that number. Blackburne, in one of his blindfold performances, after the twentieth move, announced mate in six moves more and then called off seven variations which exhausted the position.[22]

Marshall, in London, announced mate in eight moves and proceeded to accomplish it in spite of all his opponent could do to prevent it. The longest mate ever announced in blindfold play was one by Blackburne in sixteen moves.[23]

In some cases planning ahead, as was suggested above, is a simple act of memory. The player may merely recognize the situation as one previously seen and may remember the individual moves which followed and the result; or he may pass directly from the first term, the situation, to the last term, the result, recalling at the same time the number of moves, but not the moves themselves. Where the player has never reached mate from the given situation, but is able to foresee it, he must possess the ability to work through mentally all the situations which come between the one given and the final one, which calls for good powers of analysis and memory as well as experience.

Blindfold Play

The feats which have caused most wonder and admiration are those of blindfold players. Playing without sight of the board is now one of the most common forms of exhibition chess, and it has been said that almost every good amateur can play at least one game *sans voir*.

Paul Morphy, during his triumphal tour of Europe, created great astonishment by playing eight simultaneous games blindfolded. It is said by competent judges that some of his most brilliant games were those played in this way. Zukertort played twelve and fourteen games very frequently, but often remarked that the two additional ones made it much more difficult. Blackburne is one of the strongest of the blindfold players, but the greatest of all thus far in this line was the American, Pillsbury, who played as many as twenty-two blindfold games simultaneously, winning most of them. With him the number of games seemed to be limited only by the length of time required to complete them and by his physical endurance.[24]

Pillsbury, in an exhibition given at Toledo, Ohio, played twelve games of chess and four of checkers without sight of the boards, and at the same time played duplicate whist.

Such are the feats of blindfold play by the masters. What shall we say in explanation of them? Memory certainly plays a very important rôle, but it may be chiefly of the short time variety, that is, the player holds the moves in mind only during the progress of the play and forgets them immediately afterward, much as the student or the lawyer does the facts he has crammed for a particular occasion. Pillsbury, in an article, said that he had to think rather hard to recall the opening in any given game of a series five minutes after the contest ended.[25] Morphy, on the other hand, seemed to retain his games permanently.

A blindfold player, playing a single game, must have in mind at every stage of the game the position of every piece on the board, and he must have some way of knowing or of calculating the relation of each piece to every other, facts which are not necessarily involved in mere place memory. His knowledge of these positions and relations must be sufficiently clear to enable him to form combinations for attack and defense. In playing eight, ten, twelve, sixteen or twenty games simultaneously without sight of the boards, the task is, of course, immensely more difficult, since the player has not only to remember a proportionally greater number of moves (or positions) but has also to remember each move or set of moves in relation to the particular game in which it is made.

The blindfold player, playing several games simultaneously, usually employs devices to make his task less difficult. Pillsbury grouped his games and used the same opening in all games of a group. For instance, in playing sixteen games he grouped them as follows: group one contained boards 1, 5, 9, 13; group two, boards 2, 6, 10, 14; group three, boards 3, 7, 11, 15; and group four, boards 4, 8, 12, 16. It will be noticed that two groups contain odd and two even numbers, and that there is a difference of four between any number of a group and the one next to it—1, 5, 9, etc. The blindfold player usually has first move on all boards and can generally force his opponent into his system. If not, he may regroup the boards according as they do or do not fall into his system of play, or he may simply make a mental note of the boards on which eccentric replies to his opening moves have been made. Obviously, so long as the games in each group proceed without variation from the usual moves and replies, there is little chance for confusion, but very soon the game begins to vary. By the time this happens, however, the player has noted some distinctive feature by means of which to recall any game. Pillsbury put it in this way: "By the time twenty moves have been made there has been some clearing of the board and a definite objective has been developed. When I turn to the new board I say—Ah! number nine. This is the board on which we have exchanged queens; and the whole play comes back to me."[26]

In other words, the variation itself, because it involves some distinctive feature, is the cue for the recall of all the moves that have preceded it and those which grew out of it. It will help us to understand this if we recall the fact that chess is, as Binet puts it, a contest between ideas, and that each move is but a part of a series all working together toward the same end, or in other words, each move is remembered because it is a necessary part of a plan.[27]

He points out further that those who retain in mind a situation or a series of moves have the faculty of giving to the situation or the series a precise significance. A person ignorant of chess could not, of course, do this and so would be unable to hold such things in memory. Mr. R. L. Newman also, experimenting upon checker players in the laboratory of the University of Indiana, found that a long series of moves in checkers, made in the presence of his subjects, was remembered only after some form of grouping was employed and that the series was learned quickest by those who understood the purpose of the different moves.[28] The purpose caused the individual moves to hang together, so to speak.

Binet[29] concludes with M. Goetz that the memory employed in games without sight is above all a memory of reason and calculation, or more concretely, that one does not remember that he has moved his king at such and such a time, but remembers a certain project of offence or defense in accordance with which he has moved his king. He qualifies this in part, however, by the statement that sometimes individual moves which make a deep impression on the mind and awaken astonishment are recalled individually. One retains a game of chess as he does a printed line or paragraph; the meaning and not the individual letters or words are what is retained.

Both Taine and Binet have studied the question of the visual representation of the board by the blindfold player. Taine concluded that such a player sees the board and the pieces on it as in an "interior mirror." He quotes an unnamed American to the effect that at the beginning of a game he sees clearly before his mental eye, the board and the exact appearance of each piece, and that after the announcement of each move he sees the pieces in the new arrangement, in exactly the same way.[30] The method of Dr. Tarrasch is thus described by Binet:[31] At the start he represents the board in its original condition. When he makes the first move he sees the board thus modified and keeps the new impression in his mind's eye, and so on through the game, his mental picture changing with each move. Binet's correspondents, with one exception, answered that they used visual memory in playing without sight. He concludes from their answers that there are two forms of visual memory used in blindfold chess, which he designates as concrete visual memory and abstract visual memory. Players who make use of the former see the forms and the colors of the pieces and squares on the board exactly as they are. Abstract visual memory is described as follows : Most of the players see the board mentally. The mental image is localized before the player, but he apperceives at one time only the part of the board where the interesting features of the battle are taking place. The board does not ordinarily have a particular form. It is an abstract board composed of sixty-four squares. Very often the edges of the board are not seen. For some players certain diagonals, having particular importance for the game, are seen more clearly than others. Often the colors of the squares are not clearly seen, but become grayish, one color being a little brighter than the other. The form seems to be the element which is the most difficult to efface from the mental image. What Binet calls the geometrical notion often takes the place of color. Binet's correspondents are unanimous in the opinion that they represent to themselves the positions of the pieces and their spatial relations and that no combination would be possible without such representation. Charcot gives the name "geometrical visual memory" to that kind of visual memory which simply conserves the positions and the movements of the pieces.[32]

In agreement with Binet we may say that this kind of memory is the work of abstraction and results from the direction which the player gives to his attention. Form and color are neglected because they are of little importance. This abstraction, as Binet points out, is comparable to that in daily life where we gradually eliminate details and give attention only to essentials.

It seems evident from Binet's study, and from the statements of many chess players, that visual imagery in varying degrees of clearness from the most perfect representation to the most shadowy, is a very important factor in playing chess without sight, and that most players make use of it; but there is, on the other hand, data to warrant us in saying that it is not an absolutely indispensable factor. In other words, it is possible that a blindfold game could be carried on by a person entirely devoid of visual imagery. M. Goetz, in his paper published in Binet's book, says that visualization is almost entirely absent in his blindfold play and that his performance depends only on "reason and calculation."[33] For example, he knows from experience that a pawn on the king's fourth attacks one on his opponent's queen's fourth, and that a knight or a bishop on a certain square controls certain other squares; and this knowledge may be retained in verbal terms. Pillsbury, the greatest of all blindfold players, also asserted that he had little or no visual imagery and that he remembers each board and the positions on it not as a picture, but as a record.

Even in my own limited experience in blindfold play, I have found that visualization is an incidental and by no means essential factor. In my own case, in the beginning, visual images were entirely lacking, a little later they were present at times as the result of a conscious effort to call them up, and now when they are present they are so only in the most indefinite form. For instance, I have no mental picture of the board aside from its general outline, and the forms and colors of the pieces are never present, except when I have paid particular attention to them for experimental purposes. In the beginning, localization of the play was very indefinite and a replaying of the games with the board furnished many surprises both in this regard and in regard to the relative positions and distances of the pieces. At the present time the movements of the pieces and the localization of the play are fairly definite. I seem to feel the movements of the pieces, especially my own, as if I were actually moving them. Particular positions involving two or three pieces are sometimes seen in so far as the relative positions of the pieces are concerned. Normally I am a fair visualizer, but in blindfold chess my thinking seems to be largely of other sorts, and especially in verbal terms. When not engaged in actual play I frequently call up a situation with a fair degree of clearness, but when playing, verbal imagery is the most prominent in consciousness. For example, my opponent announces knight to the king's fifth. Ordinarily I do not picture the resulting position, but calculate the radius of action of the piece thus : knight on king's fifth attacks queen's seventh, bishop's seventh, etc. If it is advanced to queen's seventh it checks king at knight's first, etc., etc. It would seem that there is a closer association between the series of verbal images than between the visual images or the series composed of both verbal and visual images. My experimenting has not gone far enough, however, to furnish very much that is definite in regard to this aspect of the question. Without visual imagery the blindfold player would have to rely on word, letter and number symbols, and would have, it would seem, a much more difficult task than the player with highly developed power of visualization. In actual play, verbal memory plays an important part even for strong visualizers, for it is often by this means that they recall the actual moves that have been made when they are in doubt as to the position of any piece. My companion in the attempts at blindfold play made considerable use of visual imagery of Binet's abstract type, but used other sorts to a certain extent. I am inclined to believe that with increasing experience both of us would have made more use of verbal and other symbols.[34]

In order to determine whether it would be possible to play chess with no visual imagery whatever, the following experiment was tried. Games were played without the use of either board or chessmen. The records were kept in the German notation, but in such a way that each player could tell the number and the location of the pieces on either side. The moves and replies were thought out as far as possible with the aid of this record and in terms of the symbols used. For instance, P a 5 attacks any pawn or piece on b 6 ; Kt c 3 attacks b 1, a 2, a 4, b 5, d 5, e 4, e 2, d 1, etc. It was thus possible to calculate the relative positions of the different pieces and to attack and to defend any given position. The experiment was not long continued and visual imagery was never wholly absent, especially where attempts were made to form combinations. Nevertheless, I am convinced that it would be possible for a person to learn to play chess by means of verbal and number symbols alone. The task would be a very long and difficult one, but by no means impossible.

The Relation of Chess Skill to General Mental Ability

If chess is perhaps a tolerable index of temperament and character, is skill in chess also a reliable index of mental power in general? The reply must be qualified. Many able men are good chess players, but on the other hand there are those who live for chess, who think, talk, and dream chess, who confirm Edgar Allen Poe's observation that the best chess player may be only the best player at chess; but this number is small compared to the vast majority who indulge in it only as a pastime. Even among chess masters are to be found many who have displayed considerable ability in other lines. Dr. Emanuel Lasker, the present world's champion at chess, has taken his doctorate in mathematics. Tschigorin is a Russian government employee, Maroczy is a professor of physics and mathematics at a Budapest college, Tarrasch is a German physician, Anderson, at one time champion of the world, was a professor of mathematics, and Staunton, another world's champion and one of the best known of the older chess writers, is well known also as a writer and as an editor of the classics. Rousseau, Voltaire, Napoleon, and John Stuart Mill are said to have been strong players, and the historian Buckle an excellent one. The list might be increased almost indefinitely, but enough has been said to indicate that skillful chess players represent all walks of life, and that skill at chess is not incompatible with success in other lines. The chess player is usually something more than a mere player of chess. At the same time the cases of *idiots savants* in various forms of mental activity, and among others in chess playing, prevent the inference that skill in chess is a universally valid index of high mental endowment.[35]

5. SPECIAL PSYCHOLOGY OF CHESS

Forms of Mental Activity Required

We have now followed sufficiently, perhaps, the general aspects of the game, and can turn with advantage to its more intimate psychology. The aim of each player is, as we have said, to checkmate his opponent, that is, to bring his own pieces into such a position that the opposing king could inevitably be taken at the next move.

Each player must therefore carry out a scheme of attack, overcoming obstacles and preventing the blocking of his own plans, and at the same time guard himself from counter attack. The game in its most important portion presents in essence a succession of situations each of which calls for special examination, with reference both to its present and its future import, and the selection or invention of an appropriate line of action. The player asks himself continually, in effect, at least, what is this present situation and what ought I to do to meet it? The game throughout may be regarded as a series of reasoned inferences, expressed by moves upon the board. The present section will be devoted to an exposition of the logical and psychological relations in question.

The Stages of the Game and Their Logical Types

The game of chess proper is divided into three fairly well defined parts called the opening, middle, and end games. There are openings without number but all have been the subject of analysis for so long that one can obtain from the numerous books on the subject information limited only by his capacity to retain it. The competent player knows at least the chief openings and enough of their theory to meet any unexpected variation from the usual moves and replies.

The end game, in which the forces on either side are greatly reduced, has also received careful study at the hands of expert analysts, so that one may learn from the books to recognize certain situations and to know their possibilities. Geometrical figures have often been employed to show the possibilities of situations.

In the middle game, however, the player may no longer rely on definite directions, but is entirely dependent on his knowledge of general principles and his past experience. The former will be of service especially to the young player, but, owing to the infinite number of possibilities which may develop out of the different situations, experience in actual play is indispensable. Here the player must exercise all his ingenuity, must give rein to his creative imagination, and must follow out as far as he is able the effects of the different moves which suggest themselves. The chess player's skill is measured in terms of his ability to do all this successfully.

Opening and End Games

In the opening game and in the end game the logical type of reasoning is usually that of the categorical syllogism. In case of a typical opening it may be formulated as follows:

In all cases of the Evan's Gambit, pawn to the queen's knight's fourth is the fourth move.

This move is to be the fourth in an Evan's Gambit.

Therefore, this move should be pawn to the queen's knight's fourth.

Similarly in the end game the situation which develops recalls the procedure to be followed. If White, for example, has a king and a rook against Black's king, he must drive the latter to the edge of the board, hold him there with his king and mate with his rook. White's procedure may again be reduced to the type of the categorical syllogism.

All cases of king and rook against king are to be met by driving the latter to the edge of the board, etc.

This is a case of king and rook against king.

Therefore, this is a case to be met by driving the king to the edge of the board, etc.

All habitual actions may be reduced to this type and Professor Charles Pierce has remarked the same about all reflex actions.

The Middle Game

In the middle game, where general rules are only partially applicable, the logical procedure is mixed and will differ somewhat according to the grade of the player. In what follows immediately we shall assume the player's condition to be that of a not very skillful amateur; of the professional's condition we shall speak later. So far as general rules apply to the middle game, the play will be of the deductive type which we have just illustrated, but in the vast majority of cases it will be more complicated. The situation is not of the known sort that invites application of general rules, but of an unknown sort in which the essential features (or true meaning) must be disentangled from a mass of obscuring details, and when disentangled must be met by a move or a line of play especially selected, or invented, for the purpose. The logical type is not now simply deductive, but really a series of logical steps resembling the sort of scientific procedure which Jevons, for example, calls the "Combined or Complex Method."[36] An hypothesis is first formed, deductive inferences drawn from it, and these tested by experiment. The player finds before him a situation created by the last move of his opponent. His study of the situation gives it a certain character in his mind equivalent to the formation of an hypothesis with regard to it. He then reasons: This is a situation of such and such a sort and therefore to be met by such a move in reply. The move in reply is then tried in imagination. If it seems successful it is accepted and actually made; if it is seen to be unsatisfactory, it is rejected and a better one sought for the same purpose, or what is more likely, the hypothesis itself (the conceived character of the situation) has been changed by the evident unfitness of the move imagined.

Skill is shown in the opening and end games by the readiness with which the player recognizes the common situation and draws from memory the appropriate response. Skill in the middle game is shown by the readiness with which he recognizes the essential features of a new situation, and, in his inner experimentation, hits upon a move that fits the case, *i.e.*, proves by its appropriateness that his diagnosis of the situation was correct.

This is the condition of the commonplace player. The case of a perfect player, one with chess omniscience, whose analysis was perfect, who could see the game to the end at any stage of it, would be quite different. Having a perfect plan of procedure for every case, he would play throughout very much as the amateur plays the opening and the end games. Excellence in play ranges upward from the condition of the amateur toward that of the perfect player. To the chess master many of the situations that arise in the middle game are already familiar and the best means of meeting them known. Others will be unknown; and then the crucial point of his opponent's attack must be discovered and an appropriate response devised. His play is for the moment of essentially the same type as that of the amateur, except that he is both by nature and experience much more prompt in discovering the essential feature of the attack and much more resourceful in finding means of repelling it.

Let us, however, return to the logical type employed by the commonplace player. The type followed in the opening and end games would correspond closely to the typical logical procedure as described by James.[37]

The type followed in the middle game differs from the formal sketch of James which has in view reasoning of the deductive type. Here the essential characteristic of the situation, even when discovered, does not suggest any well known group of similar cases to which it may be referred and for which a definite mode of procedure has already been worked out. The essential characteristic can at the most suggest only a very general kind of procedure; it gives no inkling of just what should be done. The player knows that he must sacrifice the threatened piece, or withdraw it, or intercept the attack, or make a counter attack, but which of these is best must be thought out for each situation. His usual method is to try in imagination one move after another until he finds one that seems superior to all the rest. And often it is only during this experimental process that the full signification of the situation dawns upon him.

Such reasoning is concrete and practical, not put into words, or only partially so, and allied to the reasoning of animals and children.[38]

But, as Morgan well shows, the logical reasoning of man is largely dependent on the need of communication and the use of language;[39] a chess game *played* is reasoned in particulars; the same game *explained* and *defended* to a companion would be cast in verbal and syllogistic form.

Psychological Restatement of the Logical Types

This last remark touches upon an essential point to which we must give yet a little further attention, namely, the difference between the logical types of reasoning and the actual psychological processes which they symbolize. All processes of reasoning are, as psychological facts, sequences of mental states due to shifting of the focal point of attention and to processes of association dependent thereon. In the deductive portions of the game—the opening or end game, where the play is guided wholly by rule—the process is one of serial association running off under the general influence of the conception of the opening (or end game) which remains in the background of consciousness. Each move suggests the next in fixed sequence, as one might say the alphabet, having in the background of his consciousness the desire to say it.

For the middle game let us take a concrete example. Let us say that it is Black's turn to move. He glances at the board and notices the queen and knight of his opponent in position to develop a double check upon his king. Association, under the guidance of his general knowledge of the purpose of the game, freely suggests the consequences, if he cannot in some way interfere. Attention then shifts to the response to be made and association again coming in suggests the readiest means of defense. In other words, the situation, regarded from the point of view of defense and held in the focus of attention, recalls by association a number of possible moves. These associations, following, of course, the readiest lines of habit, are not by any means at random, but operate strictly within the limits imposed by Black's knowledge of the general rules of play and his present intention. Each of the moves suggested is itself brought to the focus of attention, is tried in imagination, probably by incipient movements of eye or hand, and accepted or rejected as the case may be. If accepted, it is put into execution in the same manner as other voluntary movements.

The mental action of the player in such a situation is analogous to that of the inventor. A half finished machine stands before him; his problem is clear ; he must cause such and such movement in such and such parts in order to bring about a desired result. He runs over in his mind the varieties of pulleys, cranks, gearings, cams and the like with which he is familiar, and finally selects one or the other as the most likely to accomplish what he wishes. A high grade of skill as an inventor or as a player of chess involves the utmost readiness in seeing just what needs to be done and in discovering the means of doing it. Experience helps immensely in both of these directions ; and it brings many cases under fixed rules so that they are dealt with by simple associations and correspondingly reduces the number of cases that must be treated as singular and without rule, and greatly enriches the fund of expedients that may be tried in such singular cases. When the case is so unfamiliar that experience suggests nothing, the reasoner is reduced to simple blind fumbling, on a level with that of the brutes, and rational procedure reduces to the "method of trial and error." The situation arouses an impulse to do something; there is a blundering attack; efforts that lead to unpleasant consequences are rejected;

those with pleasant consequences are repeated. Man's more complex mechanism of apperception, his wider range of associations, and his power of imaginative action all combine to reduce the cases where blind fumbling is necessary, but when these powers are of no avail there is but one method, and that is the method of lucky hits.

II. THE PSYCHOLOGY OF THE LEARNING OF THE GAME

1. GENERAL DESCRIPTION OF THE LEARNING PROCESSES IN CHESS[40]

In the preceding sections have been set forth what I conceive to be the general outlines of the mental activities involved in chess playing. It is popularly believed that chess is a very hard game to learn, that it is difficult for every one and impossible for many. To a certain extent this is true. Chess is a difficult game, but it is so because it requires a peculiar mental equipment, rather than because it calls for one of an especially high order. First and foremost is required a liking for chess. The man who finds it uninteresting may as well give it up at once. Next it requires powers of sustained attention and an excellent memory;[41] and based on these, considerable powers of analysis, and visual imagination, or its equivalent in some other sense department.

Increase in skill means increase in the knowledge of chess situations and how to meet them; or, in more psychological terms, increasing "meaning" in certain arrangements of the pieces,[42] and increased facility of association between these meaningful arrangements and certain other arrangements (moves to be made) imaginatively constructed; or, in still other terms, more adequate apperception of the situations and richer and better organized associations connected therewith. These organized apperceptions and associations insure truer and prompter apprehension of the difficulty to be met and better and prompter selection of the means to meet it. Skill is largely, though not wholly, in proportion to knowledge, and knowledge in proportion to experience.[43]

The player's progress may be divided roughly and for purposes of description into five stages, (1) The first step is to learn the names and movements of the pieces. The former is easily done, but the latter requires a trifle of practice before the pieces can be readily used in play. This is especially true in the case of the knight.[44] For successful play the moves must, in the end, become automatic, and this automatism is not reached, as the game is usually learned, in the first stage itself. It depends for its perfecting on the practice obtained in succeeding ones. This probably is the natural method in all learning, the greater interest of the advanced stages floating the learner over the drudgery necessary for complete perfection of the automatisms of the earlier. When the moves have become automatic the men are no longer pieces of wood, jade or ivory,—static things—but *forces* capable of being exerted in definite directions.

(2) The second stage may be characterized as the stage of individual moves of offence and defense during which the beginner plays with no definite aim other than to capture his opponent's pieces. Even this he blunders about, often over-looking for several moves a chance to capture a man that has been left *en prise*. My notes contain many entries showing two bishops, both unprotected, left facing each other for several moves, or a queen moved within range of a bishop or a knight. The player is able to attack one of his opponent's pieces and is able ordinarily to defend himself against direct attacks. Whichever he attempts to do he must give his whole attention to it, and even with this extreme of concentration he is able to see only the immediate consequences of the move. In general, however, his lack of conception of the aim of the game, causes him to play at random. His play lacks unity and the pieces are moved hither and thither, unsupported and unsupporting ; he has no conception of the game as a well planned sequence. Nevertheless he has hovering in the background of consciousness some idea of the ultimate object of the play, the hemming in of the adverse king, and is influenced somewhat by it.

(3) The beginner is soon able to tell at a glance what any single piece can do, but no one piece, not even the queen, is very strong unless supported by others. Hence the task in the third stage of the beginner's progress becomes that of learning the strength, not of individual pieces, but of pieces in relation to each other. He has to learn the value of groups and the value of individual pieces as parts of particular groups. There are times when a bishop or a knight or even a pawn may be so situated that its direct influence is greater than that of a rook or a queen. Many of the most fascinating of the recorded games are those in which one player has actually given away one or more of his pieces, often his queen, in order to gain the advantage of the relative positions resulting from the movement of the pieces involved.

About the time the beginner has passed beyond the first two stages of his learn-ing and during the third, the idea of checking becomes the dominating one with him and his efforts tend to centre upon that exclusively. This, of course, leads to premature attacks which usually result disastrously to the aggressor. He is also prone to fix his attention on his own plans and most likely on the particular part he is about to execute at the moment, to the neglect of all others. He suffers from inability to take in a number of details at the same time. They have no meaning except as details, and if he concentrates on one, others must, by that very fact, be neglected. He has little idea of the importance of developing his pieces, *i. e.*, making them available for future offence and defense, and of the value of position. The attack of his opponent compels some defensive play, however, and no defense can, of course, be made without the co-operation of at least two pieces, so that he soon learns something of the use of pieces in combination. He learns, for example, that often a piece may defend another and at the same time attack one of his opponent's pieces, that in some cases where two pieces are attacked simultaneously one may be withdrawn and so placed as to protect the other, and that a counter attack is often the best defense.

He has made considerable progress in this stage when he is able to give attention to the plans of his opponent beyond those that are immediately connected with his own, though in this particular, temperament plays a large rôle. That this is the usual experience, however, is testified by the fact that after a player is able to form a definite plan of his own involving some use of combination, he is often surprised by checkmate when he is within a single move of checkmating his opponent. He is unable to carry out his own plans and at the same time to give attention to anything else; he is particularly weak in defense.

In general we may say that the beginner at this stage is not able to play in proportion to his knowledge. He recognizes his errors when they are pointed out to him, but he is unable to avoid them. My records show many familiar blunders occurring over and over again. The beginner's material of knowledge is not organized and therefore not available in any situation except the most simple.

(4) The player has entered upon the fourth stage when he begins consciously to plan the systematic development of his pieces. This necessarily involves some knowledge of the value of position, which knowledge we may call judgment of position. These judgments are generalizations and are the result of the player's own experience, or have come to him in the form of general principles from the experience of others. However they may come to the player their possession is absolutely essential to further progress. Now the player no longer has to puzzle himself by attempting to consider all the possibilities of the situation, a thing he is utterly unable to do, but he applies his principle. His principles, especially those he has formulated for himself, are usually only partially true and have to undergo constant modification as his knowledge and experience increase. He knows now a number of definite situations and his plans radiate from these and are more far reaching. He is also in a position to give more attention to the moves and, indeed, to the general plans of his opponent. This is a considerable advance, for it means that the player's mental horizon has been extended very much and that he is able to disregard the non-essentials to a greater extent than before. Given positions assume more and more importance and one of the great marks of improvement is the development of "position sense."[45]

(5) As we have already pointed out, "position sense" is a result of experience, and as such is the product, we may almost say the culmination, of one's whole chess development. Nevertheless, a fairly good knowledge of the value of different

positions marks such an advance over the player who is in what we have called the fourth stage that it may be taken as the fifth in the player's course of development.

The stages mentioned above are somewhat arbitrary, and may not be followed exactly in individual cases, but they will at least give some indication of the course of the player's development, which may be summarized in brief as follows: First the names and moves of the pieces are learned. Then comes the period of blunders, of indefinite play, of premature attacks, and of concentration on single moves, particular situations or, at best, on a plan imperfectly worked out. Later, one is able to see farther ahead, to foresee results more accurately, and to give some attention to the plans of his opponent. At the same time some typical forms of attack and defense and some general principles, or supposed principles are being learned, together with some knowledge of position. Along with all of this, though appearing consciously much later, goes an ever increasing power of analysis and improvement in "position sense."

Some of the most common blunders or oversights of these early stages are leaving pieces *en prise, i.e.*, unprotected and in a position to be captured on the next move of the opponent; allowing two pieces to be attacked simultaneously by one piece; removing a guarding piece, resulting in the loss of the guarded one; allowing a piece to be "pinned," *i.e.,* leaving it in such a situation that either it cannot, under the rules, be moved at all, or only with loss of an important piece. Errors of a more general nature are overlooking the bearing and force of distant and far-reaching pieces, errors in pawn play, not correlating the pawns and pieces, blocking the radius of action of the men, forgetting the purpose which prompted the placing of a piece in a certain position and a consequent loss of time in replacing it, or a disorganization of forces, and finally, faulty combinations and unsound sacrifices. Many blunders arise at all stages of skill from haste, impatience, and impulsiveness, but they are especially numerous with beginners.

2. DISCUSSION OF THE LEARNING PROCESS

We have now given an account of the stages of learning ; it remains to speak more particularly of the psychology of the learning process. Our problem is to explain the development of a beginner, who knows merely the names of the pieces and their powers, into the skillful player who makes use of these simple elements in intricate and purposeful combinations. We have to do with the growth of skill in strictly mental operations within the limited field of chess play.[46]

Obviously, memory is the *sine qua non* of learning, but although of prime importance it is only one of the factors involved. It must be such a memory as leads to the organization of the mental materials rather than to their mere retention. One could not be far wrong in saying that mental skill is in direct proportion to the degree of this organization. How organization can best be brought about is still an open question, and indeed its answer would involve the entire psychology of pedagogy. Its ultimate nature we do not know. To a great extent the material organizes itself, *i.e.*, the organization is physiological and a matter of growth. This fact was clearly pointed out by Dr. Burnham, who holds in his study on "Retroactive Amnesia"[47] that impressions require a certain time in which to fix themselves. The growth process, fixing the impression and strengthening the association tracts, is an indispensable factor in learning. A multiplicity of impressions might be made to follow so closely on one another that none of them could become fixed. In that case, of course, nothing would be learned.

In this connection I may mention that the returns of my correspondents also indicate that short periods of rest from chess practice, varying with the individual from a few weeks to several months, may cause a noticeable increase in skill. Renewed interest and consequent greater effort in beginning again after an interval of no play may account for this in part, and it may be also that in constant playing the details accumulate faster than the mind can assimilate them, so that they confuse rather than aid the player. This seems plausible when we remember the difficulty the beginner has in applying known principles to a mass of details. Then, too, when the stress of new impressions ceases, an opportunity is given to take an inventory of the mental stock. This is not possible to any great extent when new impressions are crowding in, and the attention is fully occupied with them. On the other hand, long periods of inactivity have a very different effect. Players make blunders in the openings, their combinations are not so far reaching, and a greater effort is required. Every part of the game that requires pure memory is affected and it is often necessary to do consciously what had previously been automatic. This, however, has to do merely with the fixation of separate impressions and of ideas with their associates, and our problem is rather to account for the combination of these elements into larger and larger complexes. On the physiological side little is known. The most that can be said is that increasing complexity of nervous function parallels increasing complexity of mental function. However that may be, our explanation, for the present at least, must be sought on the psychological side.

If we omit the very earliest stages in the chess player's development, the first significant fact is the beginner's utter inability to use in actual play what little chess knowledge he possesses. His blunders are recognized at once when they are pointed out to him, but in spite of his resolution to avoid them, he finds himself committing the same ones over and over again. It seems that the more he tries to avoid them the more blunders he makes. The intensity of his effort and the deep interest he takes in the game precludes mere carelessness. His difficulties are not due to lack of attention, but to the concentration of the attention on one feature of the game to the neglect of all the others. He sees this single thing and nothing more, because it, of all the mass of impressions, has some meaning for him. Were it possible to determine the span of one's chess attention during the different periods of his progress in learning, it would be possible to give objective evidence of the progressive fusion of the different elements into larger and larger complexes. The course of development would extend from the stage in which the player is unable to see in their completeness even the immediate consequences of a single move to that in which he is able to take in at a glance the disposition of all the pieces on the board. The building up of mental complexes in learning chess and those involved in other sorts of learning are not essentially different. There is a close analogy, for example, between the chess player learning the moves and blundering through his first few games, and the child learning to read, or the telegrapher learning to send and to receive messages.[48] The letter, the telegraphic dot or dash, or the single move in chess is at first the unit of perception. Later the word, a series of dots and dashes, or the relation of two or more pieces to each other becomes the unit. The child learns later, possibly, to comprehend at a glance the meaning of a phrase or a sentence; the telegrapher to receive by phrases; the chess player to take in a whole situation at a glance. Not only has the unit of perception become larger and larger but it has become more and more meaningful.

Perhaps the anology is closer still between the chess expert and the mathematician who has merely to glance at a formula or at its first two or three terms in order to recognize its full import. Every situation in a game of chess which requires readjustment of the player's plans is a problem for him, and the quickness and the accuracy of his solution will depend upon his ability to seize upon the salient and essential features and to neglect those which have no meaning for that particular situation. Obviously the mathematician's skill, when confronted by a problem, will display itself in his ability to recognize the fundamental nature of the problem. Lindley found that an expert mathematician, among those who attempted to solve his puzzle, recognized at a glance the mathematical principle involved and solved it without difficulty.[49] He displayed what corresponds to "position sense" in chess. The chess player has this advantage. In any particular game he has built up or helped to build up his own problem and has a mental record of its progress. He has seen the possibilities of certain lines of play eliminated one by one and is thus able to concentrate on the remaining ones.

The expert chess player is not required to analyze each position as he comes to it, and, indeed, this would be impossible to any great extent. His mind grasps the situation as a whole and it has a definite meaning for him. He recognizes the salient features only and deals with them, the details having for the time being dropped out. He is in the position of the general who has to know not that in one part of the field he has a regiment of one thousand soldiers, divided into ten companies of one hundred men each, but that he has a force there sufficient to repel any ordinary attack. He has only to pay attention to the regiments and their condition when an emergency arises. The expert no longer deals with particular terms, but with general terms or concepts. These general terms have been built up step by step, their meaning changing with the ever increasing knowledge of the player, and are often represented partially or symbolically by their initial moves or general trend. More concretely, a player learns at first that a certain move is a good one because it has certain definite advantages, and this enables him to plan a little further ahead. Later he finds that this move has a great many other consequences, and perhaps this in turn modifies a general principle he may have based upon it, and this finally, may involve the modification of several other principles and result in a still more comprehensive principle embracing all of the others. Details can be organized into larger groups in proportion as they gather meaning as a group, but not before. The chess player groups his pieces and they acquire a meaning analogous to the potential meaning of the general term or the symbol in abstract thinking. Progress in chess like progress in abstract thinking of any other kind consists in the formation of an increasing symbolism which permits the manipulation of larger and larger complexes.

We are in the habit of speaking of the automatic in the motor realm, meaning by it that certain movements or combinations of movements are carried on without conscious guidance. Is there such a thing as automatism in the realm of the purely intellectual? It seems to me that this question is to be answered in the affirmative. There is something in the purely intellectual life corresponding to motor automatism, which is shown in the ability to think symbolically or abstractly, and thus to handle large masses of detail with a minimum of conscious effort. It involves the increasing ability to take in during a single pulse of attention a larger and larger group of details which means, of course, that the attention is no longer needed for each one.

An apparent difference between motor and mental automatisms, lies, however, in the fact that in the intellectual realm increasing automatism seems to involve the dropping out of details, while in the motor realm increasing automatism often means a greater perfection of the details. Careful examination, however, will probably show that in both details are dropped from consciousness and that in both they are perfected in the externalized outcome. The great feature common to both is the releasing of the attention from the details. In the intellectual sphere, as the processes become more and more complex, they are carried on by systems of symbols which tend to become more and more abstract or general. This is true of all abstract thinking, including that involved in expert chess playing. And, as in all other kinds of abstract thinking, it is essential in chess that no matter how symbolic the thinking may become the player must always have a thorough grasp of the details of the game. In other words, he must not only be able to construct his plans by the use of abstract symbols, but he must be able to translate them into the concrete and to carry them out move by move. This latter he does not necessarily do in his thinking. From one whole situation he passes directly to another whole situation. For instance in a definite situation, the first move of a long series suggests not the next move but the position after the whole series has been played. In other words, the first term does not necessarily call up the second one or the last, or some intermediate term, but the result of all the moves. This final result may be present to the mind in the form of a visual image (a mental picture) or in verbal terms. For example, the first few moves of the Evans gambit already mentioned, may cause to arise in the mind of one player a visual image of the position as it will appear after a dozen moves have been made on each side, while in the case of another player a verbal judgment of the strength or weakness of the final position may take its place. To the latter player this opening calls to mind a verbal judgment of the final position based on past experience. The formulation of principles of play, which become increasingly general, is another expression of the increasing symbolism involved in learning to play chess, but in this case in verbal instead of visual form.

The chess player's skill is measured largely in terms of his ability to use larger and larger units of thought. He has learned by means of many repetitions, a series of moves in regular sequence, later, as has already been pointed out, the first move or a given arrangement of the pieces on the board represents for him the position as it will be several moves further on. All the intermediate steps are for the moment ignored, or, in other words, "a short circuit" has been established and the association is between the first term and the last or the total result instead of each term being revived by the one immediately preceding it.

In trying to explain this from the physiological side two alternatives present themselves. It may be that an entirely new brain tract, connecting the first term with the last, has been opened up. On the other hand it is just as conceivable that the nervous impulse may travel along the same path in all cases and that in the case of a "short circuit" only the first and last terms rise into consciousness. Experiments on the learning of nonsense syllables, showing that repetitions not only strengthen the associative bonds between a syllable and the one immediately following it, but also between more remote ones,[50] seem to lend a certain support to the latter theory. This is, however, all rather speculative since neurology is able to tell us little or nothing about it. On the psychological side the "short circuiting" process seems to mean something like this. In the beginning the last term, the final result, is reached after passage through all the terms of the series. Now, ordinarily, the series is of value, and therefore of interest, not for itself, but for its result, so that little attention is given to the intermediate links, but much to the getting through. The whole strain of attention is forward. As a result of this the image before the mind may be several steps in advance of the one actually being executed, or, in well practiced series, it may be the last step itself, or even the purpose for which the series is gone through. The result is that there is a tendency to the formation of immediate associations between the earlier and later steps of the series. This suggests that conscious effort plays an important part in the establishment of the "short circuit." Bryan and Harter, in their study of telegraphic language, concluded that only by putting forth a supreme effort could one rise above the plateau of moderate attainment.[51] Still it is by no means certain that the rise in the curve would not take place in time if effort were maintained at a moderate and uniform level. In that case the rise in the curve from the plateau would mean the completion of the growth processes under the guidance of ordinary selective attention.

While chess is a type of purely intellectual learning, the fact should not be lost sight of that the emotional accompaniment is an important factor in the chess player's development as in all other sorts of acquisition, and that emotion is one of the strongest influences in fixing impressions. Ideas which are associated with strong emotions are kept before the mind for a longer period than those which have little or no emotional coloring and thus have much more chance of becoming permanently fixed. Numerous instances were noted in this study in which situations which had aroused strong emotions were continually before the mind and were so persistent as to banish sleep and to drive out all other thoughts.

In this connection mention should be made of the effect of error on one's progress. If one continues to commit errors through ignorance of the fact that they are errors, he may retard his development by falling into fixed habits of unsound play; but if they are noted as errors, and especially if they arouse a strong emotion, they are eliminated. The importance of this becomes evident when we recall that a great part of the player's progress consists in the elimination of unprofitable moves. It is easy to see, also, that emotions, so far as they are expressive of temperament and affect one's habits of play, may exercise an important influence for good or bad upon one's ability to win, as already pointed out in any earlier section.

3. AIDS TO LEARNING

By study and practice the difficulties of the beginner are gradually overcome and his faults corrected, though the latter are apt for a long time to recur at unguarded moments, and some, especially the faults of temperament (errors and oversights due to impulsiveness, rashness and quick temper, for example), may never be wholly suppressed. It is probable, indeed, that most of the faults of the earlier stages are temporarily overcome many times before they can safely be given over to the realm of the automatic, *i.e.*, they crop out from time to time when the attention is turned toward larger complexes of elements.

Of all the aids to learning, so soon as one has mastered the bare rudiments of play, there is probably nothing like actual play over the board, provided that one is willing to play slowly, study out the causes of his misfortune and profit by them. The emotional stress attending both success and failure at such a time is a great aid to memory, as has already been suggested.

The concrete criticism of a superior player is of the greatest assistance, but too many things must not be given at once, and what is given must be applied immediately in actual play in order to insure its retention.

In order to get some idea of the sources from which chess players gain their knowledge of the game and the value which they attach to them, questions were asked of my correspondents in regard to the benefit derived from problem solution, the study of standard games, end games and openings, and board play under different conditions. Most, of course, had derived most of their knowledge from actual play over the board.

The interest in problem solving is by no means universal. Many state that they have never attempted to solve problems; others, that they are not interested in them because they are artificial and mechanical and do not help one's general play. The replies indicate, however, that problem solving is widespread among players. As to its helpfulness in general play, the variety of opinion is great, varying from the statement that it is a positive detriment to extravagant claims for its utility for mental development in general. With a number of players, the problem interest, if developed at all, was developed late, *i.e.,* long after they had learned to play. It is interesting to note that few of these players think that problem solving has helped their play. Others took up problems with the beginning of play and say that they were greatly helped by their efforts to solve them. This suggests what is probably the fact that solving problems helps one in the early stages of his play, and this is in accord with my own experience. The reason for this is not hard to find. The history of problem chess shows that in the beginning the problems were merely positions taken from actual games and consequently involved all the elements of actual play. Much could then be derived from their solution which would be of general service. Since that time, however, problem composition has changed very much, and the problems now are made to conform to certain fixed rules, which have, from the standpoint of many players, made them mechanical and artificial. They have lost most of their resemblance to positions met with in actual play. No doubt they are not of much benefit to players who have had considerable experience and who are familiar with the principles involved in their solution. With the beginner, on the other hand, the case is different. He may learn something of the manner of giving check, something of the powers of pieces in different combinations, and of the value of position. They may help his powers of analysis in so far as they involve general principles which are applicable to actual play, and they may aid in improving his judgment of position. At the best, however, they are far inferior to the study of end games and to actual practice over the board. This latter statement seems borne out in part by the fact that few, if any, great problem solvers or composers are also great players.

Practically all agree that a knowledge of the openings is indispensable. The advantage is evident. It enables one to place his pieces in good positions relative to each other, to develop along sound lines, to avoid disaster in the early stages of the game, to take advantage of weak moves made by one's opponent, and what is also of great importance, it enables him to play with a minimum of effort during the early stages of a game. It should be added that knowledge of the openings and variations helps one to force the play along lines with which he is most familiar. The easiest and quickest way to get this knowledge is from the books, but many good players possess it who have given little or no time to book study. They have gained it from actual experience, and base their opening plays on principles derived from this source.

A few think that replaying standard games does not help one's play, and a still smaller number think it is a positive detriment, assigning as a reason that it destroys one's originality, and causes him to overlook advantages which slight variations from the known lines might give. There may be a real danger here, but it is more than offset by the advantages gained. Among the advantages are mentioned the opportunity to examine positions at leisure, to study comprehensive plans of attack and defense involving particular combinations, to appreciate the value of time and position, and finally to become familiar with a number of oft-recurring situations. These situations, while seldom identical, are often similar. Standard games also teach principles and aid in the development of position judgment. It should be stated, however, that the value of such games varies with the individual, and up to a certain stage is in direct proportion to his chess knowledge. The mere beginner learns little from them; the chess master also learns little from them. The one is unable to comprehend them; the other finds little in them that is unknown to him. The games take on meaning in direct proportion to the amount of knowledge that one brings to them; and their value to any individual depends on the number of new ideas he is able to carry away from them.

Playing with a weaker player is not considered a good thing by most of my correspondents. They say it makes them careless, prone to recklessness, and leads them into all sorts of extravagancies of play. Several recommend never playing with a weaker player without giving sufficient odds to make the game even. A few recommend playing with a weaker player for the reason that, by lessening the amount of attention ordinarily given to the opponent's plans, the stronger player is able to give freer play to his imagination than he would dare to do if playing with one of equal strength.

Most say that playing with many different players has made their style more flexible. A few, however, maintain that style of play is individual and that nothing can change it. This contention, as was pointed out above, is undoubtedly true in so far as fundamental traits of character enter into the game. Those who answered that playing with a number of different players has made their style more flexible, appear to mean that to a certain extent it has enabled them to overcome some faults due to temperament and that they have learned a greater variety of methods of play.

III. GENERAL SUMMARY OF THE PSYCHOLOGICAL POINTS

Chess as a strongly competitive form of human play appeals to the fundamental fighting impulse, but it appeals also to the æsthetic and puzzle-solving interests; and it affords the pleasure of "being a cause."

Visual imagination is an important element in chess playing, especially in blind-fold chess, but it is not indispensable. Motor, verbal, or auditory imagery may, and often does, occupy the chief place in the player's consciousness.

The mental qualities most utilized in chess playing are: a strong *chess* memory, power of accurate analysis, quickness of perception, strong constructive imagination and a power of far reaching combination. These are *chess* qualities, however, and skill at chess is not a universally valid index of high mental endowment.

The logical type differs in the different stages of a game and with the knowledge and skill of the player, approaching always nearer, as his knowledge and skill increases, to that of the syllogism.

The reasoning process is, in psychological terms, a sequence of mental states due to shiftings of the focal point of attention, the associations working strictly within the limits imposed by the task or purpose.

In his learning the chess player passes through well defined stages and these mark the necessary steps in his progress. The most important psychological feature in the learning of chess (and it seems equally true of all learning), is the *progressive organization of knowledge,* making possible the direction of the player's attention to the relations of larger and more complex units. The organization involves generalization, increasing symbolism, and the multiplication of associations; it insures prompter recall and increased potential meaning in the general concepts; it releases attention from details and favors consequent mental automatisms and "short circuit" processes. Thus alone is progress possible. Mental automatisms are usually perfected, one may conjecture, after advance to the next higher stages of learning.

APPENDIX: ON THE CASE OF A FEEBLE-MINDED CHESS PLAYER

During the course of this study several cases of chess playing among the feeble-minded have been reported to the writer, but it has been impossible to secure definite data except in one case. It is said that in some instances a very high degree of chess skill was possessed by men of very low mentality. An inmate of the Wisconsin Institution for the Feeble-minded, is reported to have been able to cope successfully with very strong players. Very likely the strength of these players has been very much overestimated, but the evidence is sufficient to warrant us in saying that in chess as in other kinds of mental activity a peculiar power is not incompatible with a very low average of general mental ability.

The writer has been able to study at first hand one case of chess playing by a man of low grade intelligence who is an inmate of the department for the feeble-minded and criminally insane at the Massachusetts State Farm. In the asylum records he is classed as a congenital idiot who has suffered degeneration since coming to the institution in 1891. Previous to that time he had been an inmate of other institutions for the insane. He has had and still has, though less frequently than formerly, outbursts of rage, at which times he beats his head against the wall. He says he does this because he loves his mother. He is a sexual pervert and some of his outbursts followed his separation from other inmates of the institution whom he designates as "friends." He is fifty-four years of age but looks much younger, is filthy in his personal habits, and presents a very peculiar appearance. He stoops considerably and walks with the shuffling gait characteristic of the feeble-minded. In one of the older asylum records some one has noted the fact that he resembles an anthropoid ape in appearance. His forehead is very low and receding, his maxillaries are very protruding and the posterior portions of his head are so prominent that his head resembles that of the African negro.

The term idiot is used to cover such a wide range of mental deficiency that it conveys no very definite meaning, so that it will be necessary to give a brief account of his attempts at mental work in order to convey some idea of his general intelligence. His memory for some things is fairly good, though it is not of special excellence. He remembers faces quite well and for a considerable time. He also has a fairly good memory for places, remembering, for instance, the town in which he was brought up, the different institutions he has been in, and the town in which some of his relatives live, and remembers all these by name. He has no idea of time, but holds a few dates in mind. For example, he said he came to the asylum in 1891, which was correct. He knows the names of most of the months of the year, but has no idea of their order. In January he was asked what month it was and replied that he did n't know. He was then asked if it were June and replied that it was the month before June. When asked what month that was, replied: "That is the month of October." He has had practically no schooling and can neither read nor write. When asked why he didn't go to school when he was a boy he replied that he was too thick-headed to learn. He repeated this on several occasions.

The following questions were asked him: If you had two apples and I gave you two more how many would you have then? How many are five times five? If you worked for me five days and I gave you a dollar for every day you worked, how many dollars would you have, To all these and to other questions he gave the same answer: "Don't know." Questions in regard to his name, the names of others his age, and other simple questions he answers intelligently or with his indifferent "Don't know." In this regard he may be compared to a young child. There is this difference, however: he does not show the curiosity of a child, and displays very little mental initiative. He is like a child, however, in another respect: he is very fond of toys, picture books, and especially of neckties. He asks for them repeatedly, but only apparently when he notices them. He enjoyed playing with my watch and with my ring and asked for the latter several times. When told he could not have a thing or promised it later he always replied "Thank you." He is unable to tell time by the clock or watch, but almost always knows the hour of the day, which he is no doubt able to determine from the regularity of the institution life. In reply to a question he said that he is twenty-one years old and that he had been that age for a long time.

In regard to his chess playing I should say at the outset that he is not a strong player, and that an average player of a year's experience could probably play as well or better. It should be remembered, however, that he has never studied the game at all, has never played regularly, and has not played with many different players. There was no way of determining how long he had known the game, except from his own statements and these are, of course, not very certain. He said he learned about three years ago, that no one had taught him the moves, but that he learned them by watching others play. He has played checkers for many years, but there is no trace in his game at present of interference of association from this source. As is to be expected from the circumstances under which he learned, and played, his play shows very little variety, although there was some improvement in this regard as well as in general chess ability during the time I had him under observation. He has considerable familiarity with certain situations and can be relied on to meet them in certain ways. He usually meets a threat, for example, at once and by dislodging the threatening piece if possible. An analysis of his games shows a number of oft recurring moves such as Kt-R3, Q-B3, P-Q3, and advancing a pawn one square to serve as a guard for a piece or a pawn to be advanced at the next move. Attacking a piece with a pawn, and "forking" two pieces are favorite methods of attack with him. He makes his moves very rapidly and apparently with little or no time for consideration, but usually waits very patiently for his opponent to reply. If the effect of a move of his opponent is not very remote, he notes it almost immediately. For instance, on one occasion when a bishop attacked both of his rooks he announced at once that one of them was lost, and on another occasion when his queen was attacked by a knight, he announced at once that she was lost, a fact which his opponent had not yet appreciated. It may be, of course, that he had anticipated the dangerous move.

He had a great deal of difficulty with a set of chessmen of a pattern different from those he had been using. In the new set the king was larger than the queen, while in the old set the reverse was the case. He was utterly unable to use them until, at his request, a piece of colored cloth, which had been tied around the old queen, was fastened to the new one. After that he had little difficulty with the new set.

At times he seemed to see a situation very quickly, but to be unable to retain it in mind when he attempted to meet it. For instance, when trying to get out of check, he moved his king back into check several times, that is, he would find a move impossible, recall it and then a little later attempt it again.

On the whole it is not too much to say that his game compares quite favorably with those of players whose advantages in the way of instruction, study, and practice have been much greater than his, and there is no reason to doubt that with more practice and instruction he would be able to improve his game considerably.

Our conclusions from the study of this case must be, it seems to me, that chess skill is not an index of general intelligence, that the reasoning involved in chess playing is reasoning within very narrow limits, and that a considerable degree of chess skill is possible to one who is mentally deficient in almost every other line.

The following records of games played by this player will indicate to those who are familiar with the game something of his chess ability. The games are chosen as fairly representative of his play during the time he was studied, which extended a little over two months, with an interruption of three weeks between the last observation and the one just preceding it.

Game No. 2.

White (feeble-minded player)	Black.	White	Black (Feeble-minded player)
1 P-Q4	P-Q4	1 P-K4	P-K4
2 P-K3	Kt-QB3	2 Kt-KB3	Q-KB3
3 Q-KB3	P-K4	3 P-Q3	Kt-KR3
4 P-QB3	Kt-B3	4 B-Kt5	Q-QB3
5 Kt-KR3	QB-Kt5	5 KtxKP	Q-K3
6 Q-Kt3	Q-K2	6 B-KB4	P-KB3
7 P-KB3	B-R4	7 BxKKt	PxB
8 QPxP	KtxP	8 Kt-QB4	Q-QB3
9 P-KB4	Kt-QB3	9 KB-K2	P-QKt4
10 QKt-R3	KKt-K5	10 B-KR5 (ch)	K-Qsq.
11 Q-B3	BxQ	11 P-Q4	QxKt
12 KtPxB	Q-R5ch	12 Kt-QR3	Q-B3
13 K-K2	Kt-KB3	13 P-Q5	Q-Kt3
14 KKt-Kt5	KB-B4	14 O-O	B-QB4
15 Kt-QKt5	O-O	15 Q-K2	B-QR3
16 P-QR3	P-KR3	16 P-K5	P-QKt5
17 P-Kt4	B-QKt3	17 KPxP	BxQ
18 KtxKBP	RxKt	18 R-Ksq.	QxP
19 P-QR4	P-QR4	19 RxB	QxQKtP
20 PxP	BxP	20 R-Ksq.	QxKt
21 K-Qsq.	R-K2	21 R-K8 (ch)	RxR
22 B-Q2	B-Kt3	22 RxR (checkmate)	
23 B-Ksq.	Q-R4		
24 KR-Kt	QxBp (ch)		
25 K-Q2	QxP (ch)		
26 K-Kt2	QxR		
27 Kt-Q3	QKtxKt		
28 PxKt	BxQP		
29 R-Q1	QxKB		
30 B-Kt4	Q-QB5 (ch)		
31 K-Ktsq.	Q-Kt6 (ch)		
32 K-B	Q-Kt7 (checkmate)		

NOTES

1. It is a pleasure to acknowledge my indebtedness to Professor E. C. Sanford for the suggestion of this topic of study, and for generous assistance in following it out; to Dr. C. A. Drew and others at the Massachusetts State Farm for courtesies extended ; to those who in the capacity of assistants have contributed much to this study; and to all who have answered my questionnaire on chess or assisted in securing answers to it.

2. The history of chess may be followed in Forbes's History of Chess, and in Dr. Van der Linde's book on its history and literature.

3. Binet, Alfred: Psychologie des grands Calculateurs et Joueurs d' Echecs, Deuxième Partie, Paris, 1894.

4. Lasker's *Chess Magazine,* Vol. 1, No. 1, Nov. 1904. p. 48.

5. Patrick: The Psychology of Football. *Am, Jour, Psy.,* Vol. XIV, 1903, pp. 368–381.

6. Groos: The Play of Man, New York, 1901. pp. 173 ff.

7. Groos: *op, cit.,* p. 190.

8. Lindley: A Study of Puzzles, *Am. Jour. Psy.,* VIII, 1897, pp. 431493, especially p. 437.

9. Groos: *op. cit.,* pp. 369 ff.

10. Groos: *op. cit.,* p. 385.

11. In order to supplement my own observations and those of my assistants, a questionnaire was submitted to chess players of different grades of ability. The list of players answering is a fairly representative one and contains the names of some of the best amateurs of the United States and Canada. Some of the data from this source are specifically included in this study, but in many other cases the substance of the views expressed has been incorporated without more acknowledgment than is here made. About 100 answers in all were obtained.

12. Lindley: *op. cit.,* p. 437.

13. This instinct in man, we are told, is being gradually overcome or suppressed. It would be interesting to note, however, whether in the contests which still give opportunity for it, there is any lessening of the desire to win, and whether individuals change at all in this regard. The fact probably is that the instinct is changing its form with social pressure, but losing little of its native power.

14. Binet: *op. cit.,* p. 236.

15. Binet: *ibid.*

16. A player of perfect "position sense" could play any number of games *ad hoc* without recalling anything.

17. Edge, F. M.: Exploits and Triumphs in Europe of Paul Morphy, N. Y., 1859. p. 164.

18. Edge: *op. cit.,* p. 187.

19. Edge: *op. cit.,* p. 187.

20. Graham, P. Anderson: Mr. Blackburne's Games at Chess. London, 1899. p. 207.

21. *British Chess Magazine,* Vol. XX, p. 399.

22. Graham: *op. cit.,* p. 209.

23. Graham: *op. cit.,* p. 211.

24. The physical endurance required for play in such contests is something little realized by the uninitiated. Morphy, at Paris, played for ten consecutive hours without eating or drinking anything. Paulsen, who played as many as ten games blindfold, played twelve consecutive hours on one occasion with no refreshments of any kind except a little lemonade.

25. Pillsbury: The Chess Player's Mind. *Independent*, Vol. LII, p. 1104.

26. Pillsbury: *op. cit.*

27. Binet: *op. cit.,* p. 264, p. 274.

28. Mr. Newman's article has not been published, but the manuscript was placed at the writer's disposal through the kindness of Prof. E. H. Lindley of the University of Indiana.

29. Binet: *op. cit.,* pp. 270 ff.

30. Taine: On Intelligence. New York, 1899. pp, 38, 39.

31. Binet: *op. cit.,* pp. 276 ff.

32. Binet: *op. cit.,* p. 311.

33. Binet: *op. cit.,* pp. 340–351.

34. It may be conjectured that the necessary concentration of attention on the *relations* of the pieces rather than on the pieces themselves is partly responsible for the incomplete development of visual imagery.

35. See in the appendix to this study an account of a fair chess player of otherwise feeble intelligence.

36. Jevons: Lessons in Logic. New Ed. London and New York, 1905, p. 258.

37. James: Principles of Psychology, N. Y., 1899, Vol. II, pp. 330 ff.

38. It is what Romanes calls reasoning in particulars. Romanes: Mental Evolution in Animals. N. Y., 1900. p. 337.

39. Morgan: Introduction to Comparative Psychology. London and N. Y., 1902. pp. 293 ff.

40. My sources of information here are my own introspective notes while learning to play, and those of four assistants, together with the replies of my correspondents.

41. These last may not seem absolutely essential in view of the case to be described in the appendix, but even from that case I shall hope to show that this statement is justified.

42. Stout: Manual of Psychology. N. Y., 1899. pp. 84 ff.

43. I say "not wholly in proportion to knowledge," because skill represents only that part of knowledge that can be readily and effectively applied. Our general problem in this section is, therefore, to describe, as far as we are able, the way in which experience becomes transmuted into skill. Our immediate concern is with chess skill, but if we are successful in our study of that, we shall be justified in certain inferences with regard to many other sorts of learning which, like it, are matters of mental as opposed to purely physical training.

44. Knowledge of checkers is at first a source of many interferences. The player is tempted to move his pawns diagonally, has a tendency to keep his pieces bunched so that his opponent cannot "jump" them, is on the lookout for vacant squares on which to plant his pieces, and has a tendency to clear the board as soon as possible. He also finds it difficult to remember that the pieces can retreat after having been once advanced.

45. *Vide,* p. 277.

46. Numerous studies have been made on memory, attention, and other complex mental processes and a considerable number on learning, but these latter have been concerned chiefly with motor training. Bryan and Harter's study on the learning of the telegraphic language among the earlier studies, is the nearest approach to the present one, but it deals more especially with a sort of learning which is of a mixed motor and sensory type, whereas the skill here in question is almost wholly central. In that study learning on the sensory side consisted in the formation of fixed associations between complex sounds and the corresponding words; in our case the learn-

ing process involves the formation of complex groups rather than that of fixed associations of symbol and word. Nevertheless much of what Bryan and Harter discovered in reference to this latter sort of learning is strictly applicable to the form with which we are dealing, especially their chief generalization, namely, that advance in skill depends upon the formation of a "hierarchy of habits." Among the more recent studies, that of Swift, on Beginning a Language, in the Garman Commemorative volume (Studies in Philosophy and Psychology by former students of Charles Edward Garman, Boston, 1906) may be mentioned as dealing like this with a form of mental skill.

47. Burnham: Retroactive Amnesia, *Amer. Jour. of Psy.*, Vol. XIV, 1903, pp. 382–396.

48. Bryan and Harter: *op. cit.*

49. Lindley: *op. cit.*, p. 470.

50. Ebbinghaus: Ueber das Gedächtniss. Leipzig, 1885.

51. Bryan and Harter: *op. cit.*, p. 50.